HOLLYWOOD FACTION

HOLLYWOOD FACTION

reality and myth in the movies

Bruce Crowther

COLUMBUS BOOKS
LONDON

Copyright © 1984 Bruce Crowther

First published in Great Britain in 1984 by
Columbus Books,
Devonshire House, 29 Elmfield Road, Bromley, Kent BR1 1LT

Design and production in association with
Book Production Consultants, 47 Norfolk Street, Cambridge CB1 2LE

Typeset by Goodfellow & Egan Limited, Cambridge

Printed and bound by Alden Press Limited, Oxford

British Library Cataloguing in Publication Data

Crowther, Bruce
    Hollywood faction.
    1. Moving-pictures—Social aspects—
    United States   2. Moving-pictures—
    Political aspects—United States
    I. Title
    302.2′343′0973   PN1995.9.S6

ISBN 0-86287-097-6

CONTENTS

AUTHOR'S NOTE

I am not a historian; this is not a history book.

This book is about the movies. Specifically, it is about those movies which depict real eras, events and individuals in American history.

Historical events recounted here are necessarily condensed; any reader seeking more information on American history should turn to a good history book. Some suggestions are listed in the bibliography.

The bibliography also lists books on various aspects of films, many of which I found both thought-provoking and useful when preparing this book.

I have also benefited from conversations with a number of people, some of whom have read portions of the typescript and whose comments and criticisms have proved invaluable.

Nevertheless, the interpretation in this book of incidents and individuals in history, and, of course, the movies themselves, is mine alone.

Should any errors of fact have crept through into the final draft, these too are my responsibility.

Bruce Crowther

ACKNOWLEDGEMENTS

The idea for this book emerged from conversations with
DAVE TUCK,
who also assisted during research and writing. I am most grateful for his help
and, similarly, I gratefully acknowledge the help of Louis Billington, who read
the first draft typescript, and Steve Baskerville, Dustin Mirick and John White
who read parts of it; Edward Abramson and Hilton Tims listened to me; all
made invaluable suggestions. I received co-operation and help from Teresa
Coleman and Iain Smith of Enigma Productions and from Leslie Halliwell,
while the library staff at the University of Hull and at the British Film Institute
were as smoothly efficient as always.

B.C.

FOREWORD

The history books have it all wrong. America was not born when a Genoese adventurer, financed by the King and Queen of Spain, sailed over the edge of the Old World and touched the fringes of a new continent. No, America was not born then, so Goodbye, Columbus.

Neither was the nation born in anger and dismay generated by an arrogant king and his government who thus lost an empire far greater in potential than anything the British gouged out of India and Africa.

No, America was born after a war between brothers, fought upon native soil, over an issue only dimly comprehended then and even now, but which, as every student knows, has some vague connection with slavery.

How do we know this was when and how the nation was born?

Because Hollywood has told us so through the sheer volume of its output. Hundreds of films have been set in and around the Civil War, while only a handful have dealt with the three-and-a-half centuries between Columbus and the firing on Fort Sumter. Hollywood has thus reflected the important position the War holds in the consciousness of the American people.

Or is the importance attached to the Civil War by the people a reflection of the attention paid to it by writers and scholars and, especially, by film-makers?

The Civil War is not, of course, the only perod of American history from which Hollywood has drawn inspiration.

There are the Old West, two World Wars, the bullet-strewn years of Prohibition, the Depression, the Dillinger Days, Korea and Vietnam, the space race and much more besides.

Then there are those real-life individuals who have attracted film-makers: gangsters and statesmen, villains and heroes, sometimes both roles embodied in one man: Wyatt Earp, Billy the Kid, Alvin York, Al Capone, Douglas MacArthur, Huey Long, Joe McCarthy, John Kennedy, Chuck Yeager, Richard Nixon and many others.

But are the resulting films historically accurate? Indeed, what is the truth about history? Our understanding of the past changes as our perception of the present is adjusted. Films about, say, World War I, vary enormously in their approach according to when they were made.

Conversely, the past influences the present both by its enduring institutions and its framework for thought.

Film-makers, however innovative they might be, observe certain conventions, some of which are imposed by the medium in which they work, others by their own education and background. Seldom, however, do they appear overawed by the need for historical accuracy. Perhaps they are subconsciously acknowledging that there is no guarantee that any aspect of history is accurate. Every historical account, whether on film, in a book, a newspaper report, or an oral statement, is adjusted, amended and altered by the reporter, or by the recorder, or by both.

Accuracy, then, becomes a matter of relativity. If history itself is not especially reliable, then is it justifiable to complain if Hollywood is also inaccurate when it depicts historical events?

That some changes need to be made in bringing historical events or figures to the screen is not disputed. The film-maker is obliged to make his work coherent within its time span. It is necessary to simplify and to concentrate. The film-maker cannot assume that his audience is made up of people with historical knowledge or interest, thus further simplifications are needed and with them an inevitable diffusion of reality.

But given that technical or artistic constraints, conventions and needs may force change, should no limits be imposed?

Surely, when there is deliberate misrepresentation of reality for no good cause, questions must be asked.

Any feature film, however indifferent it might be, may well be seen by more people in any given community than would voluntarily read a history book. If the film is inaccurate, those members of its audience who have no other knowledge nor any interest in reading a history book might well take the film as a real and truthful account. If the film is a major production it will be seen by millions of people throughout the world. Inaccurate renditions of history may thus become part of a popular misconception about the past.

As moviegoers out-number historians, this other version of American history determines much of what the rest of the world thinks about America and its role in world events. To a considerable extent, it also conditions what America thinks of itself.

There is another point to consider: people and nations are supposed to learn from past mistakes. If they don't, the old adage runs, they are doomed to make the same mistakes again. If popular conceptions of the past have been altered, whether by films or through other means, how will people and nations know which mistakes to avoid in the future?

If there is a known truth or, at least, a consensus view of events, a film-maker who imposes his own vision must be open to criticism, perhaps even to suspicion. If the changes are made because new information has come to light, that is one thing; it is quite another matter for changes to be made solely to make a story more exciting, or to ensure the villain gets his comeuppance,

10

or the hero gets the girl, or to enable the film-maker to impose a political or sociological point of view which has nothing whatsoever to do with the events being depicted on-screen. Some of these motives for change are trivial; the last is not.

Nevertheless, too-tight constraints cannot be imposed. A film-maker cannot be denied the freedom to interpret individuals and events in a way which will highlight those facets of the individual or event which provided the stimulus to make the film in the first place.

Clearly, this book can encompass neither every event in the history of the American nation, nor every factually-based motion-picture. What follows is an exploration of some of those events and individuals deemed sufficiently important by film-makers to warrant their attention in major features.

The choice of films for examination and analysis is occasionally arbitrary but the guiding factor has not been to prove points or support preconceptions. It is simply a question of whether the films have been seen by a mass audience, either at the movies or on television.

More than 800 films have either dealt with or touched upon the American Civil War; those examined in the first chapter were seen by millions of people in many lands who used them, consciously or not, to form a conception and understanding, right or wrong, of the Civil War and the period of Reconstruction. Whether they are good, bad, or indifferent films is not especially relevant.

The same guiding principle is observed in later chapters whether dealing with Indians or gangsters, politicians or soldiers, policemen or astronauts.

A wholly accurate film seen by a handful of people is commendable but in the wider scheme of things has little impact. A multi-million dollar blockbuster that is seen by millions in cinemas, or on late-night TV or on video, and is grossly inaccurate can and does shape and condition false attitudes towards America.

The House UnAmerican Activities Committee, a malignant body which is discussed in some detail in Chapter 9, was aware of the importance of popular accessibility: 'We are less interested in a film that has Communist context, where a few hundred people will come and see it. We are more interested in an ordinary John-and-Mary picture where there is only a drop of progressive thought in it.'

Setting aside, for the moment, the self-revelation contained in these words, a certain truth can be observed.

The power of a film to influence or condition thought and perceptions about America should not be underestimated.

In the following pages, the degree to which Hollywood has changed history is examined, as is the reason why it has done so. Also sought is an understanding of the effect such changes have had upon perceptions of the nation, past and present.

A further question lies beneath the surface: does it matter?

Without wishing to pre-judge this last point, it has to be acknowledged that with a former Warner Brothers contract player in the White House, no one can afford to overlook the possibility that the fate of the world may well rest in the hands of a man whose view of his nation, the rest of the world, and life itself, is based not upon reality but upon the myth created by Hollywood.

CHAPTER ONE

'Like writing history with lightning.
And it's all true.'
(President Woodrow Wilson on
The Birth of a Nation)

David Wark Griffith fervently refuted accusations of racism, but no modern audience can see *The Birth of a Nation* (1915) without thinking otherwise. Unfortunately, most of the film's huge and enthusiastic contemporary audience was much less perceptive and in consequence racial issues and relations in America suffered incalculable harm.

It is difficult to attribute the majority of the changes Griffith made to historical events to any cause other than latent, if not blatant, racism. There was certainly no need to change history merely for the sake of dramatic effect. The Civil War had drama enough, as the hundreds of films which touch upon it testify. Certainly, adjustments were needed in order that the era covered by the film (the duration of the American Civil War and the period of Reconstruction) could be satisfactorily condensed. Additionally, the story had to be made comprehensible to audiences with only pictures and written title cards to aid them, but this does not justify Griffith's changes both to known facts and to the social, political, and moral atmosphere of the era he was depicting.

The decision to make any changes at all is surprising, given the fact that *The Birth of a Nation* was made at a time when so many people who had lived through the era under scrutiny were still alive. In the last year of the war, a boy of fifteen might well have taken up arms for the Confederacy, if not for the Union. He would have reached early manhood during Reconstruction and have been only sixty-five when the film was released. Additionally, pictures taken by the remarkable war photographers Mathew Brady and Timothy O'Sullivan had ensured that many people were familiar with the 'look' of the Civil War. The war's effect upon families who had lost relatives, and damage to the nation's economy caused by both the war and Reconstruction, were similarly well-known. None of this appears to have mattered to Griffith, and audiences were equally unconcerned. For the immigrants in the audience who had entered America in their millions between the end of Reconstruction and 1915, and whose knowledge of the period was understandably sketchy, the film appeared as an illustrated history lesson. Later audiences for historical films, especially those dealing with wars, would suffer the same temporary blindness.

The racism and sectionalism at the root of Griffith's prejudices were probably unconscious, so deeply interwoven as they were in his background, and in any other film of the time would have been relatively unimportant. What makes the racial bigotry and historical manipulation exercised in *The Birth of a Nation* significant is the fact that this film is in all other respects a work of genius which created a lasting impression in the minds of its original audiences. Across the nation and throughout the world, people saw this impressive saga unfolding before their eyes and they believed it. Why should they not? The President of the United States, Woodrow Wilson himself, declared that the film was 'like writing history with lightning. And it's all true.' If the President said it was so, then who would deny it? This was long ago, when Presidents spoke only the truth – or so people thought. Today, in post-Watergate disillusionment, audiences might take a healthily sceptical view of such declarations, but not then. Voices were raised against the film, of course, and in the resulting furore the President's remark was withdrawn – but it had had its effect.

Most of Griffith's interpretation of Reconstruction bore out popular but false assumptions about the era. In essence the period of Reconstruction, which ran from the end of the war in 1865 until 1877, was a time when the victors attempted to define political relationships which would now exist between the former Confederacy and the Federal government.

Other issues arose, few of them clear-cut, and all added to the confusion of the times. One such issue was the future of the newly freed slaves. There was no question that they should take up full citizenship. The majority of Northerners were not integrationists; abolishing slavery was one thing, building an interracial society was another.

An important issue which concerned politicians during Reconstruction was the complete reorganization of the once-proud society below the Mason-Dixon line. The South had been provincial, even parochial, educationally and industrially backward, opposed to reform, and incurably romantic. All but the last of these qualities had to be drastically revised if the South was to grow along with the rest of the nation. That last quality, the South's romanticism, remained and proved to be the feature most attractive to film-makers for whom romance usually outweighed social and political implications.

Not everyone accepted *The Birth of a Nation* as a historically accurate documentation of the times. Those who complained, however, while vociferous enough to cause the President to recant his fulsome praise, were mostly either black or committed Abolitionists and their intervention was dismissed as inconsequential, or prejudiced, or both. For the majority, the film was taken as gospel. It was seen as true not because it delivered facts but because it showed the people what they wanted to believe and confirmed the nation's mistaken understanding of its own past. Inadvertently or not, D.W. Griffith had stumbled upon the public need to believe in legend.

Griffith based his film upon two books by the Rev. Thomas Dixon, *The*

Clansman (which title he used initially for the film) and *The Leopard's Spots*. He believed both books to be accurate, probably because they confirmed his own views, just as his film confirmed the beliefs of others. Seymour Stern, authorized biographer of Griffith, suggests that additional source material was drawn from documents on public record and from Woodrow Wilson's *History of the American People*, perhaps accounting for the President's conviction of the film's veracity.

After the film opened, Griffith decided to change its title from *The Clansman* to *The Birth of a Nation*, an action which simultaneously demonstrates his shrewd awareness of the significance of his film and of the era it depicted, and a sharp grasp of the commercial potential of the medium.

The film begins shortly before the Civil War and quickly establishes the main characters: the Stoneman family from the North and the Camerons from the South. The brotherhood implicit in the concept of nationhood towards which the states had striven for so long is underlined in the opening section of the film. The two Stoneman boys travel to the South where they spend time with the Cameron's sons with whom they form close ties.

In its next section, the film deals with the war between the states. The young men join their respective armies and two die – a Stoneman and a Cameron. Another Cameron, Ben (Henry B. Walthall), is wounded and sent to a Union hospital as a prisoner. There he meets Elsie Stoneman (Lillian Gish), a nurse, whose picture he had earlier admired. Then the war ends and President Lincoln (Joseph Henabery) is assassinated. Thus far, there is little cause for objection to Griffith's conception. Only carefully selected and limited aspects of the war are shown but this is a fair and reasonable condensation of events whose time span must inevitably exceed the narrative time span of the film.

What is less than acceptable is that the film makes no comment on the magnitude of this, the first 'modern' war. This was total war and the use of relatively sophisticated weapons helped bring about a death toll exceeding that which America was to suffer in both world wars. Neither are there any hints of the appalling individual acts of violence carried out by Union soldiers upon their Confederate cousins, both in and out of uniform, or those with which Johnny Reb retaliated. In Griffith's conception of the conflict there is no place for the Andersonville prisoner-of-war camp in which Union soldiers were treated in a manner which foreshadowed the horrors of Singapore's Changi jail in World War II.

A more serious omission, even within the necessarily limited framework of the film, is that there is never any real explanation of the reason for the war between the States. Slavery, a significant, if not the crucial factor, in the dissension between North and South, is barely touched upon.

The institution of slavery alone did not rive the Union apart. The North's rapid industrialization and economic growth, which swiftly left the agrarian South far behind, was a factor for dissent. Additionally, there was a growing determination among Northerners not to allow slavery to spread to the

Territories which would soon join the Union. If it did spread, the *status quo* which delicately balanced slave states and free states would be upset. Economics and political weighting, not moral values, were at the core of the dissension which led to war, yet none of this is clearly defined in the film.

It is when the film moves into its third section, the era of Reconstruction, that it graduates from the sins of omission and takes grave liberties with the truth, despite Griffith's claim to have been impartial in his dramatization of historical events. Even if it is allowed that Griffith's fictions are inadvertent, reality is further distorted by his prejudices.

During this section of *The Birth of a Nation* the story functions well, if predictably, on a personal level. Elsie Stoneman meets Ben once again while her brother Phil (Elmer Clifton) meets Margaret (Miriam Cooper), the Camerons' eldest daughter. Young love triumphs, if only temporarily, over immediate adversity. There may be nothing especially original in this thread of the story, but it is no less acceptable for that.

On the political level the film is much less satisfactory. The Hon. Austin Stoneman (Ralph Lewis) is a leading northern politician and a determined Abolitionist. He travels south to begin the process of Reconstruction which will lead to the restoration of the former Confederacy to full statehood. But Stoneman does not support the policies of the assassinated President. Forgiveness is not in his book. He is blindly indifferent to the carpet-baggers from the North who manipulate the elective process by encouraging newly-enfranchised blacks to vote for their puppets. Those blacks who continue to support their former masters and fail to vote as required by the carpet-baggers (men so rootless and shiftless that they can allegedly carry all their assets in a carpet-bag) are reviled and persecuted, sometimes killed, for their faithfulness to the planter aristocracy. The co-operative blacks also persecute the disenfranchised whites and when elected to the state legislatures behave like animals, or, at best, like primitive children. Socially, they are feared as potential rapists and, worse still in this racist lexicon, are shown to be actively intent on permanent miscegenation. Rape may be bad, but interracial marriage is a fate worse even than the fate worse than death.

To combat this threat to white womanhood, Ben Cameron decides to frighten off the blacks, who are shown as naturally childlike and superstitious, by dressing in a white hood and cloak. Thus his success endows the Ku Klux Klan with an air of chivalric nobility which is entirely artificial, whatever its apologists might say about the reasons for its first incarnation in 1866–7.

A major variation from the truth of Reconstruction comes in the film's depiction of how blacks acquired power. Recently freed and newly enfranchised former slaves were always very much in the grasp of white politicians, and not just those from the North. Southern political leaders, temporarily removed from office, never completely lost control.

Despite the continuing conflict between Americans from northern and southern states, the conditions imposed by the victors were extremely gener-

16

ous. The terms under which seceded states could re-enter the Union were anything but onerous and it was not long before white hands were once more, legitimately, holding the reins of power. Most southern states were back in the Union within a few short years, all within a decade. Once the states were re-admitted, the new leaders were found to be the same old political horse-traders as before and were again closely allied with the planter aristocracy. It was a simple matter for them to remove the blacks from their brief and illusory position of authority and to subjugate them once more. Blacks may have been freed from slavery but what followed was an appalling denial of their rights as human beings. Segregation and discrimination were imposed and underlined with violence and murder in order that the South could swiftly return to a condition as close as possible to that which had gone before.

The North chose not to interfere, thus highlighting the sham of proclaimed differences between the Union and the former Confederacy. With a few notable exceptions, many Northerners were akin to their Southern neighbours in their view that the condition of inferiority of blacks was not a matter of justice but was merely the natural order of things. Griffith does nothing to dispel this view and goes even further down the path of white supremacy; the blacks in *The Birth of a Nation* are not a lasting danger to the stability of the nation, nor are they detrimental to the conduct of the legislative process. Blacks threaten whites just by being black. In case any member of the audience is in any doubt, a title card flashes on to the screen a ringing declaration that the binding together of North and South is in 'common defence of their Aryan birthright'.

Griffith was far from unusual in his attitude towards the black man. Fear of dilution of the 'pure' blood of white people through miscegenation has been a fundamental preoccupation of racists and bigots throughout the history of white society from the moment of discovery that there existed such a seem-ingly alien thing as a non-white race. What is unfortunate about this common-place failing finding a home in Griffith's mind is that he was a film-maker of astonishing genius. Had he been a mere celluloid hack his personal prejudices would have been no more important than those of any backwoods redneck. But he was special, and as a result his prejudices were spectacularly reinforced by the breathtaking virtuosity of *The Birth of a Nation*.

The film is a brilliant synthesis of recently developed techniques and innovative ideas. Some of his techniques had been used before by other film-makers, but never to better effect. When Griffith brought his genius to bear upon these camera tricks they became something more than mere gimmickry and the overall effect was startling in its impact.

The nature of the audience for *The Birth of a Nation* and for other films of its time is important in assessing the measure of this impact. Many were poor and ill-educated (an unfortunate corollary both at the time and later). In major cities such as New York and Chicago a substantial portion of the average audience was made up of immigrants and their new, native-born families. Some immigrants even used silent-film title cards as a teaching-aid to learn the language of their new homeland. As already noted, they had little or no knowledge of America's past; no alternative concept of the nation's history jostled in their minds with the images on the screen. Few among these ill-educated masses chose to question the accuracy of what Griffith showed them.

Most important for the film's effect upon American audiences was the fact that it struck at nerves tautened by impending dangers from overseas and from within. Europe was sliding into a war which might soon draw in a reluctant America; there was trouble with Mexico; strikes disrupted the industrial expansion which was rushing the nation headlong into prosperity.

By 1915, the black problem had been buried for many years: not solved, not forgotten, just buried. The impact the film had on audiences showed that these other threats to the nation – distant wars and labour agitation – were but minor difficulties which created surface tensions. The real problem was the one few outside the South spoke of openly; *The Birth of a Nation* not only spoke openly but also loudly and authoritatively and provided an emotional catharsis for a nation's guilt at its concealed prejudices. It also provided support for those who believed that any action was justified if it seemed likely to lead to a situation in which the white race could be freed from fears of contamination.

Among these supposedly legitimate actions was tacit acceptance that lynching is a satisfactory means of maintaining racial superiority, purity and control. Such an argument is propounded in the contentious third section of the film. Herein, Stoneman's aide and friend, Silas Lynch (George Siegmann, who was also assistant director), a mulatto and by implication an evil man, is appointed lieutenant-governor and undertakes the task of causing blacks to rise up and take advantage of their new rights under Emancipation. Lynch tries to force Elsie into marriage while one of the Cameron girls, Flora (Mae Marsh), chooses suicide rather than face the sexual advances (here automatically interpreted as intended rape) from a renegade black, Gus (Walter Long). The Ku Klux Klan lynch Gus and generally set the South to rights; peace and harmony are thus restored. In Griffith's world this means that the blacks resume their proper place as a subjugated labour force and northern and southern whites intermarry to assure the continuation of national accord.

Apart from the few vociferous protestors, who included the NAACP (National Association for the Advancement of Coloured People), audiences did not question the implications of such assumptions. There was no reason why they should have done. Only a few years earlier the Jack Johnson race riots had resulted in violence, killings and blacks on the rampage. And lynchings were commonplace throughout the turn-of-the-century years. Between the end of Reconstruction and the release of *The Birth of a Nation*, a period of thirty-eight years, almost four thousand blacks were lynched in the South alone.

Any film which touched upon such topics was bound to have an impact upon

On the white cloak tails of Griffith's supposedly
noble gang (in *Birth of a Nation*) the real Klan
rose again.

audiences conditioned by life in American society; a film of the scope and imagination of *The Birth of a Nation*, could, and did, with its sweeping excitement and sustained power, sear receptive minds with certain attitudes and misconceptions that lasted a lifetime.

The film ran for a dozen years to ecstatic audiences in the South and the Ku Klux Klan, disbanded but not forgotten, rose again on the white cloak-tails of Ben Cameron and his friends. As historian Martin Simcovich has reported, Imperial Wizard of the Modern Klan William Joseph Simmons made his decision to reform the old Reconstruction Klan after reading the film's pre-release publicity. The film had opened in Los Angeles as *The Clansman*, then moved to New York in March 1915 under its new title. As publicity built towards the film's release in Atlanta, Georgia on 5 December 1915, Simmons revived the old order. He publicized his action in November and obtained a State Charter for the Klan on 4 December. Simmons was rewarded with a rush of people eager to join the Klan. Even if the film had been honest, this would have been deplorable. As the film is a mixture of misrepresentation, vicious prejudice and blatant lies, its effect upon public opinion and behaviour was even more reprehensible. However, the re-emergence of the Klan cannot be blamed upon the film alone; latent racism was there all along, needing just a spark to set it afire. This was what the film provided: the spark to re-ignite the Klan's fiery cross.

For blacks in the South, a revitalized Klan can have come as no surprise. They knew what was happening all around them. For a while it simply came out into the open, before going underground again. The Klan was then, and remains today (for there has been yet another public rebirth in the 1980s), a brutally racist organization with more kinship to European fascism than to the spirit of American democratic ideals.

Inevitably, all this colours the film beyond the point of endurance for today's filmgoers. It should be possible to step back from the film and look at it detachedly, ignoring evidence of Griffith's naiveties, his paternalism, and his bigotry. Sadly, the reality of life for many southern blacks, even in the 1980s, makes such detachment impossible.

Griffith was a Southerner who brought to his brain-child a considerable measure of the childhood conditioning which helped form his attitudes. His father served as a colonel in the Confederate army and was wounded in action. The young Griffith absorbed, and later mirrored, attitudes rife through-out the South.

If a determined effort is made to accept that he was a victim of the times in which he lived, that his views had been formed by a childhood environment over which he had no control, and if eyes and mind are closed to the worst excesses of *The Birth of a Nation*, it is just possible to avoid unjustifiably overlooking Griffith's undeniable genius as a film-maker – but how can *Gone with the Wind* (1939) be explained?

Made a generation later, David O. Selznick's film displays most of the

historical defects of Griffith's before it. True, the overt racism of this interpretation of the era is largely omitted, although the film has more than its
share of contented darkies singing happily in the fields as they toil away for Ol'
Massa. Like its predecessor, *Gone with the Wind* makes little or no attempt to
define the causes of the conflict. For a considerable part of its length, although
set against the savage backdrop of the war, it too is a saga or torn families and,
above all, a love story.

No member of the film's first audiences can have entertained any doubt that
this was its main thrust. The ballyhoo which surrounded the casting of Rhett
Butler (Clark Gable, always odds-on favourite) and Scarlett O'Hara (Vivien
Leigh, not even in the running until she was presented to Selznick) confirmed
that this was *the* love story to end them all. Even though filming began before
casting was complete, there was never any doubt that Rhett's and Scarlett's
love-affair would provide the solid core of the film. From the outset, historical
accuracy was doomed to a seat at the back of the wagon. Not that this
mattered very much to the audience for *Gone with the Wind*. They knew what
they wanted, and a history lesson was not it.

The horrors of the war itself appear with some measure of impact in the
later film much as they had in the earlier. The long and still impressive crane
shot of dead and dying soldiers at Atlanta station remains in the memory
(even though it fails to be reinforced by small-screen television showings). Yet
there is no sense of compassion accompanying the impression the scene makes
upon the mind. There is a degree of involvement in the scenes in the makeshift
hospital, but here the camera's concentration upon the principal characters
diminishes what could have been a powerful and moving account of the results
of the fighting upon the nation's young men. Nowhere does an injured,
maimed, or dead man receive the reverence afforded both visually and
musically to Scarlett's destroyed home.

As for the condition of the blacks, just as Griffith grossly distorted reality,
so Selznick patronizingly glamorizes the truth. (Selznick was, of course, the
producer of *Gone with the Wind*, but the circumstances of this film's making
the frequent departures of writers and directors, make this very much the
producer's rather than the director's film.) Selznick's blacks are 'real', in as
much as the actors in the roles really are black. Hattie McDaniel, who plays
the part of Scarlett's Mammy, became the first black recipient of an Oscar.
Undoubtedly there had been advances on Griffith's use of blacked-up whites,
but the treatment of the on-screen characters showed that in Hollywood, as
elsewhere in the country, little had changed in the intervening quarter-
century. America was still failing to respond in either letter or spirit to the
Emancipation Proclamation of Abraham Lincoln.

Gone with the Wind was not alone among films of its time in failing to
respond adequately to the reality of the black experience in the aftermath of
the Civil War. *Tennessee Johnson* (1943) tells the story of Lincoln's presidential successor and even before production began it ran into serious problems

from an increasingly vocal black community. The original screenplay showed Andrew Johnson as supportive of the infamous Black Codes, which did more than anything else to subjugate former slaves in the years following Emancipation. Johnson's opponent, Thaddeus Stevens, upon whom Griffith loosely modelled the character of Austin Stoneman in *The Birth of a Nation*, was shown not merely as a downright bad hat but also as a friend and probable aide to Lincoln's assassin, John Wilkes Booth.

In response to the outcry, the screenplay duly underwent a number of hasty rewrites which eliminated much of its offensiveness to blacks. What remains is a reasonably accurate impression of Andrew Johnson's life, with the central role extremely well played by Van Heflin. However, the film sank swiftly from sight and shows no sign of emerging from its obscurity.

Neither this film nor *The Birth of a Nation* nor *Gone with the Wind* reflects the reality of the treatment of blacks in American society. Where blacks appear their condition is subject to errors of facts, judgement and taste. In the manner in which the films of Griffith and Selznick amend historical fact to suit the required thrust of their story-telling, both show a blatant contempt for the truth about blacks.

Interestingly, if predictably, both films display a marked prejudice in favour of the South although very probably for different reasons. Griffith's film favours the South because he was a Southerner and the books upon which he based his story were strongly southern-orientated. Selznick's film was similarly based upon a South-favouring novel (Margaret Mitchell, the author, came from Atlanta); moreover, by 1939 film-makers were aware of their audiences' emotional leanings, and the romantic appeal of the South was undeniable.

The visible surface of the South was of courtliness, gentlemanly behaviour and deep-seated honour among men, which gave southern society a flair and charm not readily apparent in the industrialized North. Additionally, southern men were thought constantly to idealize and idolize women. This somewhat gilded view of the Southerner and the South had quickly become an established cinematic stereotype, just as the white colonaded mansions nestling 'midst magnolias, hooped skirts, tight breeches and exaggerated speech-patterns had. It was not Selznick's intention to shatter such mythic beliefs. The vicious bigotry of many Southerners, and the abject poverty in which many whites lived out their lives, often as deprived as the exploited and brutalized black slaves, could remain unexamined a while longer.

Although much more calculatedly commercial beneath its shell of big studio glossiness, *Gone with the Wind* is, however, the lesser culprit in regard to its failure to tell the truth, if only because it is much less concerned with the political aspects of Reconstruction.

The Birth of a Nation was a commercial gamble and an artistic *tour de force*, yet in its grossly racist view of the American Civil War and Reconstruction Griffith's film is diminished. Unquestionably, however, it belongs in an infinitely superior class to its successor when assessed on technical and purely filmic terms. As a direct result of its maker's breathtaking command of technique and its visual grandeur it became immeasurably influential. Until the film was released moving pictures were regarded by many as a cheap form of entertainment suitable only for the ill-educated masses and a grubbily inferior working-class alternative to the higher cultural form of the theatre (an attitude of mind still entrenched in both the USA and Britain).

Griffith's film transcended all that had gone before in the new medium and showed the middle class, the intellectual elite and those who governed that this particular form of popular entertainment was not only art but was also capable of influencing, if not actually changing, the way the people thought. *The Birth of a Nation* certainly did change attitudes towards films and set standards both for other film-makers and for audiences. The standards it set for film-makers were those of Griffith the artist; the standards set for the public were those of Griffith the racist.

By the time *Gone with the Wind* appeared Americans and the rest of the world had undergone almost a quarter-century of indoctrination at the hands of the makers of Hollywood's feature films. Even if *Gone with the Wind* had been a work of art it could not have had the impact of Griffith's film. As it was, a marvellous example of Hollywood superschlock, the public took it at face value and laughed and were thrilled and wept when cued by Max Steiner's music, but were not swayed. The Ku Klux Klan did not make an appearance in Selznick's film but even had it done so it seems unlikely that a resurgence of interest would have ensued. In 1939, black Americans were not regarded as the threat they had once been, and would become again, to white complacency. But if *Gone with the Wind* did not cause a positive shift in public attitudes and behaviour, it did serve to underline erroneous beliefs about the American Civil War and Reconstruction – beliefs that had been fixed in the minds of many by *The Birth of a Nation*.

The period of history dealt with by both films was not the beginning of America. Before the Civil War was a century of discovery and adventure, of revolution and commitment to democratic ideals. Before that had been an even longer period of exploration and settlement. Nevertheless, in many respects, Griffith's choice of title for his film was most apt. Modern America must owe much to every moment of its history, yet the conflict and transformation of the Civil War and Reconstruction was more important even than the work of either the Pilgrim or the Founding Fathers. The war rent the nation apart; Reconstruction began the healing process. Eventually, the repaired whole was stronger than the original and even though many of the nation's flaws were merely hidden beneath the surface, where they remain to this day, it truly was the time when the modern nation was born.

The accuracy of Griffith's title apart (and Selznick's too, for that matter), the nation's birth was dishonestly depicted. If Hollywood could deal so ruthlessly with the historical reality of such an important period in the nation's history, what hope was there for other, lesser, moments?

Not that Hollywood paid too much attention to what had gone before, apparently concluding intuitively that Columbus and his valiant and misunderstood efforts to find what lay over the edge of the world were not something out of which to fashion either an art form or a money-making business. Neither did the Pilgrim Fathers offer the stuff of which dreams are made. As for the Founding Fathers – too dull by half.

Nevertheless, these earlier times have attracted some film-makers, although not many have chosen to tell tales rooted in historical fact.

CHAPTER TWO

'. . . one of the rare men who succeed in becoming
great, without ceasing to be good.'
(Karl Marx writing about Abraham Lincoln)

To an uninvolved spectator obsession can be many things: inspiring, fascinating, exhilarating, irritating, tedious. If film-makers are to be believed,
Christopher Columbus, who was massively obsessed, was incredibly tedious.

Like many fifteenth-century navigators, Columbus was convinced that the
riches of the East could be reached by means other than a long and arduous
overland journey. Unlike his fellows, who were trying to find an eastward sea
route from Europe, he suggested sailing West. He made his suggestion to
John II, King of Portugal, in 1484 but after consideration his wild scheme was
discarded. Later, King John began seriously to reconsider the idea, but by
then Columbus had drifted away from Portugal. Then in 1487, Bartolomeu
Dias sailed far enough around the tip of Africa to raise hopes that an eastward
sea passage could be made. It no longer seemed necessary to put Columbus's
dangerous theory into practice.

Christopher Columbus (1948) was made by a British film company, the J.
Arthur Rank Organisation, with a Hollywood star of the first magnitude in the
title role. Yet despite Fredric March's powerful presence the film quickly runs
on to the rocks. Heavy on expository dialogue, the film does attempt to show
the background against which Columbus's obsession glowed, but of all the
qualities discernible in men in the grip of obsession, here tedium reigns.

The reason why Columbus had left Portugal was to hawk his theories
around the crowned heads of Europe, eventually ending up at the court of
Ferdinand and Isabella. They celebrated Spain's long-awaited victory over the
Moors by granting this ambitious visionary a chance to put his theory to the
test.

In 1492 Columbus set sail; he had three ships, money, the honorary rank of
Admiral, and he had also changed his name to Cristóbal Colón (from
Cristofero Colombo di Terrarossa).

Fortunately, grandiose ambition and arrogant belief in his own infallibility
were not Columbus's sole attributes. He was also a courageous man. He
needed courage, self-confidence and a measure of ingenuity to face down an
increasingly mutinous crew. Having made a fundamental error in his calcu-
lations (he believed the globe to be smaller than it is and hence distances

25

shorter than they are), he had to fake the log and lie to his crew about how far they had sailed.

Eventually, five weeks after leaving the Canaries, land was sighted. Columbus had done it: he had reached the Far East – or so he thought; in fact he had landed on an island in what later became known as the Bahamas. A few days later, when the explorer came ashore again, he believed he was on the mainland of Asia; in fact he was on Cuba. Despite later voyages to these and other islands, indeed to the very end of his life, Columbus believed he had discovered a new route to Asia. He never knew that he had touched the fringes of a New World. If he had sailed a few more miles and set foot on the mainland, America today might bear another name.

Even Amerigo Vespucci, after whom the new continent was named, had not discovered North America; his sightings were of what is known as South America. Setting aside, somewhat ungenerously perhaps, much earlier voyages by Scandinavians whose courage overshadows even that of their fifteenth-century successors, the first European to sight the North American mainland was the Englishman John Cabot in 1498.

All these and other voyages of exploration to the New World contain the ingredients necessary for stirring motion pictures: a determined hero who overcomes indifference and disbelief, sea voyages with all the attendant dangers of storms and recalcitrant crews, to say nothing of disease, followed by triumphant success and great riches. In the case of Columbus there were even such added dramatic elements as dishonour, imprisonment and a lonely, poverty-stricken death. Surprisingly, these explorers have received virtually no attention from makers of feature films even the most renowned adventurer of them all having to be feted, however unsatifactorily, by a non-American production.

Columbus, if his filmed story is believed, was a tough, single-minded eccentric, with a shaky grasp of mathematics and an inability to do anything very well apart from sail ships. Certainly, all this was true. His abilities on-shore were decidedly suspect, his mismanagement of affairs at the colony on Hispaniola leading to his being clapped in chains and hauled back to face the anger of the King and Queen of Spain.

But to achieve what he did, to venture where no European was known to have gone before, at a time when not all men had set aside fears that it was possible to sail off the edge of the world, suggests a man of considerable stature and imagination, even if he could not make that extra leap which would have allowed him to believe in the existence of a New World. He deserved a better fate than he received, either at the hands of Ferdinand and Isabella, who later relented and financed other voyages, or at the hands of the makers of *Christopher Columbus*.

A far greater omission by film-makers who have touched upon these times has been their disinclination to depict or even hint at the slaughter and plundering with which early European explorers and adventurers laid waste so much of Latin America.

Columbus was relatively harmless in this respect but his successors lay about them with appalling lack of concern for their fellow human beings in this New World. These are events which film-makers have chosen to ignore, perhaps because they are too massively infamous to depict on film, perhaps because it is something which Americans of European descent do not care to think about.

It was almost a century after Columbus that Europeans made a serious attempt at settling the New World. At first they were unsuccessful. The settlement at Roanoke in 1587 ended in the disappearance of the entire community. The next attempt, at Jamestown in 1607, was much more encouraging. This toehold on the vast, and at the time unimagined, continent, was touched upon in a feature film which dealt with the life and exploits, real and invented, of John Smith, an English adventurer. Unfortunately for anyone interested in life in this period, *John Smith and Pocohontas* (1953) is concerned primarily with Smith's love for an Indian maiden and takes as its source material the legend rather than the few known facts.

A few years later, in 1620, came the first of the great religious escapes from the Old World. The Pilgrims, who set sail from Plymouth in England, sought a land where the Church would be free from interference by government. A short stay in Holland had not proved entirely satisfactory as they did not want their descendants to grow up as anything other than English. To enjoy those two basic needs, religious freedom and the chance to remain English, it was necessary to travel to the New World.

Here again are strong elements to interest film-makers, but *Plymouth Adventure* (1952) concentrates its attention upon the captain of the ship rather than his passengers. The other aspects of the story are dealt with honestly enough but the characters, however impassioned they might be, come over as wild-eyed zealots. Additionally, with Spencer Tracy playing the leading role of the ship's captain attention is taken away from the men and women whose beliefs and hopes are the reason for the journey.

The subsequent arrival of the Puritans has been paid scant attention by feature film-makers, apart from those intent on parading exploitative tales of witchcraft in New England. Hollywood has never been comfortable with religion, especially in extreme forms. With few exceptions film-makers have leaned towards either tedious preaching or displays of devil worship, preferably laced with as much nudity as times have allowed. This is especially true of religion in New England, which has the dubious distinction of featuring frequently in contemporary porno movies.

As with Columbus, film-makers have been less than generous with these early settlers. Although firmly imprinted upon the minds of American schoolchildren, their story has failed to ignite imaginations in Hollywood – despite the fact that the first Americans showed, like Columbus, remarkable courage in facing up to unknown hazards in what cannot always have appeared to be truly a Promised Land.

The next century-and-a-half of America's early history has been sparsely treated by film-makers. The French and Indian War of 1754 and the growing conflict with England provides the setting for a number of films which are usually westerns in all but location. This war is touched upon in *Northwest Passage* (1940), which supports its main plot with the bloody activities of Rogers' Rangers, a guerilla band who massacre Indians while helping the regular British army dispose of the French. The main plot concerns the search for a north-west passage to serve as a trade route, but killing Indians is a patriotic sideline. The film is full of tough, gritty moments, and stars hard-bitten Spencer Tracy, but its morality is decidedly suspect. The massacre appears to have been inserted for dramatic effect and has an unsettling effect on present-day consciousness in the light of changed attitudes towards the Indian. Then, as later, the Indian was an obstacle in the white man's path and had to be removed as swiftly and often as violently as a fallen tree might be hacked aside. Although dubiously motivated, the killings shown here stay closer to the ruthless truth than many 7th Cavalry epics of the same era of film-making.

Conflict with the British prior to the Revolution has received rather more attention than other seventeenth- and eighteenth-century events, but few of the resulting films display many signs of attention to historical accuracy, or of profound thought. Fur-hatted John Wayne in *Allegheny Uprising* (1940) is not too dissimilar from the stetsoned Duke in the previous year's *Stagecoach* despite a century's difference in period. Neither are attitudes towards the Indian noticeably different.

Despite its general air of having been made hastily during a long weekend in Los Angeles' Griffith Park, *Allegheny Uprising* is very loosely based upon an insurrection in Pennsylvania in 1763. The dialogue, almost all of which is highly forgettable, includes a variation on the infamous General Sheridan statement, that the only good Indians are dead ones (this despite the fact that at the time in which the film is set the General had yet to be born). In later films, especially in the 1950s and 1960s, this line would usually be spoken by a villain; here it is spoken by one of the heroes.

Unlike most such films, and in particular the later westerns, *Allegheny Uprising* does at least make a token attempt at displaying the nationality-mix of these early years of the new nation's history; the line about dead Indians is delivered by English actor Wilfred Lawson in a somewhat shaky Scottish accent. Unfortunately for the overall effect, the Duke ignores such niceties and drawls his way through the script in his blithely customary fashion.

The Colonial period is also dealt with in *Fort Ti* (1953), a yawn-a-minute tale set around Fort Ticonderoga which even the new gimmick of 3-D could not save from deserved obscurity.

Sincere and well-meaning though it is, Disney's *A Light in the Forest* (1958) only flits across the surface of the complex relationships between the white settlers and the Indians of this same period.

Throughout these years the new nation, while still a British colony, was forming the attitudes which would later drive it to seek independence. In none of these films is there any clear indication of what was building in men's minds. A casual member of the audience could be excused for thinking that nothing happened in these times but a considerable amount of Indian killing interspersed with long moments of hard labour as log cabins were constructed ready for burning by the next batch of Indians.

The extensive settlement of the West Coast by the Spaniards is rarely touched upon in films. When it is, the form usually tells a straightforward adventure yarn set vaguely in the late seventeenth or early eighteenth century. These films are mostly forgettable if enjoyable romps through the Barbary Coast or sword-and-cape epics such as *The Mark of Zorro* (1920 and 1940).

The American Revolution and the War of Independence received rather more attention but film-makers have proved curiously unwilling to explore the full possibilities of this formative period in the nation's history. *The Scarlet Coat* (1955) deals with the story of Benedict Arnold while *Johnny Tremaine* (1957) takes a somewhat simplistic look at the War from the viewpoint of the younger generation. This is a Walt Disney film with high production values, and although there are signs of a serious attempt to retain historical accuracy the end result is curiously dispirited and, given the age of its cast and target audience, predictably unsophisticated.

Revolutionary times were examined by D.W. Griffith in *America* (1924) and by John Ford in *Drums Along the Mohawk* (1939). Griffith's film attempts to tell the entire story of the Revolution in as fair and unbiassed a manner as possible. The fact that the film was sponsored by the Daughters of the American Revolution probably gave him a few tricky moments but he overcame any obstacles placed in his way.

The film was banned for a time in Britain but was eventually admitted and enjoyed some success, albeit retitled *Love and Sacrifice*. The political complexities underlying the differences between the colonists and the agents of the British government are carefully delineated and it is clear that a serious attempt is being made to tell a faithful history.

Equally serious, if much more action-orientated, is Ford's *Drums Along the Mohawk*. The film uses as its basis a novel by Walter Edmonds which was meticulously researched, and its background and historical placement are impeccable. Necessarily, the novelists's preoccupation with veracity was bent a little to allow him to construct a coherent narrative. Equally necessary, if somewhat more ruthless, were the film-maker's changes. The producer, Darryl F. Zanuck, worried over the film for some time after he had bought the rights to the book. Some of his thoughts, captured in notes written during a script conference, show that he was concerned chiefly with retaining the spirit of the book, its characters and the period. If that was achieved, he considered, the book could and should be forgotten.

Although concerned with a novel, however factual it might be, and not with real history, Zanuck's comments clearly suggest the attitude of mind of film-makers of the period. Hollywood was in the business of providing entertainment, not education.

Between them, Zanuck and Ford certainly provided an entertaining film with *Drums Along the Mohawk*, but it is also largely successful in its attempt to show the reality of pioneer life and the struggles needed to establish a frontier community, even if the frontier of this period is no farther West than New York's Mohawk Valley. The conflict which develops between the agrarian communities of the region and the unreasonable behaviour of the far-distant British government is highlighted with the appearance of the combined forces of those pioneers who side with the Crown and the Indians. Pressure increases until the independently-minded settlers have no choice but to fight back. As far as the film is concerned, while tough and demanding and costly in terms of human life, property and progress, the fight is a relatively simple affair. The independents win the day against their British-backed former compatriots and the new nation is ready to be born.

In fact, the events upon which the novel was based were not so clear-cut and decisive. The colonist's struggles against the Indians and the British, both separately and as joint enemies, were much less clearly conclusive than displayed here. The struggle dragged on sporadically for several years and it was not until late in 1781 that the fighting, which had begun in the spring of 1775, finally ended. Obviously, events had to be foreshortened and crystal-lized for the film but in their over-simplification much coherence is lost and the reasons for the war are reduced almost to the level of resistance, by an already self-governing nation, to oppression from an alien regime. In a very real sense, the revolutionaries become a guerilla army fighting to establish rule by a Popular Front.

The role of the British in *Drums Along the Mohawk* is quite clearly that of double-dyed villains; so much so that the studio worried over the possibly detrimental effect it might have upon morale in Britain in the months immediately preceding the outbreak of World War II.

There is no indication in this film, nor in any film set in the era, that the various confederacies of Indian nations were very powerful and an important factor in the outcome of the war. If the confederacies had managed to avoid fighting among themselves and had remained steadfast in their alignment with the British, the outcome of the war might well have been different if only in its time-scale. Ford avoided cluttering up his narrative with any such suggestion, doubtless jointly motivated by a need for clear-cut, flowing action and realization that to hint at potential Indian superiority would detract from the undoubted courage and determination of the men and women of this pioneer community. In the central roles of Gil Martin and his wife Lana, Henry Fonda and Claudette Colbert conveyed this strength and spirit, even if they do manage to stay rather too neat and tidy most of the time.

This period of American history has received none of the attention it deserves. There is no equivalent to *The Birth of a Nation*, prejudices and all; neither is there a *Gone with the Wind*, with or without its false glitter. It is strange that film-makers have remained so detached from and uninterested in the moment of the true historical birth of the American nation.

The War of Independence over, this new nation was created on the American continent. The first of the truly great figures in American history had emerged before the War and rose to national prominence during it. After the War he became an internationally-known figure but Hollywood has shied away from making George Washington the subject of a major bio-pic. Washington's Secretary of the Treasury did receive the full treatment in *Alexander Hamilton* (1931), but the result was uninspired. Fiscal policies and problems are not the stuff of which gripping cinema is made, not without much melodramatic manipulation, and this film sticks reasonably close to the faintly dull truth. It is intensely patriotic, perhaps a much-needed quality at the time it was made, with the nation already deep into the Depression. Washington does appear in the film, of course, in the unlikely guise of Alan Mowbray. An Englishman who made a corner in playing butlers and diplomats, Mowbray was definitely not the heroic type, yet Hollywood used him as Washington on at least one other occasion.

One notable hero of the War who did receive the Hollywood treatment was John Paul Jones, but the result is a travesty of what is a fundamentally interesting life story. *John Paul Jones* (1959) appears to have begun with good intentions but somewhere along the way someone must have suffered from cold feet. An attempt at curing this affliction is made by an over-generous application of a remedy Hollywood has often used before and since: hiring a few stars for cameo roles.

In 1773 the intrepid Scots-born sailor, played by Robert Stack, inherits a Virginia plantation from his brother and has an unhappy love-affair with Dorothea Danders (Erin O'Brien). When war with the British breaks out he returns to the sea and is promptly sent to Europe. In Paris he meets Benjamin Franklin (Charles Coburn) and also a French lady named Aimée de Tellison (Marisa Pavan), with whom he falls in love. Marie-Antoinette (Susana Canales) is persuaded by Franklin and Aimée to give Jones command of a ship with which to fight the English.

His efforts to build an American navy are largely ignored by his government, which sends him to Russia where a predictably amorous Catherine the Great (an improbable role for Bette Davis) betrays more interest in his swordsmanship than in his seamanship.

Eventually, however, the good sailor convinces his government of the validity of his arguments and is allowed to lay the keel upon which will be built the future US Navy.

Turgid, and badly written, acted and directed, no one could have imagined any of this nonsense to be even faintly close to the truth – except that John Paul Jones really was a determined individual upon whose efforts the Navy was built. Like other important figures of this era, he deserves better.

By the dawn of the nineteenth century the American continent was being opened up, thus providing more scope for film-makers. Even so, Hollywood's enthusiasm for the period remained unfired.

At the time of Washington's inauguration as President less than 6 per cent of the population lived west of the Appalachian-Allegheny ranges. True, lands to the west were not all free and awaiting anyone who took the trouble to reach them. The western continental extremities were closed to the new American nation, with Mexico thrusting up into what are now the states of Texas, Nevada, Utah and California. The French held most of the Middle-West but surprisingly proposed selling the lot to President Jefferson's emissary in 1801. Robert Livingston, the American minister to France, wanted to buy New Orleans, through which much of the emerging nation's trade passed.

Instead of merely agreeing to sell New Orleans to the Americans, Napoleon also offered Louisiana, which he had only recently acquired from the Spanish. Napoleon's reasons lay in his forthcoming war with England: he foresaw difficulties in holding on to a territory far across the ocean, and he needed the asking price of 15 million dollars. Thus America acquired a tract of land which stretched northwards from the Gulf of Mexico to the Canadian border and which spanned the lands between the Mississippi and the Spanish-held territory on the West Coast. Into this vast, uncharted and sparsely populated region went the explorers and trappers. Both breeds of men needed to be extraordinarily tough in mind and body for the hardships which faced them.

The adventures they encountered during the early years of the nineteenth century contained all bar one of the ingredients film-makers need. The missing ingredient is the conflict generated between men, or between a man and a woman. These men, especially the mountain men, spent much of their life alone grimly surviving potentially lethal weather and terrain to trap animals for furs and occasionally to guide explorers and map-makers. Such tales clearly held much appeal for cinematographers and in the few instances when films of mountain men have been made it is the scenery which remains most in the mind. *Jeremiah Johnson* (1972), with Robert Redford, and *The Mountain Man* (1979), which stars Charlton Heston, are probably the best known and it is significant that they are films of the 1970s. To survive, the mountain men had to adopt Indian ways, which would have been an unthinkable admission for most earlier film-makers.

Similarly unacceptable to film-makers, and stars, of the past was the fact that the real mountain men were unkempt, unclean and generally unpleasant individuals who had to be all the things a big-name movie star is not in order to survive. John Colter, Jim Bridger, Hugh Glass and their fellows were hard-bitten characters with none of the finer qualities that separate the savage from so-called civilized man. As depicted by Heston and a somewhat too clean Redford, the movie mountain men are really pussycats deep down, while Colter, Glass and company were mean mountain-lion all the way through.

32

Explorers have had a similarly poor response from Hollywood, with the exception of Meriwether Lewis and William Clark, perhaps the most famous of all, who received recognition in *The Far Horizons* (1955). Their expedition of 1804–6 captured many imaginations, if not always to good effect. Some of the hardships they endured were severe enough to deter rather than inspire settlers from following in their tracks. Their story contained many of the elements of the rousing adventure enjoyed by the mountain men plus the bonus, as far as film-makers were concerned, of there being two of them. This allowed dialogue to be written and, unfortunately as it turned out, to be spoken. A further bonus was that they were acquainted with an Indian lady named Sacajwea, the Bird Woman, who was married to a French-Canadian trapper named Charbonneau. All this was enough to capture Hollywood's attention if not its imagination.

The script for *The Far Horizons*, which stars Fred MacMurray and Charlton Heston, is staggeringly inept but is, thankfully, rich in unintentional humour: 'Oh,' Lewis remarks to President Jefferson at one point in the proceedings, 'congratulations on the Louisiana Purchase.'

The war with Britain which began in 1812 is another early American conflict which has failed to spark much enthusiasm in Hollywood. There were, however, two bites at the same apple with *The Buccaneer* (1938 and 1958). Another film which took a simplistic look at the same events was *Mutiny* (1952), which settled for being an unpretentious maritime adventure yarn.

The maritime angle was paramount in both versions of *The Buccaneer* for, as its title suggests, the story concentrates on the role played in the Battle of New Orleans by the French-born pirate Jean Lafitte, portrayed by Yul Brynner (Fredric March having taken this role in the original). In terms of historical ambience, neither film offers too much to grumble at, although the physical appearance of Andrew Jackson in the remake is more than a trifle off-base. Charlton Heston's usual careful attention to detail slipped and, as he candidly recounted in his published journals, he based his make-up on Jackson's appearance in a portrait painted fourteen years after New Orleans. By the time the error was discovered it was too late to change and the film was stuck with a 46-year-old General who looks sixty. It was a strange mistake for Heston to have made as he had earlier played Jackson in *The President's Lady* (1953). In any event, it was a trifling matter when contrasted with the real-life disaster which resulted in the Battle of New Orleans being fought in January 1815, when, unknown to the participants, the war had ended the previous month.

Wound into the storyline of *The Buccaneer* is a love-affair between Lafitte and Annette Claiborne (Inger Stevens), who is the daughter of the Governor of Louisiana (E.G. Marshall). Inadvisedly, given his relationship with Annette, Lafitte scuttles a ship on which her sister is sailing and hangs the captain. The captain's daughter, Bonnie Brown (Claire Bloom), obviously the indecisive type, cannot decide whether to love or hate Lafitte for this. Later, after Lafitte has proudly told the British that he will not fight for them because he is a patriotic American, Andrew Jackson offers him a free pardon in exchange for his help in the defence of New Orleans.

Following various complications, including a narrowly avoided lynching, all of which owe almost nothing to reality and just about everything to an apparently desperate need to pump some romance into the tale, Lafitte gives up Annette, collects his pardon and, with his Bonnie, sails over the ocean.

At the end of the first quarter of the nineteenth century American thoughts were beginning to turn towards securing their part of the world against outside interference. In particular, they were concerned at possible intervention by European nations; this led to the establishment in American political thinking of the Monroe Doctrine, which regarded any non-American attempts at colonization in the Americas as a positive act of aggression against the United States. Although apparently arbitrary at the time, the principles involved have stood the test of time.

Although not directly a matter of application of the Monroe Doctrine, American sensitivity to outside interference in the Western Hemisphere prompted President Kennedy into acting over Cuba in 1963. President Reagan's response to the introduction of potentially discordant thinking in Grenada was similarly aligned with these principles, albeit an apparently massive overreaction.

At the time of President Monroe's declaration the problem was very clear. There were still non-Americans on the mainland and, worryingly, their spread was extensive. Mexico stretched high up into the lands north of the Rio Grande. Prominent in this vast region were the Texans, Americans living relatively amicably inside Mexico. Gradually, however, the Texans began to seek self-determination and this in turn worried the Mexicans. If Texas became independent it was inevitable, they rightly supposed, that annexation to the United States would follow. This would place a very large and almost impassable obstacle between the southern part of Mexico and those regions to the north of Texas which also came under Mexican rule.

In 1836 the Mexican General Santa Anna decided that the only way to prevent such problems was to nip in the bud any incipient revolution. He duly led a force of men northwards towards Texas where the independently-minded Americans were under the leadership of Stephen F. Austin. The Texans had originally held fast to a declaration to remain loyal to the Mexican constitution. Now Santa Anna was in the process of overthrowing this constitution and by March he was dictator of Mexico. The Texans decided they would no longer remain loyal, even to the old constitution. Now, nothing short of complete independence would do for them. Texas declared itself free and independent and, in expectation of trouble, the redoubtable Sam Houston was appointed commander-in-chief of the army.

The fighting spirit of the Texans had already made itself apparent four months earlier when they drove the Mexican army out of Gonzales. This was where Santa Anna intended restoring control of the region and he moved his army towards a small Texan garrison in a broken-down fort at San Antonio. The fort, in reality a lightly defended former mission, was named the Alamo.

The Alamo was then commanded by William B. Travis, who had with him less than 200 men – although some of them were sterling fighters such as James Bowie, J.B. Bonham and David Crockett. By the time the siege began, there were more than 3000 Mexican soldiers ranged outside.

Inevitably, the fort was taken but only at the cost of every American combatant. Elsewhere in the region, at Goliad, another battle was fought and once again overwhelming odds led to defeat for the Texans. This time many surrendered but almost all were subsequently massacred.

These two defeats, the high loss of life and the heroism displayed, especially at the Alamo, proved to be the spur which drove the Texans to ultimate victory.

The Mexicans had overwhelmed the Alamo on 6 March, the Goliad massacre took place on 27 March, but on 21 April Sam Houston attacked Santa Anna's army at Buffalo Bayou on the San Jacinto River. The Texans routed the Mexican army, every man was either killed or captured. Santa Anna himself was among the prisoners. The was was over and Texas was independent.

Perhaps more than any other incident in American military history, the Alamo is remembered with greatest pride although initially the response was one of acute anger. The cry 'Remember the Alamo!' was simultaneously a call for liberty and a cry for revenge. Hollywood could not have asked for a better story.

The Alamo has been touched upon in a number of films, among them *The Man from the Alamo* (1953), which bent reality in order to have as hero a man who had survived the battle. *Davy Crockett* (1955) was aimed at the adolescent market and proved a huge commercial success, as did its theme song, but this film concerned itself with Crockett as frontiersman and all-round hero rather than with examining the mythic stature he achieved through his death.

Few interpretations of Crockett portray him either as a loving family man or as a gently humorous individual, both of which he was. Similarly, his role as a political figure of no mean standing only rarely receives mention. When it does it is only in passing reference, not as a matter of any significance. Yet it was partly as a result of some disaffection with political and economic life back home that he decided to travel to Texas. Crockett had become a member of the state legislature in Tennessee and was later elected to Congress, but he subsequently fell out with President Andrew Jackson with whom he had fought in the War of 1812. This led to his defeat during a re-election campaign and it was then that he decided to head West. In Texas he hoped to develop his role in American political life and also make a few dollars in the expected boom.

The Last Command (1955) tells the story of Alamo victim Jim Bowie and his lethal hunting knife. *The First Texan* (1956) traces the life of Sam Houston with not too much concern for precise historical detail. All are adequate western fare but none is especially good. It was left to *The Alamo* (1960) to recount the saga in all its heroic detail.

It has long been a tradition of the British to turn defeats into victories and over the years the Americans have done the same with the Alamo. Perhaps predictably *The Alamo*, which was produced and directed by John Wayne as well as starring him as Davy Crockett, went over the top in a powerful display of all-American machismo. The film is sparing in its adjustments to historical reality, although any story about a group of men of whom none survive has to rely upon some measure of creative imagination.

At least one man is thought to have left the Alamo immediately prior to the Mexican attack. As recounted by Lon Tinkle in his study of these events, a certain Louis Moses Rose appears to have done exactly that. Given that Rose had been with Napoleon at Moscow, he must have had a remarkable instinct for survival.

With the sounding of the *deguello*, the bugle call which indicated that the Mexicans did not plan on taking any prisoners, the men at the Alamo knew what to expect. There were, however, about half a dozen women there, a few children and a couple of black servants. They were hidden in the chapel which also served as a hospital. Although this makeshift first-aid station also housed Jim Bowie, who had cracked several ribs trying to move a heavy gun into place, the Mexicans allowed the occupants to live – all except Bowie, who took more than a handful of Mexicans with him when he died.

Despite their survival, the women and children could not cast much light on events outside the chapel. For that a combination of eye-witness accounts from Mexicans, Travis's reports, which were written until shortly before the final assault took place, and some logical reconstruction has to be made. There can be no doubt that extraordinary heroism was displayed by every man at the Alamo.

With some of these provisions in mind, any screenplay of such an event has to be inventive but *The Alamo* appears to be reliable concerning personal relationships and behaviour during the siege and massacre. The changes that have been made are relatively trivial, yet the overriding air of the film is that if this were not a true story then nothing need be changed to make it into a typically unbelievable extravaganza of Hollywood super-heroics. The blame for this, if blame needs apportioning, lies primarily with John Wayne. By 1960 he was already an integrated part of the American West. He had seldom gone this far back into history, although he had appeared in the Revolution-era *Allegheny Uprising* (in which he wore a costume remarkably similar to the one he dons for *The Alamo*, although not quite as clean), but for the most part he stayed in the last quarter of the nineteenth century and became synonymous with The Cowboy. By starring himself in this film, Wayne unintentionally unbalanced the entire production. Audiences had already accepted him as

Supercowboy, yet here both they and Wayne himself have to contend with the fact that he is not John Wayne, the character he played in all his other films. Now he is Davy Crockett, a part of the nation's historical fabric. Wayne, the Great American Western Legend, confronts Crockett, the Great American Hero. Neither for the first nor the last time, Legend wins.

Minor errors abound in *The Alamo* but few really matter very much. Once Wayne had been cast as Crockett it was perhaps understandable that he should be given the task of blowing up the fort's ammunition supply by throwing himself, complete with flaming torch, into the arsenal. It was not Crockett who tried this, but Major Robert Evans – and he failed, being shot down before he could make it. It is not particularly important, this variation on reality, but there may be a kind of truth here. If John Wayne really had been at the Alamo *he* would not have failed to blow up the arsenal. But then, he probably would not have been defeated either, not by some old Mexican named Santy Anny.

Rather more than most modern nations, America appears to need its heroes. Hollywood has happily obliged, although in the case of Davy Crockett most of the work was done before film-makers came along. Some other individuals elevated to the role needed rather more effort but Hollywood was equal to the task. The same effort had to be applied to some events which were considerably less heroic than the Alamo.

The events immediately prior to the Civil War were picked up, looked at, shaken around quite a lot, then cobbled back together again in *Santa Fe Trail* (1940). This improbable saga centres upon Jeb Stuart (Errol Flynn) and George Armstrong Custer (Ronald Reagan) behaving heroically in Kansas to the general detriment of a demented John Brown (Raymond Massey) while various historic figures look on: Robert E. Lee (Moroni Olsen), James Longstreet (Frank Wilcox), Jefferson Davis (Erville Alderson), Phil Sheridan (David Bruce) and George Pickett (William Marshall). With so many names that have been drilled into the subconscious of Americans (and not a few which have entered minds farther afield), the film was bound to be thought truthful by audiences. It is not. Mostly inaccurate in matters of fact, on the few occasions when it does stick to the truth the hopelessly unbalanced atmosphere is laughable.

Custer is portrayed as a close friend of later Civil War hero Jeb Stuart when in fact they never met. West Point, where they are shown together, must have excelled itself that year if Hollywood is to be believed. In one class are Custer, Stuart, Sheridan, Longstreet, Pickett and Hood – every one made general before his career was over.

Although such adjustment of historical fact irritates it does not do very much harm. Some matters, while not actually harmful are unnecessarily mischievous: the vilification of John Brown, for example. On his death someone remarks, 'So perish all such enemies of the Union', which is curious given that much of what Brown advocated was later carried out by Abraham

Lincoln. A contemporary would not have known that, of course, but it is not enough to say that it is consequently legitimate for him to speak in this way. The line has about it the clear ring of a scriptwriter needing to justify his vilification of a man who was nowhere nearly as black, or as crazy, as he was so often painted.

John Brown as wide-eyed, grey-bearded loony is a long time dying. He was still being represented in this way as late as 1971 in *The Skin Game*, a film which otherwise had merit in bringing something of the reality of slavery into what was essentially a comedy-western. This contrasts sharply with *Santa Fe Trail*, in which there is a black family who aver a preference for slavery over the kind of freedom John Brown is offering.

Occasionally sequences in *Santa Fe Trail* are factually correct: Lee tackling Brown at Harper's Ferry and Stuart conferring with Brown under a white flag are two such instances. But the overall air created by the film generates disbelief that such inaccuracies could have been foisted upon a public remarkably well informed about this particular period in its history.

Although secondary to Stuart here, Custer is a character to whom Hollywood has regularly turned, mostly in connection with his post-war activities, as will emerge in a later chapter.

If the legends of Davy Crockett and George Custer proved to be simultaneously attractive and liberally scattered with problems for film-makers, much more difficult was the story of that great and noble legend Abraham Lincoln.

Apart from turning up occasionally as a peripheral character, he was the subject of three major biographical films. *Abraham Lincoln* (1930) was directed by D. W. Griffith and starred Walter Huston in the title role. *Abe Lincoln in Illinois* (1940) was based upon Robert Sherwood's stage play and stars Raymond Massey. In *Young Mr Lincoln* (1939) the great man is portrayed by Henry Fonda.

Although perhaps the least of the three in terms of its script and central performance (Huston was excellent, Massey unforgettable) it is *Young Mr Lincoln* which has gained most favour with audiences and scholars (of both film and history). This may well be due to the fact that it was directed by John Ford in the midst of a great run of fine films. In the same year he directed *Stagecoach* and *Drums Along the Mohawk*, and the following year *The Grapes of Wrath*.

The historical accuracy of the Ford-Fonda portrait of the Great Emancipator's early life does nothing that is noticeably unfaithful (dare any film-maker, even in the iconoclastic 1980s, tamper with this particular giant?), but the historical veracity of the film is undermined by the degree to which the film-maker has assumed the audience's knowledge of the main character's life, both at the times depicted and in later years. It is in this second assumption, that the audience knows what is to become of Lincoln, that the film is most unsettling.

The director regularly makes use of a dual-audience device by having Lincoln address groups of people: gathered at his home, in the town store, in the court-room. Lincoln thus addresses his immediate audience and, through and beyond them, the audience for the film. The words he speaks, however, have a very different effect upon these two audiences.

At his first such speech he declares, 'Gentlemen and fellow citizens, I presume you all know who I am. I'm plain Abraham Lincoln. My politics are short and sweet, like an old woman's dance.' The audience in the film believes he speaks literally, he *is* just plain Abe Lincoln; the audience for the film understands much more. They know what he will become, they know that he is not just plain Abe. He is the nation's greatest man, albeit still in embryo. There is, therefore, a deeper political and philosophical message implicit in words and actions at all times which cannot be ignored. Indeed, the audience (for the film) is not expected to overlook them. The film-maker's intention is that this secondary layer of understanding should be incorporated into the images on the screen. This even extends to the choice of Henry Fonda for the leading role. Certain screen actors bring with them particular political and sociological preconceptions which audiences cannot fail to pick up. John Wayne is a patriotic extremist; Henry Fonda a liberal. Even if this patina was not fully formed at the time Fonda made *Young Mr Lincoln*, subsequent viewings are consequently affected. The combination of Fonda portraying Lincoln is highly potent and no member of the audience can fail to respond appropriately.

Among the problems of the film is the absence of any clear understanding of what motivated the young man into taking his chosen course through life. What little motivation is shown quickly fades, to be replaced by a vaguely-outlined form of divine intention.

At his first appearance Lincoln is already a political figure but we are never too sure what it is he is campaigning for. Politics, it seems, are just a means of attaining his later role as his nation's mystical leader. The nuts and bolts of his political philosophy are not shown; the audience is not allowed to examine them and make up its own mind as to their worth. The fact that he became what he did is assumed to be enough. If *that* is so, Ford appears to say, then his politics must have been right from the start.

Unfortunately for the strength of the film, this failure to offer up Lincoln's politics for examination means that the mental processes by which he moved towards the concept of emancipation are not shown. The question of slavery is almost completely absent from the film, the only reference coming in a scene in which Lincoln the lawyer explains why a poor white man might have felt obliged to leave home in order to escape an even greater poverty, inflicted as a result of the arrival of black slave labour.

The way in which slavery should be treated also caused problems in Griffith's *Abraham Lincoln*. The opening sequences show the crew of a slaver in the notorious Middle Passage throwing overboard the dead body of a man fortunate not to live long enough to have to suffer a lifetime of slavery in the bright New World. There are few attempts later in the film to relate this grim moment to the philosophical purpose of the adult Lincoln.

Young Mr Lincoln, while sticking close to historical reality, underlines and even extends the myth by confirming Lincoln's predestination. Yet this is a quality which became apparent only after the event; predestination before the event is nothing more than hope or ambition. After the event, with a little juggling, most human activities can be made to seem pre-ordained. It is at best unfortunate that a man of such extraordinary gifts, such single-minded devotion to high ideals, such strength of character and determination, should have all his success attributed to nothing more than predestination. The implication is that it really did not have very much to do with him. Was he really just an earthly receptacle for some heaven-sent gift of the gods? Didn't the man, the real Mr Lincoln, have any part to play in his own destiny?

The real man does get a chance to emerge above the legend in some passages of *Young Mr Lincoln*, most particularly in his relationship with Ann Rutledge (Pauline Moore), whose death simultaneously marks him as tragic hero and underlines his almost monastic simplicity. His subsequent marriage to Mary Todd (Marjorie Weaver) is thus clearly defined as second best, a pragmatic decision to settle for the attainable because his one true love was now out of reach. Certainly, this film shows Ann to be the only person with whom Lincoln can hold a conversation without it turning into a speech, even though some of these are really monologues which he addresses to her grave. It is in such moments that something of the man begins to emerge from behind the legend that Ford's film never questions.

More than any other American, Abraham Lincoln was deeply and passionately concerned with the problems of national identity and the need for maintaining and strengthening the Union. He believed that his destiny was inextricably bound up with that of the nation and that it was his mission to ensure that the Union would prevail. Even the Civil War, which must surely have torn him emotionally and spiritually, was seen by him as a test of the strength of the ideals of the Founding Fathers.

The definitive film about Abraham Lincoln, especially in regard to his attitude towards slavery and the role of blacks in American society, has yet to be made. Perhaps film-makers have been put off by the complexities of both the issues and the man. Certainly, his response to slavery was anything but simple and underwent one major reversal. At one point, he had been prepared to look aside from slavery and permit its existence in the South if to do so meant preservation of the Union. At this time he held that the principle of slavery was wrong but he was not prepared to risk the Union by asserting his opposition. When the Civil War came he gradually shifted his stance. Although previously ambivalent towards the Abolitionists, he was determinedly against extending slavery into the territories which had yet to become states of the Union. However, he held that the states should make their own plans for emancipation, which he must have known some would never do. For slave-owners obliged to give up slaves he offered compensation, and he suggested Federal aid should be granted to former slave states. At all times, until forced into military necessity, he believed in a softly-softly approach to the problem. Even when he had moved towards complete abolition of slavery, he never accepted the principle of an integrated society. Rather, he retained some of his earlier ambivalence and looked forward to seeing blacks depart to form new colonies on other continents – a form of repatriation.

Perhaps the problem for film-makers lies in the mythology which has grown up around Lincoln since his law-partner biographer helped begin the process. It is strange that film-makers, who have readily taken on the task of debunking latterday notable figures in the nation's history, have not chosen to look closely at Lincoln. In his case, they are unlikely to find any serious flaws but the exercise could prove interesting if only in highlighting those of Lincoln's qualities which have been so sadly missing in his successors.

Although the question of slavery played only a limited part in any of the Lincoln films, it formed the *raison d'être* for television's *Roots* (1977). Certain aspects of Alex Haley's search for his origins were subsequently questioned but none can deny the powerful impact this series had upon audiences, especially in America. Perhaps as part of the continuing refusal of man to think about those things he deems unthinkable, white Americans reacted to *Roots* as if they had never suspected the existence of anything like this in their shared past. (German audiences displayed similar responses on seeing film and television versions of the slaughter of the Jews in World War II.)

While black Americans had never forgotten, *Roots* managed to show to whites not only what their forebears had done but also to demonstrate why blacks could not forget. Whether the series changed anyone is unknown; but it did make people think about facts they had hitherto chosen to ignore. If it did nothing more, *Roots* thus served a great purpose. That it created such an impact is an indictment of the preceding three-quarters of a century of film-making which had failed to tell the truth about slavery. That *Roots* was made at all suggests that in this respect at least, American television has a moral edge over Hollywood.

That it *needed* to be made suggests that America still has a long way to go in its internal race relations before the nation can expect to fulfil the dreams and hopes of Abraham Lincoln.

CHAPTER THREE

'The truth is what gets the most applause.'
(from *Buffalo Bill and the Indians*)

Despite the wide-open spaces there is often a strangely constricted air about Hollywood's West: most films are set between 1865 and 1890, before John Ford most look as if they were made in Griffith Park (after Ford all appear to be have been located in Monument Valley, even if they were not), and most storylines are concerned centrally with the Outlaw and the Lawman – oh, yes, and Indians.

The role of the native American in feature films has been an unhappy one. True, there have been occasional attempts to show an image other than that of the unspeakably sadistic, painted savage, but most have failed.

Film-makers have seldom troubled to display the reality of the sociological structure of the Indian nations, let alone attempted to depict honestly their tragic role in American history. Even the rush of pro-Indian movies in the 1950s owes more to guilt-purging than any desire to be truthful.

Not that any of this is an original failing of Hollywood's. The myth of the Indian, together with those of the Outlaw and the Lawman, owes its origins to a preceding barrage of pulp fiction. These fictions were based in their turn upon a highly dubious social history and grossly misleading military records. In the case of the Indians, these falsifications served a positive purpose for the white man. The Indian had to be a brutal savage, intent on rape, murder and mutilation, a creature less than human and with no saving graces. He *had* to be, otherwise what reason did the white man have for the relocations, incarcerations and massacres he inflicted?

Not every early film which depicts the Indian follows this pattern, although in most he is an all-purpose baddie, who simultaneously adds a touch of exotica to the background. During the 1920s occasional efforts were made at giving the Indian a more sympathetic appearance. Most notable of these 'noble savage' films is *Ramona*, which was re-made in 1928 having already appeared in three earlier versions (and it was to appear yet again in 1936), *Laughing Boy* (1929) and *The Vanishing American* (1925), which was also unusual in being set in the twentieth century, with the central character returning from World War I to confront the contemporary problems facing his people. However well-intentioned, and undoubtedly it was that, today *The Vanishing American* can be seen to contain elements of racism. The film-maker, although clearly saddened by the thought, obviously believes that the white man is superior and must therefore replace the Indian. Despite such failings, when set against the standards of the day the film is a notable landmark, throwing into harsh relief the countless travesties with which it was surrounded and by which it would be followed for the next quarter-century. The film's serious purpose was undermined by the decision to cast Richard Dix in the central role, an unfortunate precedent for the pro-Indian films which began in the 1950s. They did not star real Indians either.

In this later cycle the fact that the audience was meant to sympathize and even identify with the Indian was hammered home by the casting of such non-Indian box-office attractions as Jeff Chandler, Burt Lancaster, Chuck Connors, Anthony Quinn and Rock Hudson. Sympathetic Indian maidens were similarly cast in order to set up a predictable response. Jean Peters, Audrey Hepburn, Paulette Goddard and Loretta Young all played such parts, while Debra Paget built a career on them.

The storylines for this cycle were often spun around real-life Indians or events in Indian history: Cochise, Sitting Bull, Geronimo, the massacres at Sand Creek, Washita and Wounded Knee all came in for treatment of one kind or another but rarely with either sympathy or perception.

During this period, and before and since, most real-life Indians and Indian-orientated events were built into stories whose main thrust concerned non-Indians. Several of these films centred upon two heroes of the mythic West for whom reality and legend are hopelessly intertwined in film and real life: George Armstrong Custer and Buffalo Bill Cody.

Custer has been a main character in an inordinate number of films. As mentioned in an earlier chapter, he featured peripherally in *Santa Fe Trail*. Similarly peripheral was Custer's appearance in *Little Big Man* (1970), although by then his image had undergone a marked change. Initially Custer was falsified as a great national hero; later he was equally falsified as a vicious villain. Neither version tells the whole truth.

The fascination with Custer, who led a battalion of two hundred men to bloody and unnecessary death at the Battle of Little Big Horn, can be most readily and logically explained as another piece of psychological blame-shifting. If Custer can be proved to be a man of honour misled by venal superiors (earlier films) or to be a psychopath with a homicidal hatred of Indians (later films) then it is easy to conclude that his activities against the Indians were at best a mistake or at worst an act for which neither the US Army nor the Government can be held responsible.

The Custer of fact was a West Point graduate of 1861 who ended the Civil War as brevet major-general. After the war, and having transferred from the volunteers to the regulars (with a corresponding drop in rank), he established a reputation as a harsh disciplinarian. Narrowly avoiding dismissal for the manner in which he treated his own men, Custer, now a lieutenant-colonel, was put in charge of the newly established 7th Cavalry.

In November 1868 he and his men attacked a group of peaceful Cheyenne camped on the banks of the Washita. In the next few hours Custer and the 7th carried out an orgy of killing at the end of which 11 warriors and 92 women and children were dead. A further 53 women and children were taken prisoner and the Indians' pony herd, estimated at more than 600 animals, was slaughtered. Custer's actions were in response to clear and specific orders from General Sheridan, who had by then delivered his infamous statement that the only good Indians were dead ones. Sheridan publicly glorified Custer after the Washita massacre, which was thus transformed into a courageous military operation.

The chief of this particular group of Cheyenne, Black Kettle, was one of the few survivors of the Sand Creek Massacre which had taken place almost exactly four years earlier, on 28 November 1864. On that occasion the perpetrators were 'Colonel' Chivington and his Colorado Cavalry. Chivington was a Methodist preacher and his men were civilian volunteers of dubious morals and reputation. Court-martialled for the atrocities committed at Sand Creek, Chivington was acquitted but relieved of his command. The Sand Creek Massacre formed the gruesome climax to the film *Soldier Blue* (1970), in which Chivington was renamed Iverson.

The total number of Indian dead at Sand Creek was about the same as at the later Washita massacre: 28 men and 105 women and children. It was, however, much bloodier, and Indians were mutilated both before and after death, a commonplace occurrence. Only 7 prisoners were taken. The army lost 9 men at Sand Creek, as against 21 at Washita. For Black Kettle, the Washita replay of Sand Creek held one major difference. This time, he did not survive.

By the peculiar standards of the day the Washita massacre made Custer's name, but clearly he was only one of many who treated Indians brutally. The orders under which he acted show a clear line of descent from the kind of thinking that had motivated Chivington. The Indian was still an obstacle in the way of the white man's advance. Civilization would not be halted, even if it took genocide to clear the way. But Custer was not a mindless cog hiding behind the soldier's last resort of 'just obeying orders'. He was well aware of the benefits to be gained from fame. He had ambitions, both political and commercial. Politically, he hoped to gain the nomination of the Democrats at the National Convention. Commercially, he was acutely aware of the mineral deposits beneath the lands occupied by the Indian and had begun taking steps to ensure he acquired an adequate share.

When, in June 1876, he had an opportunity to further his career by confronting the Cheyenne and Sioux massed on the banks of Little Big Horn he knew it was too good to miss.

Unfortunately for Custer, his intelligence was faulty: the information upon which he based his plans suggested that only a small number of Indians were present, and there was no suggestion that many of them were fighting men. Undoubtedly Custer thought he was approaching another Washita: a few warriors, women and children, all blithely unaware of his intentions. He was wrong on all counts.

As a result of his misunderstanding of what lay ahead he split his men into three groups. He took one battalion, which numbered 201 men and scouts, directly into the camp; the other battalions took the wings. All but one of Custer's men, a Crow scout, were killed. The other battalions were pinned down and although they lost comparatively few men, 36 and 11 respectively with perhaps a further 60 wounded, they were unable to help Custer.

The Cheyenne and Sioux, who were gathered under the political leadership of Sitting Bull and who had many notable war chiefs including Gall, Two Moon and Crazy Horse, numbered about 6,000. They lost only 33 men.

Unfortunately for the Indians, they lost much more than a handful of men by defeating Custer. All memories of Sand Creek and Washita, and any justification those events might have given the Indian, were forgotten by white Americans. The deaths of Custer and his men, immediately termed a massacre by the East Coast press for whom semantics was a way of concealing what was really being done to the Indian, brought more than anger and indignation: righteous fury was the overriding emotion. Any subsequent confrontations during the next fourteen years, until the massacre at Wounded Knee in 1890, were tacitly accepted as justifiable genocide.

The character of Custer on-screen has varied considerably over the years. The Custer of Ronald Reagan in *Santa Fe Trail* is a mild-mannered, amiable young man who is a patriot and a good soldier. As the film ends with the outbreak of the Civil War, his attitude towards the Indian is never displayed.

When the same studio, Warner's, made *They Died With Their Boots On* (1941) only one year after *Santa Fe Trail* a very different Custer emerges. This was due in considerable part to the actor chosen for the role. Errol Flynn, who had played Jeb Stuart in the earlier film, stars, and his Custer is a development of the swashbuckling, light-hearted adventurer he had established in various costume dramas including the excellent, if historically hopeless, *Adventures of Robin Hood* (1938). Flynn's Custer is everything any young boy could aspire to: noble, heroic, dashing, without a drop of homicidal intent or venal ambition in him. His defeat and death are a result of bad luck and political chicanery in which he has no part. Essentially, the film is a *Boy's Own Paper* adventure yarn set in an Old West which also owes its origins to the comic books.

The Little Big Horn débâcle is given a somewhat more realistic treatment in the fictional rendition depicted in *Fort Apache* (1948). Here, renamed Colonel Thursday and portrayed by Henry Fonda, Custer is an arrogant individual with the unqualified conviction that the Indian must be destroyed to permit mankind to progress. In this context, mankind begins and ends with the whites. Although men like Sheridan and Chivington undoubtedly thought this way, Custer's motivation was much less overtly genocidal. He was driven by the profit motive.

By its title, *Custer of the West* (1968) suggests a broader canvas upon which the film's hero is to be strategically placed. From being a relatively minor figure in the US Army, albeit one venerated by many who read of his exploits in the contemporary press, he has here become a part of the greater myth of the West. Nevertheless this version of events, despite the involvment of the director Robert Siodmak (making his last film) and its Super Technirama 70 format, has no more respect for the truth and is clearly aimed at an audience which neither knows nor cares about reality.

By the time of *Little Big Man* Custer had been sufficiently tarnished in the public's mind to qualify for treatment as a homicidal maniac. Thus, despite a sympathetic view of the Washita massacre, the end result falls in line with the view that it was not the American people who were responsible for the slaughter of the Indian nations, it was just a handful of lunatics of whom Custer is a conveniently well-known example.

Even more mythic than Custer is Buffalo Bill. Indeed, perhaps more than any other figure of the American West it is he who is most inextricably bound up in a confusing mass of contradictory information. Long before the movies took him up as a suitably heroic figure for further manipulation, he had been reconstructed through the pulp fiction of several writers beginning with the astonishingly prolific Ned Buntline.

William Frederick Cody gained his nickname while working as a hunter with the Kansas Pacific Railroad. Perhaps 'hunter' is a misleading term with which to describe the men who slaughtered millions of buffalo with no regard for either conservation or the Indians who depended so much upon these animals. Cody once managed to kill 69 in a day, thus qualifying for the nickname of Buffalo Bill.

Later, while working as an army scout, Cody struck lucky. The company commander, Major Frank North, was a self-effacing man and when the well-known writer Ed Judson, who used the pen-name Ned Buntline, wanted to write a dramatic story about him he refused. Instead, North suggested that Buntline should write about Cody. Buntline did so, with Cody's idly unconcerned approval.

The resulting story was the first of hundreds of similar tales which seized the imagination of the public. These tales owed everything to the imaginations of Buntline and his successors, which proved to be even more eager and as readily inflamed as the public's. They owed absolutely nothing to the reality of Cody's very ordinary existence.

The stories were so successful, however, that Cody found himself in great demand and quickly realized that he must dress and act the part: that is, he had to dress and act the way the stories claimed he did. Cody's involvement with these fictions was so thorough that when a Buntline story was made into a stage play the hero was played by none other than Buffalo Bill himself. At one point Cody broke away from showbiz in order to take up Indian fighting once more, this time allegedly contriving to kill Yellow Hand at War Bonnet Creek while dressed, however improbably, in the costume he wore for his show.

Buffalo Bill's Wild West Shows were a popular attraction throughout America and in Europe, but from being a millionaire at the beginning of the 1890s Cody was reduced to bankruptcy by 1913. His show, which had become a joint venture with Pawnee Bill Lillie, had to be sold. Buffalo Bill, by now with his veins full of the spirit of showbiz, took what little money he had saved from the wreckage and did what any self-respecting Indian fighter-turned-showman would have done at this point in the nation's history: he went into the motion picture business.

It is to Buffalo Bill's everlasting credit that his first film venture was an attempt to depict events at Wounded Knee with a reasonable degree of accuracy. Unfortunately, as Kevin Brownlow has reported, after a limited number of showings the film vanished into the archives of the Bureau of Indian Affairs. Perhaps 1913, only twenty-three years after the event, was too soon for the truth to be told.

The complexities of Buffalo Bill's life, the consistent intermingling of myth and reality which took place even while the man himself was still alive and for which he must take a considerable measure of responsibility, were displayed in all their hopeless confusion in *Buffalo Bill and the Indians, or Sitting Bull's History Lesson* (1976). Starring Paul Newman as Bill and with a tacit, senile Sitting Bull (Frank Kaquitts), the film was based upon Arthur Kopit's stage play which set out to make its audience aware of the reality of the horrors inflicted upon the Indian through the device of having Bill slowly accept the same truth, and simultaneously reveal truths about Vietnam.

The intertwining of different strands of fiction – dime novels, the Wild West Shows, theatre, and, eventually, fiction in the form of film – completely overwhelms any vestige of the truth that might have been left at the end of the last century. What remains, however, is enough of the reality of the differences between the white man and the Indian to show that there never was any chance for co-existence. Conflict was inevitable and given the nature of the two sides, so too was the eventual outcome.

Buffalo Bill and the Indians was directed by Robert Altman and through its deliberate use of the Wild West Show as a setting, complete with an audience determined to be entertained and not educated, and with a fictitious Indian, William Halsey (Will Sampson), and Ned Buntline (Burt Lancaster) himself as interlocutors, the film makes no pretence at separating truth from legend. Equally, however, it underlines the impossibility of transmuting the legend that already exists into anything approaching the truth. And, anyway, as Buffalo Bill observes in the film, 'The truth is what gets the most applause.'

Although the Vietnam allegory vanished during transition to the screen, Altman's version of the legend is harder-edged than any other filmed attempt but for all that he cannot approach any closer to the truth than could the makers of *Buffalo Bill* (1944), in which Joel McCrae plays the character as a thoroughly romantic hero. But Altman's version succeeds in spite of itself because it knows it must fail. While not making a virtue of failure it implies that its inability to discover the truth beneath the many layers of fiction is in itself a form of the truth. This truth is that there never was any substance to the legend.

Although the common enemy in the Custer and Buffalo Bill films is the Indian, in most of these sagas he is very little advanced from the all-purpose baddie with whom film-makers peopled many a B-western throughout the 1930s and early 1940s.

The native American, the Injun of countless horse-operas, was unalterably transformed by Hollywood. From a natural man living in close harmony with the land, which he regarded as holy, and for the most part leading a peaceful nomadic life, he became a wild, painted, untamable savage. In showing the Indian in this light, however, Hollywood was not creating a false image out of its own imagination, any more than it had done with Custer and Buffalo Bill. In this instance Hollywood perpetuated a myth already created by land speculators, the US Government, and anyone for whom the Indian represented an obstacle in the way of achieving the American Dream. He could and would be moved, by force if necessary. Inevitably, force did become necessary and any extremes thought desirable by the authorities of the day were sanctioned, sometimes unofficially but all too often with official approval and participation.

As described earlier, when the time came for Hollywood to make amends to the Indian it did so by allowing its most glamorous stars to play Indian roles. That none of these actors was Indian seemed not to matter – it was the thought that counted, even if the thought did contain undertones of paternalism and prejudice.

A few real Indians had begun making appearances in films. Will Sampson in *Buffalo Bill and the Indians* is one; Chief Dan George is another. He played to good effect in *Little Big Man* and delivered a delightfully camp performance which effectively upstaged Clint Eastwood in *The Outlaw Josey Wales* (1976). Iron Eyes Cody has made numerous films and in *Sitting Bull* (1954) played the part of Crazy Horse, the great Sioux warrior (despite being a Cherokee). Even if film-makers were trying to rise above the level of 'the only good Indian is a dead one' they had not yet passed the point of 'all Indians look alike'. The title role in *Sitting Bull* went to J. Carrol Naish, who comfortably added an Indian to his endless gallery of Arabs and Orientals. He was, in fact, of Irish descent. That was only one of several adjustments made to reality in this film. Presumably out of a need for a serious political statement, the film has Sitting Bull meet President Grant. In fact he did nothing of the sort. Immediately after the Little Big Horn battle the Chief set out for Canada in fear of reprisal. Later he was tempted back with the offer of a pardon. He should have known better; the white man, long expert at breaking his word and his treaties, clapped him in prison.

Even movies set in recent times have suffered from the unwillingness of film-makers to look for Indian actors. *Jim Thorpe, All-American* (1951) stars Burt Lancaster as the Indian who was America's greatest-ever all-round athlete. He won Olympic gold medals in both the pentathlon and decathlon in the 1912 Helsinki Games before being stripped of his honours for having once played professional baseball. Ira Hayes, a hero of Iwo Jima in World War II, has been the subject of two films; in one he was played by Tony Curtis, in the other by Lee Marvin.

The comparative successes of men like Iron Eyes Cody, Chief Dan George and Will Sampson are certainly steps in the right direction, however uncertain and inconclusive they might be. They are undoubtedly an improvement over the fate of Indian actors like Chief Thundercloud (real name Victor Daniels – trust Hollywood to change *that*) who was afforded the indignity of playing the lead in *Geronimo* (1939) without receiving any billing, or Jay Silverheels who for many years tagged along a respectful two paces behind the Lone Ranger.

When John Ford decided to make *Cheyenne Autumn* (1964) the project was openly offered as an apology for earlier forays into Indian territory. As Ford remarked to Peter Bogdanovich in an interview for *Esquire* in April 1964: 'I've wanted to make this for a long time. Y'know, I've killed more Indians than Custer, Beecher and Chivington put together . . . I wanted to show what they were like.' His wishes did not have much impact on the casting department. The five main Indian characters are played by Victor Jory, Gilbert Roland, Ricardo Montalban, Sal Mineo and Dolores Del Rio. There is not an Indian among them, although as three out of the five are Mexican an element of mildly racist typecasting is apparent.

Cheyenne Autumn traces the true story of a band of Cheyenne (played in the film by Navajos) compelled to live in near-starvation on their Oklahoma reservation who decide to head for their far-distant Montana homelands.

This was in 1877, and news of the breakout created panic among farmers and townspeople in the vicinity. Even people many thousands of miles away were afraid. Their misconceptions, however compelling, were based upon nothing more than the fictions created to justify the relocation on a reservation of men and women and their children who had done nothing to deserve their fate except be Indian. The army was sent in pursuit and soon began picking off stragglers.

At the start of their truly epic journey, the Cheyenne band, which was led by Dull Knife and Little Wolf, numbered 297. By the time they reached Nebraska their pursuers, admittedly not all on the trail at the same time, numbered 3000 civilians and 10,000 soldiers.

Eventually, split up, tired, dispirited and with many of their original party dead or sick to the point of death, the Cheyenne gave up. By now public opinion had been swayed by their efforts and people had gradually come to realize that the Indians were not on the rampage but were simply trying to return home in peace. The degree of sympathy was not, however, enough to permit freedom to be granted. The reservation was still the fate of the

Cheyenne but, as the Indian historian Vine Deloria Jr. has observed, they were at least freed from the fear of physical extermination.

While John Ford's film follows these events with reasonable accuracy, the reasons for the Cheyenne's decision to return, the impulse which drives them, and the motivation for the immense fortitude with which they approached their task, fails to make itself apparent. Unrelated and historically dubious episodes are inserted along the way. These allow a few star names to get into the act and also accommodate audiences who might not be sufficiently gripped by the unfolding saga.

Ford might have believed he was ready to make amends to the Indian but, like that of most other film-makers, his desire to make an Indian movie which tells the truth was inadequate when faced with Hollywood's need for the perpetuation of myths and legends.

A need to prolong and occasionally to re-create myths has also pervaded that other notable figure of the West, the Outlaw.

Almost every man, and every woman, who broke the tenuous law of the Old West seems to have found a place in Hollywood's gallery of Western characters. The worse the crimes, whether in terms of money stolen or men killed, the bigger and better the ballyhoo. Head and shoulders above all others in this particular gallery of rogues come Jesse James and Billy the Kid.

Jesse, together with his older brother Frank, have ridden through unnumerable versions of their life stories. Few have taken much time to worry over accuracy, although *The Long Riders* (1980) almost made amends for earlier glorifications such as *Jesse James* (1939), starring Tyrone Power and Henry Fonda, *The Return of Frank James* (1940) (Fonda again), and *The True Story of Jesse James* (1957). Despite crisp direction by Nicholas Ray in the last of these, the story is anything but true and it continued the established tradition of making these strange heroes physically handsome. This time Robert Wagner and Jeffrey Hunter play the brothers. (Four years later Nicholas Ray and Jeffrey Hunter worked together again, when Jeffrey played Jesus Christ in *King of Kings*.)

Cast as Jesse and Frank in *The Long Riders* are the brothers James and Stacy Keach, while the three brothers Carradine play the Youngers, the Quaids play the Millers, and the Guests play the brothers Ford. This attempt to give the film a certain degree of familial realism, to say nothing of giving it a massive publicity hook, is just one part of a serious attempt to show the true story of these men who made a career of robbery and murder yet managed somehow to capture the imagination of the people of their own times to such an extent that they were folk heroes long before they were dead.

In most of the films, including *The Long Riders*, part of the blame for the James boys' depredations is laid at the door of the Civil War, which dislocated family and morals. The injury to their mother, when her home was attacked by Pinkerton detectives who believed Jesse and Frank were present, is another factor much favoured by apologists.

50

None of these film-makers seems to have noticed that the dislocation of family and morals caused by the Civil War affected just about every young male in America at the time. They did not all turn to crime and of those few who did, none was as quick or as eager as Jesse and Frank James to begin robbing and killing.

Much of the activities of the James boys took place in Missouri, a border state during the Civil War. Collectively neither for the North nor the South, individual Missourians took one side or another and feuded endlessly. Bloody violence was very much a way of life.

During the war Frank was with Quantrill's guerillas and took part in the infamous Lawrence massacre, when about 200 people were killed and the tiny Kansas town all but razed to the ground. Jesse got into the war as a sidekick of one of Quantrill's equally unpleasant associates, 'Bloody' Bill Anderson, and also participated in a massacre, this one at Centralia. Thus, by the time the war was over, the James brothers were well set in their killing ways and went about their tasks with little or no compunction for human life or the property of others.

As for their injured mother, who variously loses limb or life in the Hollywood versions (she actually lost an arm), her fate may have hardened the brothers' resolve to avenge themselves on the Pinkertons (or even to steer clear of them) but it certainly did not set them on their unlawful course through life. It did, of course, provide a nicely sympathetic touch which film-makers could not fail to exploit.

After the war, much external capital found its way into Missouri with the banks and railroads among the most obvious examples of this outside influence. When Jesse and Frank took to robbing banks and trains, the local people saw this as a justifiable activity and their enthusiastic support and absence of protest gave the boys an aura of respectability and helped manufacture a wholly unjustified Robin Hood-style legend.

Billy the Kid has been subjected to even more apologias than the James-Younger gang. An ugly, scrawny, mentally subnormal and altogether unprepossessing specimen of humanity, Billy has been portrayed on film by a string of Hollywood actors, none of whom could be termed ugly, while some were the glamour-boys of their day: Johnny Mack Brown, Roy Rogers, Robert Taylor, Jack Buetel, Paul Newman, Kris Kristofferson and Audie Murphy have all taken a turn and their physical appearance usually matched the historically inaccurate character they gave to Billy. Bob Steele, who churned out a half dozen Billy the Kid cheapies for Madison in the 1940s, portrayed the outlaw as a close cousin to the Range Rider. Only Michael J. Pollard, in *Dirty Little Billy* (1972), comes anywhere near the appearance and manner of this squalid little psychopath who has acquired the superficial gloss of a true American hero.

Billy the Kid contrived to be a legend before he died, which was no mean feat as he was dead before reaching the age of twenty-two. He was born in

Billy the Kid . . . all the charm of an upright rodent.

Only Michael J. Pollard in *Dirty Little Billy (right)* came close to this real-life squalid psychopath.

52

New York City in 1859, the second son of Patrick and Catherine McCarty, who were Irish immigrants. His given names were Patrick Henry but he was called Henry to avoid confusion with his father. Such confusions did not last long however as McCarty Sr. was lucky enough to die before he had a chance to discover exactly what he had sired. Young Henry's mother married again, this time a man named William Antrim, in Santa Fe, New Mexico. The Antrims moved to Silver City where Catherine died in 1874. Henry, by now fifteen years old, did not hit it off with step-papa so he promptly left home. After a couple of mildly lawless escapades he became a cowboy, calling himself Kid Antrim. In 1877 he killed a man who insulted him, always a good pretext for a quick and lethal revenge in the real West, just as it is in the Hollywood version.

The following year the Kid met an upper-crust English rancher, John H. Tunstall, and a strange and devoted friendship was formed. About this time the Kid used another name, William H. Bonney, which has stuck like glue to the present day. He was also known as Kid Billy and, for the first time, Billy the Kid. A range war was afoot in Lincoln County, New Mexico where Tunstall had his spread and in early 1878 the Englishman was murdered. During the next few months a great many people bit the Lincoln County dust as Billy, now on the payroll of rancher John S. Chisum (whom John Wayne would one day portray on-screen) managed to notch up roughly one killing for every year of his life.

The Lincoln County killings were big news and the President of the United States, Rutherford B. Hayes, appointed a new state governor in the hope that he could eradicate the troubles. The new governor was General Lew Wallace, who must have had other matters on his mind at this time because his massive novel, *Ben-Hur*, was published the following year. The governor met secretly with Billy and tried to do a deal. He failed and the lethal lad was duly arrested and charged with a couple of murders to keep him out of mischief. A few weeks in jail was enough for the Kid, who unheroically passed the time by informing on old comrades, and one night he slipped through the bars and made off.

For another year he co-led a gang of nasties who terrorized the region until a new county sheriff was appointed. Pat Garrett was made of sterner stuff than his predecessors and the Kid was captured, re-imprisoned, tried and sentenced to death. Once more he escaped, once more Pat Garrett took to the trail. This time, perhaps unwilling to let the saga drag on through more trials, more imprisonments, more escapes, the sheriff and his posse saved the county any more expense by killing the Kid.

Photographs of Billy reveal him to have been a sawn-off runt of a man, buck-toothed and possessing all the charm of a temporarily upright rodent. The best-known of the photographs was originally printed back to front, thus making the Kid appear left-handed, which he was not. Subsequent reprints of the photograph rarely troubled to correct this falsehood and Hollywood compounded it by entitling the Paul Newman version of the Kid's adventures *The Left-handed Gun* (1958).

Even the most cursory glance at the Hollywood versions of this man's life story demonstrate how little regard was shown for veracity. Handsome, romantic, gentlemanly, always giving the other fellow a better than even break, usually named William Bonney (a much *nicer* name than plain Henry McCarty), often misunderstood and much put upon, he was soon so deeply hidden beneath the heroic gloss that the dirt no longer showed through.

Some of the earlier accounts of Billy the Kid's exploits which appeared in the dime novels of the late nineteenth century owe their origins to a book published a year after his death. This was entitled *The Authentic Life of Billy the Kid* and was ostensibly written by Pat Garrett, the man responsible for his death. Presumably Garrett wanted to make a buck or two and enhance his own reputation, so it is not surprising that the runty little psychopath was made to appear considerably grander than in real life. After all, Garrett would not have wanted to be thought responsible for gunning down (in the dark) an unprepared deadleg who, had he lived one hundred years later, would undoubtedly have lived a life of similarly short duration mugging old ladies and pushing drugs on New York's Lower East Side.

That Hollywood perpetuated Garrett's gloss comes as no surprise. The requirements of the motion-picture industry in presenting such tales are perhaps best underlined by comments made by King Vidor, who directed *Billy the Kid* (1930) with Johnny Mack Brown in the title role. This film originally ended with the death of Billy, but previews showed that audiences did not like its heroes to die so a new ending was made in which Billy marries his sweetheart – just like any other B-western hero. 'You see,' Vidor commented in a *Los Angeles Times* interview in 1930, 'the public doesn't want the truth. Why should I try anymore to give it to them?'

Why, indeed? And few of Hollywood's film-makers since then have seen any reason to be more truthful. The movies, like the American people, need heroes regardless of the cost to truth and reality. It is unfortunate that the need has proved so strong that heroes have been manufactured from such improbable base material. Were there no law-abiding figures who could be idolized?

Well, yes, of course there were some. Unfortunately, the wearing of a tin star was no guarantee of either heroism or honesty.

Just as outlaws became the subject of endless Hollywood films, so too have lawmen provided the skeletons of hundreds of tales which, when fleshed out, do not look very much different. On whichever side of the Law of the West these men stand, the end result is usually that someone is shot to death. The fact that some killers wear badges while others do not appears to be sufficient reason for justifying wholesale murder. This is not to suggest that the lawmen of the Old West were mere gunmen who were paid to kill. Many were courageous individuals who did a dangerous job well, often for poor reward, but they were not all like that.

In some respects, Hollywood's hazy line between the good and the bad is justified in that many lawmen and outlaws were kindred spirits who came from broadly similar social backgrounds. It was often a matter of luck which dictated where they stood in relation to the law. Some stood on both sides, occasionally at the same time. If an outlaw was offered a roof over his head and enough money to keep him in steak and whisky, then he might well settle for a badge instead of a mask.

This blurred distinction between the law and the lawless meant that hero and villain were uncomfortably related. Oddly enough, some of the most dubious became the best-known in Hollywood. High on the list of lawless lawmen came 'Judge' Roy Bean and Marshal Wyatt Earp.

Bean, self-styled 'law west of the Pecos', had totted up an impressive number of infractions of the law, including two or three homicides, before he set up court in a bar-room in the town of Langtry. Nursing a lifelong passion for Lily Langtry, the Jersey Lily, the Judge doled out 'likker' and law, often at the same time, in his dual-purpose home. Eventually removed from the office he had taken upon himself without authority, for one infringement too many, he managed to edge himself into the film industry by staging a fight between British heavyweight champion Bob Fitzsimmons and Peter Maher in 1896 which was photographed in Kinetoscope, the newly devised apparatus invented by Edison and Dickson.

Brought to the screen in roaring style by Paul Newman in *The Life and Times of Judge Roy Bean* (1972), the old reprobate comes over as merely rascally and rumbustiously humorous. As to historical accuracy, screenwriter John Milius entered a note at the beginning of the published version of his screenplay: 'To pompous historians – any similarity to historical characters, living or dead is purely accidental. If this story is not the way it was – then it's the way it should have been and furthermore the author does not give a plug damn.' Ah, well.

Perhaps a more accurate interpretation of Bean, and certainly nastier, was the Oscar-winning performance by Walter Brennan in *The Westerner* (1940) (although adding humour to the tale of the dubious judge was not without justification: any man who could exonerate a pal for killing a Mexican on the grounds that the victim should not have chosen that moment to walk in front of the gun, or of acquitting another crony for killing a Chinaman because there was no entry under 'Chinamen; killing of' in his well-thumbed *Revised Statutes of Texas* must have had some sense of humour, however misplaced and macabre).

There has been very little, if any, equivocation in Hollywood's treatment of that other dubious law-enforcer, Wyatt Earp. Almost without exception, Earp has been portrayed as a zealous defender of the law and a man of honour and distinction at a time when such men were desperately needed to prevent the West from descending into anarchy. There can be no doubt that Earp was almost all the things various screen portrayals have suggested, although the whiter-than-white honesty does seem to stretch the truth uncomfortably far. A touch of larceny here and there clearly helped him eke out the rather meagre pay afforded peace officers in Dodge City and Tombstone, the two towns in which Earp built his reputation and with which his name has ever after been most closely associated.

Apart from his brothers Virgil, Warren and Morgan, Wyatt was also assisted from time to time by another of the West's larger than life villains-turned-hero. Doc Holliday divided his time randomly between drinking, dentistry, gambling, gunfighting and the pursuit of ladies. Another Earp brother, James, helped Wyatt too, but usually in a non-combative capacity.

Although Wyatt tried to interest film-makers in his story in the 1920s, it was not until after his death that the possibilities of the story, be it true or legend, made themselves apparent. Of the many versions of the story, the best-known are *My Darling Clementine* (1946) and *Gunfight at the OK Corral* (1957).

In *My Darling Clementine* Earp is portrayed by Henry Fonda as an ordinary man caught up in extraordinary times. Directed by John Ford, who had met Wyatt in Hollywood, the film makes a serious bid to demythologize the lawman. In the process, however, historical accuracy suffers a few serious blows. Not the least of these is that Doc Holliday dies in the final shoot-out. Holliday is portrayed here by big and brawny Victor Mature; given the fact that among all his other problems Doc had consumption, this is a strange piece of casting. Doc was not in fact killed at the OK Corral gunfight; he eventually died some six years later in a sanatorium where attempts to allay the disease which was slowly killing him were jeopardized by his determination not to give up hard liquor.

Other variations from reality include having James Earp (Don Garner) appear as the youngest of the brothers when he was in fact the oldest; additionally, the film shows him being shot to death, thus starting up a feud between the Earps and the Clantons. James, who had been severely wounded in the Civil War, was closely associated with his brothers but his wartime injuries prevented his ever becoming involved in their gunfighting activities. He died of natural causes in 1926.

Old Man Clanton (Walter Brennan) kills Virgil Earp (Tim Holt) and is later himself killed at the Corral. Clanton had in fact been killed some months before the gunfight at the OK Corral, while busily rustling cattle. This was a pastime he indulged in from time to time, as did Wyatt Earp, and very likely set up antagonism between the Clantons and the Earps that had nothing to do with law and order. As for Virgil, he did not die until 1906, twenty-five years after the shoot-out, and then it was from pneumonia (although some three months after the OK Corral he was gravely injured by five unidentified gunmen).

There are many other instances of inaccuracies in the film, and while some can be justified on the grounds of presenting a more balanced structure, too many exist to give cause, even justification, to events depicted later.

Gunfight at the OK Corral was similarly careless with reality. At the core of the film lies the friendship beween Wyatt (Burt Lancaster) and Doc (Kirk Douglas). The homicidally-inclined dentist certainly trailed the lawman around the country, but it was out of self-preservation rather than friendship. Doc had once helped the lawman out of a tight spot and believed this meant that Earp owed him a favour or two. For a man almost always at odds with the law, this was a useful card to have up his sleeve.

As in Fonda's earlier portrayal, Lancaster's Earp is a solid, peaceful man who yearns for the quiet life and only takes up his guns when sorely tried by those who seek to disturb his rest. In common with most other portrayals of the lawman, and most other heroic peace officers for that matter, the villain is always given an even break in this version, a sure-fire way in the real West to end up dead fast.

Women in these films have only background roles to play and although neither version touches the truth, one does flirt discreetly with reality. In *My Darling Clementine*, Wyatt has a refined lady-friend named Clementine (Cathy Downs), while Doc has a friend named Chihuahua (Linda Darnell) whose racial ancestry and morals are sufficiently dubious to guarantee her death before the end. In the 1940s, heroes did not marry anyone who was not pure white, physically and morally. In *Gunfight at the OK Corral*, Wyatt has a relationship with gambler Laura Denbow (Rhonda Fleming) while Doc's love interest is provided by a certain Kate Fisher (Jo Van Fleet).

In real life Wyatt was married twice or, more probably, three times, his first wife dying a few months after the wedding during a typhus epidemic. His stay in Tombstone was brightened by an intimate relationship with a lady whom he might well have married, although records are slightly vague on this point. She died in 1888 and he married for what was probably the third and certainly last time in 1897, shortly after refereeing a fight between Jack Sharkey and the same Bob Fitzsimmons who had drifted through Judge Roy Bean's life. Doc's affairs of the heart were two long-standing relationships, one with Lottie Deno, a pretty gambler, the other with a whore named Big-Nose Kate Elder. The confusion of names, occupations and relationships in *Gunfight at the OK Corral* suggests that everything was put in a hat, shaken up, and drawn out at random.

These details, like those surrounding the sequence of events, are relatively trivial; yet since the overall effect is to change the manners, morals and mores of the principal characters they cannot be ignored. This is especially true of *My Darling Clementine*, in which the Earp-Clanton feud is attributed to something very different from the conflict of interests between the two families.

As with countless other Hollywood films setting out to portray real-life people, in whatever walk of life, the changes raise important questions. Not least of these is why, if so many changes needed to be made, it was thought desirable to make a biographical film in the first instance; why, once they had decided to make the movie, the film-makers did not take some measure of responsibility on behalf of their audience for the facts concerning the people and events they were depicting.

In the case of films portraying men who have become all-American heroes, the motives for changing known facts assume much greater importance and serious doubts are raised concerning the morals and mores of the film-makers themselves.

Much more justifiable, if only on the grounds of ensuring exciting cinema, are changes made to such matters as the nature of gunfights in the real West. They were usually short and curiously static affairs. Men stood still, not to make easy targets but because most handguns were hopelessly inaccurate (and in the case of Navy Colts were extremely heavy) and their operators were not very good shots anyway. It was also necessary to stand quite close to one's opponent otherwise those bullets that did not miss might not reach their targets.

Doc (1971), which stars Stacy Keach as Holliday, compacted the OK shoot-out into seven seconds, which was probably about the right length of time. The much longer versions shown in most films, and especially the marvellously choreographed affair in *Gunfight at the OK Corral*, are clearly ridiculous, but given the conventions of the genre (to say nothing of the fact that the film's title was designed to bring into the cinemas people who wanted and expected rather more than seven seconds of gunplay) they are accceptable because they do not change history.

The case of Wyatt Earp is another example of errors of fact and interpretation pre-dating Hollywood's intervention. In 1907 former lawman Bat Masterson (whose story has also been told in movies) wrote a series of articles for the Boston magazine *Human Life* in which he extolled the virtues of frontier lawmen and gunfighters, among them Wyatt Earp and Doc Holliday. Since Bat presumably wanted his own activities to be free from slurs, none of these pieces is at all critical. The popularity of these articles, together with an additional piece about Bat himself written by Alfred H. Lewis, the magazine's editor, proved that the public wanted to read what it believed to be the truth rather than the truth itself.

Behind all these western heroes, Lawman or Outlaw, lurks the Superhero – the Westerner himself. This archetypal, if non-existent, individual came to life largely through the efforts of three men whose work in different fields helped establish a stereotype of an honourable, clean-living solitary for whom the law of the gun is a last resort. But if the gun is used, it becomes in his hands a pure instrument of moral, not legal, justice. The myth thus created exists today in the active pro-gun lobby in America: that a gun is only as good or as bad as the man behind it. As an argument, this is as thin as the line between the Old West's lawmen and outlaws.

The three men who created the Westerner were Frederic Remington, whose paintings showed the West as most people believed or hoped it to be;

Theodore Roosevelt, who wrote *The Winning of the West*, a so-called 'history' which extolled the virtues of land-grabbers and the killers of Indians; and Owen Wister whose novel, *The Virginian*, first published in 1902, set the precedent for every subsequent book and film which portrayed the Westerner as a quietly-spoken gentleman who defended women, children and the under-dog against all-comers, which usually meant anyone who threatened the continued existence of the free and open ranges.

The fact that between them these three men could number less than ten years' experience of the West mattered not one iota. They created an image which everyone who saw Remington's paintings or who read the words of Roosevelt and Wister carried in their minds until the day that Gary Cooper ambled leisurely on to the motion-picture screen and drawled his first 'yep'. After Cooper the image was complete. Or so it seemed until John Wayne added a further variation of his own which had its origins in Duke's fierce patriotism.

In reality, those early pioneers were neither John Waynes nor Gary Coopers. They were a mixed bunch, some good, some bad but mostly honest, hard-working, enduring people from all corners of far-distant Europe who had emigrated to the New World and kept right on moving until they found a place they chose to call home.

Many immigrants stayed in the cities where they first set foot, particularly New York; others kept on going from city to city until their money ran out. But for many of those for whom the land had provided a meagre existence back home, it was land they sought in America. Their westward journeys, once they were actually in America, were no less arduous than the voyages which had brought them from their European homes. They faced long treks over difficult terrain, sometimes with the aid of horses, often on foot with what little horse- or mule-power they had being reserved for their pathetically few possessions. They faced appalling weather conditions, injury and sickness with no medical assistance, inadequate clothing and limited food supplies. They occasionally had trouble with hostile Indians, to say nothing of the depred-ations made by other pioneers who were either better armed or more desperate than they were themselves.

The pioneer has turned up in many Western movies but usually to provide background colour or to serve as a plot device. The covered wagon train, so beloved of B-western film-makers, was rarely seen, certainly not in such well-organized and huge numbers as featured in *The Covered Wagon* (1923). The national and language-mix is usually omitted – virtually everyone speaks in a variation of the Cooper drawl. Occasionally some attempts were made to depict specialized pioneer groups, as in *Wagonmaster* (1950), in which wagons carry Mormons towards their promised land. Few moviegoers would suspect that many Italians went West, yet between 15 and 20 per cent of the four million Italian immigrants ignored the cities where their fellow countrymen settled and pushed onwards against the frontier.

Most Hollywood wagon trains do carry a Scandinavian family – probably, one suspects, because the accent is easy to imitate and recognize. A much more sensitive depiction of Scandinavian settlers came in two Swedish films which show the hard slog of the would-be farmer and his family. Although slow-moving, *The Emigrants* (1970) and its sequel, *The New Land* (1972), faithfully record the reality of life in Sweden which drove people out, and the irresistible attraction of what has been described as the distant magnet of America. Life in Minnesota, where these Swedes eventually settle, is not easy. Death and privation accompany them for many more years but the reaffirmation of human hope which these two films constantly display is something which is sadly absent in all but a tiny few of the innumerable films in which Hollywood has sought to depict those pioneering days.

One creditable attempt to record this life faithfully came in *Heartland* (1979), which is based upon the books and letters of Elinore Randall Stewart who lived and worked with her husband on inhospitable land near Burnt Fork, Wyoming at the turn of the century. The grim existence and the harsh struggle for survival through bitter winters and all manner of physical and psychological hardships is vividly portrayed in a warm and moving film which manages to avoid the sentimentality which dogged several television movies and Disney productions telling similar tales.

It would seem that for most film-makers, especially in Hollywood, the pioneer is just too dull. Ploughing fields, planting seeds and harvesting crops is not the stuff of which movies are made, certainly not movies set in the mythical West. Adventure and excitement are demanded and consequently invented. The movies filled a need, although in doing so they destroyed the reality of one of the greatest experiences of modern America – the pushing back of the Western Frontier – and replaced it with myths of Indian-killers and gunfighters whose suspect activities were thus glorified.

At best this is an unfortunate exchange. Despite the artificial glamour everyone has thereby lost something, most of all the American people who have to accept a heroic heritage built upon robbery, murder, genocide and the rule of the gun.

At the turn of the century America was becoming a new world in many ways, not least of which was the realization that the Old West was gone and that the future lay in the cities. For many Americans this was an unacceptable truth and they clung hopefully to the myth that the West would go on forever. To the best, and often to the worst, of their abilities, film-makers have perpetuated that myth.

It was not just the fact of the passing of the Old West that troubled Americans. The Frontier was much more than an invisible barrier beyond which civilized man had yet to pass. The Frontier was a mythic boundary, a mirage which all strove to reach. But like all mirages it either retreated at the same pace as man's approach, or vanished entirely only to reappear somewhere else and just as far off.

61

When the entire country was settled, coast to coast, the Frontier had to be sought elsewhere, and if the industrialized cities were not the same, they were at least as hazardous. A few film-makers have sought to convey the problem of this transitional period, especially in the form of westerns which show life in the West as the motor-car replaces the horse and the muddy streets of cowtowns are paved. *The Good Guys and the Bad Guys* (1969) and, most especially, *Ride the High Country* (1962) approached this awkward transition with sympathy and understanding.

Yet the truth remained; those days were past. The British release title for *Ride the High Country* caught the flavour of the times most aptly: *Guns in the Afternoon* says it all.

As the West died, the cities flourished. Millions of immigrants flooded in and industrialization paved the way towards a richer and brighter future, albeit one with much less to excite the imaginations of frontiersmen, pioneers and Westerners. Industrialization also paved the way for several occurrences that would give Hollywood much food for films, if not for deep thought on matters of historical significance. One of these events was something which few Americans wanted, because it threatened to drag the nation out of isolation. Inevitably, World War I would thrust the nation firmly and irrevocably into the centre of the world's stage.

CHAPTER FOUR

'Troops are like children, they need discipline. We
must shoot a man now and then.'
(from *Paths of Glory*)

Although many immigrants pushed Westwards into farming lands, many more
stayed in the cities, closer to their point of arrival in America. For some the
decision was deliberate: they wanted to be with their own kind who were
already resident there. Others had the decision thrust upon them: they had no
money and needed work immediately with which to feed themselves and their
families. To reverse a statistic mentioned earlier, out of 4 million Italian
immigrants who entered America between 1865 and 1915, at least 80 per cent
stayed in the cities and major towns. In the same period, from the end of the
Civil War to the beginning of World War I, people of other nationalities
flooded into America. A further 4 million came from Germany, 2 million from
Scandinavia, over 3 million came from Russia, and from Great Britain and
Ireland more than 5 million. Expansion of the cities was rapid; more often
than not, the physical expansion of accommodation and services was not rapid
enough. Some, especially New York and Chicago, swelled to bursting point.
Overcrowding and inadequate sanitation led to sickness and disease; too many
people seeking too few jobs brought exploitation of the work-force. Where
work could not be found, some who had been upright and honest in the Old
Country turned to crime.

For many, the gleam of hope with which the New World had beckoned now
flickered and died. Not surprisingly, film-makers have been attracted to the
drama inherent in the story of the immigrants but the results have rarely been
accurate portrayals of life and conditions in the ghettoes. All too often, the
resulting films have been poor-boy-makes-good melodramas which perpetuate
the American Dream with no hint of the nightmare into which many plunged,
there to remain for the rest of their lives.

Hester Street (1975) concentrates upon east-European Jews in New York
City in 1896 and is both humorous and faintly romantic but has an underlying
irony which dispels sentimentality. Humour in this film, as in real life, is a
means by which the Jews made light of the grim conditions under which they
learned to live in the New World.

There is little humour in *The Godfather Part II* (1974), but there is a sharply
perceptive view of the life of the Italian immigrant after his arrival in New

The Godfather, Part II recreated teeming turn-of-the-century New York streets . . .

. . . accurately reflecting the reality caught by the photographer Jacob Riis in 1902.

Museum of the City of New York

York. By showing life and conditions back home, the film also succeeds, as did none of the gangster movies of earlier generations of film-making, in giving purpose and meaning to the lawless life some immigrants chose to follow. The re-created streets of turn-of-the-century New York, teeming with life and only just managing to avoid squalor, are filled with people almost all of whom are honest citizens. The film thus avoids the cliché with which Hollywood has insulted Italian-Americans for generations.

A marked change in American domestic life occurred in the early years of the twentieth century. Consumer-orientated manufacturing expanded rapidly, offering improvements in the standard of living to many Americans across the nation but especially those located in the classier neighbourhoods of major cities. Necessarily, the goods bought by these consumers had to be manufactured fast and cheaply, and accordingly a new class of poorly paid, inadequately clothed and housed toilers was created. These people, largely immigrants from either Europe or the Orient or from the poorer states of the Union (which usually meant blacks from the South), sweated away in factories, workshops, backrooms of apartment houses and even in their own homes. American society therefore consisted of a large and often grubbily distasteful underbelly swathed in a glittering gown of new-fangled gadgets and status symbols.

The material object desired by many, and granted even to the (better-off) masses thanks to men like Henry Ford, was the automobile. The love-affair which Americans began with the car in the early years of this century cut across class and age. Even women liked it, although it was and remains essentially a male virility symbol, rivalling that other great American penis-substitute – the gun.

The change in attitudes at the turn of the century both within and towards the commercial and industrial worlds is mirrored in Orson Welles's *The Magnificent Ambersons* (1942), which brilliantly depicts the social change generated by new products and attitudes. More than any film of any era this reflects the preoccupations of middle-America and the nature of the class structure within what was claimed by many to be a classless society.

Also lasting in its effect upon America, and especially in its relationship with the rest of the world, were grave events in which America would be involved in a military capacity, first in Mexico and then in Europe.

When Woodrow Wilson took office as President in 1912 he was acutely aware of the problems on America's south-western border. The Mexican Revolution had erupted in 1911 when Francisco Madero, who had deposed Porfirio Diaz, was defeated and assassinated by Victoriana Huerta and his men. Huerta promptly set up a viciously reactionary government; never wholly stable, Mexico was now dangerously volatile. It was at this point that Wilson came to office and despite his undoubted intellectual ability quickly showed himself to be a diplomatic blunderer of epic proportions. His initial problem was deciding which of the many factions involved in the unrest south of the Rio Grande he should support.

The Huertistas were opposed by revolutionaries who were themselves divided into two dissimilar but not opposed factions. In the south was Emiliano Zapata; in the north, and therefore closest to the border with the United States, was Venustiano Carranza.

Wilson offered to help Carranza but was shunned so the President, intent on displaying where his sympathies lay, exercised some ill-timed and ill-advised gunboat diplomacy against the Huertistas. Then a split occurred in the northern elements of the revolutionaries and Wilson took it upon himself to support Carranza's outspoken and charismatic lieutenant, Francisco 'Pancho' Villa. Apart from annoying Carranza, Wilson overlooked the fact that Villa, while generally supportive of Zapata's land reform ambitions in the south, had the mentality and inclinations of a hill-bandit.

In choosing to back a bandit, Wilson unwittingly set a precedent many of his successors in the White House would follow through to the present day as Central America established itself as a permanent irritant in the nation's most sensitive region. Too often, faced with backing left or right-wing extremists, predictable decisions have been made which bear little or no relation to the needs of the people of Central America.

In 1915 Wilson switched support back to Carranza, recognizing him as leader of the Mexican *de facto* government. This angered Villa, who showed his displeasure by killing rather a lot of Americans, first on his side of the border and then, the greatest affront of all, across the Rio Grande in the United States itself. Villa may well have had an ulterior motive: if America had been provoked into intervention in Mexico, Carranza would have been discredited.

In 1916 Wilson did intervene, sending General John Pershing into Mexico, but the General was recalled by mid-January and in March of that year, Carranza became President of Mexico.

These activities in Mexico, many of which were carried out on horseback, contained most of the elements of the traditional Western movie with the added bonus of exotic locations and characters and a surface smear of political motivation. Not surprisingly, film-makers were attracted; several films have been set during this period, although most have chosen to be non-specific about individuals, using all-purpose central characters who could be any one of the principals involved in the revolution. In most cases, only the period and location are retained and the films are peopled with fictitious characters upon whom the plot hangs. The main exception is Pancho Villa, who turns up in many films, most often being depicted as bandit, somewhat nobly motivated, rather than revolutionary. In this respect, probably accidentally, Hollywood came closer to reality than did the American government.

Among the films featuring Pancho's tale is *Viva Villa!* (1934) which makes a token effort to explain the revolutionary impulse. Wallace Beery as the central character captures some of the complexity of this man for whom the attractions of banditry considerably outweighed the responsibilities attached to leading a revolutionary movement.

Later films swung between faithful interpretations, such as *Viva Revolution* (1956), which was made by Mexicans in Mexico, and straightforward transposed westerns like *Villa Rides* (1968), in which the bandit is portrayed by a faintly bemused Yul Brynner who is effectively upstaged by Robert Mitchum as a gun-running aviator.

General Pershing pops up from time to time, usually as a very minor character. He appears in *Cannon for Cordoba* (1970), which is very loosely based upon the real events surrounding the General's 1916 intervention.

Emiliano Zapata appears much less frequently than Villa, although the one main film about his life proved to be that which came closest to an understanding of the political reality of revolution in general, if not of Mexico's in particular. *Viva Zapata!* (1952) owes much more to the political climate of America at the time it was made than that of Mexico forty years before.

The concept which drives Zapata (Marlon Brando) to support Madero (Harold Gordon) strays far from the real revolution, for in 1952 advocation of anything even remotely akin to communism was death in Hollywood. Joseph McCarthy was a power in the land and was giving lessons in headline-grabbing to his fellow red-hunters, the members of the committee investigating subversion in Hollywood. The producer, Darryl F. Zanuck, was unwilling freely to hand out ammunition which could be used to attack the studio, the film, or Zanuck himself. Self-preservation in Hollywood in the 1950s was just as important as it had been in Mexico in the times in which *Viva Zapata!* is set. The director and co-writer, Elia Kazan, was already adopting an ambivalent stance towards interference by the Committee on Un-American Activities in his affairs. Even the other writer on the project, John Steinbeck, who had been fiercely urging a Zapata movie for many years, found his enthusiasm waning and his sense of political direction deserting him.

Historical accuracy takes a hammering and, as Paul J. Vanderwood has observed, Francisco Madero is subjected to much down-grading, largely through the activities of the Mexican government's appointed censors. Zapata too is re-adjusted, becoming a liberal democrat who is frequently at odds, politically, with an entirely fictitious character. This is Fernando (Joseph Wiseman), a sinister foreign interloper who by implication can be interpreted as an *agent provocateur* of vaguely Stalinist cast. Thus, Cold War ideology and attitudes slipped back in time to before the Russian Revolution and altered historical facts and attitudes.

Hollywood had made a foray into earlier Mexican history with a major film dealing with the life of Benito Juarez. Unfortunately, *Juarez* (1939) also adjusted history. In this film Paul Muni stars as the Mexican leader who opposes the imposition of a European-controlled ruler by overthrowing the regime of Maximilian von Hapsburg. The adjustment in this case is concerned not so much with facts as with aligning Juarez with his contemporary, Abraham Lincoln. The motivation of the studio concerned, Warner's, was a desire to ensure that its depiction of political events in Mexico at the time of the American Civil War carried clear and unmistakable mirror-images of what was happening in Europe in 1939. Impressive motivation, perhaps, but at the cost of extensive falsification of the historical truth.

American actions in Mexico are linked to the war which had begun in Europe in 1914 in *They Came to Cordura* (1959). Once again the 1916 punitive expedition which chased Villa is used as a pretext for a tale concerned with non-revolutionary matters. The film examines the US Army's need for heroes at a time of national emergency. As America prepares to involve itself in World War I, Major Thomas Thorn (Gary Cooper) seeks out five men to recommend for the Congressional Medal of Honour. They can thus be used as symbols by the Army. Although fictitious, the film had some serious comments to make on the meaning of courage and vividly contrasted the differences between heroism in action and true, lasting human values. None of Major Thorn's nominees is worth a light as a man, despite his undoubted heroism in battle. Very much a film of its time (post-McCarthy and post-Korean War), *They Came to Cordura* is defiantly non-gung-ho, even if it does have a somewhat unbelievable cop-out ending. Double-dyed villains of the calibre of these men would never be turned into nobly-motivated good guys merely because Major Thorn gives them a good end-of-combat report.

By the time America had straightened out its dishevelled foreign policy towards Mexico, other more ominous matters were taxing President Wilson and Congress. The war in Europe was dividing Americans predictably and naturally along lines of national origins.

The Central Powers, the Triple Alliance of Germany, Italy and Austria-Hungary, were favoured by German Americans and Italian-Americans. Americans of British descent favoured Britain, France and Russia, the Triple Entente. Others took sides negatively rather than positively. Irish-Americans favoured the Central Powers through long-standing hatred of the British; Jewish-Americans did not favour Russia because memories of the pogroms which had driven many from their homes were still too fresh in the collective memory.

For Woodrow Wilson, times now became even more trying as he strove mightily to keep America out of the war. *Wilson* (1944) gives a reasonably accurate account of the President's life, covering his years from Princeton to his failed hopes for a powerful and lasting League of Nations. Wilson had never been held in especially high esteem by the American people. His election victory in 1912 gave him 82 per cent of the electoral vote but only 42 per cent of the popular vote. The great popularity of the man shown in this film is largely a device to give justification for the status to which he is lifted by the film-makers. He has to be seen to be popular, given the fact that the film was made in the midst of America's efforts in World War II: a war, it is hinted, that might never have happened had the American Senate ratified the Treaty of Versailles in 1919, thus allowing America to enter the League of Nations.

Very well played by Alexander Knox, Wilson becomes something he was not; as

Charles Alexander has commented, the film is 'an interesting example of Hollywood's power to destroy one set of myths, only to replace them with another.'

Wilson's efforts to keep America out of the war in Europe were countered by Germany's increasing use of submarines with which they waged the war at sea. In April 1915 a British vessel was sunk with great loss of life, but although one of the dead was American Wilson made no protest. When in May of that year the British liner *Lusitania* was sunk, with 128 Americans among the 1200 dead, Wilson demanded reparation and succeeded in obtaining German agreement to restrict submarine warfare and to give warnings of attack.

Throughout the following year Wilson attempted to mediate but by March 1916 relations between America and Germany had deteriorated. Still determined to secure an acceptable peace, Wilson continued with his efforts and at the end of the year had succeeded in persuading the two sides to declare their terms and conditions for a cease-fire. The Germans were unco-operative and early in 1917 announced that they would sink any ships, including neutrals, in the approaches to the British Isles or in the Mediterranean. Left with no alternative, Wilson broke off all diplomatic relations.

Then the British intercepted a telegram from the German Foreign Secretary Zimmerman to the German minister in Mexico. The telegram, the authenticity of which has since been questioned, called upon Mexico to take up the struggle and seek to recover from the United States those lands that were now Texas, New Mexico and Arizona.

The Alamo had not been forgotten and Americans were predictably angry. On 12 March Wilson ordered American vessels to be armed. Six days later three American ships were sunk without warning and on 2 April 1917 America declared war on Germany. The Selective Service Act was brought into force and by 1 June almost 10 million Americans had registered for the draft. Much of the credit for the speed and efficiency with which this happened rested with a junior officer named Douglas MacArthur.

American intervention was only just in time. A beleagured Britain was low on food; supplies would have lasted only a few more weeks. On the Continent, the armies of the Triple Entente were devastated by appallingly high casualties; out of sixteen French divisions, fourteen had mutinied. As for the Russians, in October 1917 they had something to think about which they naturally found more important than anything that was happening in France and Germany.

Before America entered the war the nation's ambivalence towards events in Europe was apparent through the films being made; once in and 'over there' a marked change took place. Soon, film-makers were as committed as any of the nation's allies could have wanted. After the war was over it would be different but patriotism was now the order of the day.

Film-makers had initially buckled down to the task of showing prospective cannon-fodder that war was for heroes; that God was on 'our' side; and that the enemy was in league with the Devil.

War as heroic conflict was not, of course, the only position adopted by film-makers. Several film clowns saw a potential for humour although only Chaplin, sweetening a sharper centre, fully realized this, with his delicately balanced *Shoulder Arms* (1918).

Some anti-war sentiment was displayed before America was in the war. Thomas Ince's *Civilization* (1916), which includes references to the sinking of the *Lusitania*, and *War Brides* (1916) showed women refusing to bear children whose fate would be to perish in battle. That the anti-war films misjudged the prevailing mood can be determined from the fact that *War Brides*, which was made by and starred Alla Nazimova in her first screen role, had to be withdrawn from circulation during 1917 on the grounds that it endangered the nation's morale.

As soon as American soldiers were marching boldly to the front, film-makers saw to it that most of the remaining films of the period took a more positive and uplifting attitude and avoided giving grounds for concern at what lay in wait in the trenches.

Lest We Forget (1918) has a noble American lady spy giving her all for her country while major film-makers D.W. Griffith and Cecil B. De Mille weighed in respectively with the patriotic *Hearts of the World* and *Till I Come Back to You* (both 1918).

Hearts of the World, which stars Erich Von Stroheim, was instigated and underwritten by the British War Office. War footage from newsreels was incorporated into this film and into *The Kaiser, the Beast of Berlin* (1918) in an attempt to provide a measure of authenticity. In such films as these the German soldier, the Hun, was thoroughly despicable whether portrayed by Germanic Erich Von Stroheim or such Hollywood stalwarts as Walter Long (mercifully free of the black make-up he had worn as Gus in *The Birth of a Nation*), who torments America's sweetheart Mary Pickford in *The Little American* (1917), and Lon Chaney, who made the appropriately titled *False Faces* (1919).

With the ending of the war in November 1918, America's film-makers hastened on to other things as the bottom dropped out of the war-movie market. *The Four Horsemen of the Apocalypse* (1921) made money, but that was due to its leading player, Rudolph Valentino, rather than to any change in the mood of audiences.

It was, however, only a few years before Hollywood returned to the theme of World War I for a major production. More surprising than the relatively brief lapse of time was the nature of this film.

The Big Parade (1925) begins as an outwardly romantic drama in which the war provides an exciting and realistic background. Although falling well short of being anti-war, once it gets into its stride *The Big Parade* makes a deliberate attempt to show war realistically within the accepted conventions of film-making of its era. Most credit for this must go to the film's director King Vidor.

70

Marching to the beat of a drum in Griffith Park,
Los Angeles (*The Big Parade*) . . .

The Kobal Collection

. . . while the real thing looked even more
theatrical – German troops in the Lorraine.

Netherlands State Institute for War Documentation

Texan-born Vidor was an MGM contract director with nothing of especial merit to his credit when he was offered a property entitled *Plumes*. This was a semi-autobiographical novel written by Laurence Stallings, who had served as a Marine captain with the AEF and lost a leg at the battle of Belleau Wood. A former journalist, Stallings had also used his wartime experiences as the basis of a highly successful Broadway play, *What Price Glory?*, which he wrote in collaboration with Maxwell Anderson.

Stallings' attitude towards the war was decidedly mixed, in common with that of most of Hollywood's film-makers both then and later. His concern appears to have been primarily to describe war as it really was, yet he never failed to observe patriotic conventions. To a considerable extent the film which Vidor made, despite being a significant personal statement, retains this dichotomy of intent.

The Big Parade begins with the swift establishment of the three principal male characters, none of whom fulfils the standard Hollywood type for war stories. Slim (Karl Dane) is a steelworker recently come from building skyscrapers (actor Dane had similarly just made the transition from studio carpenter to actor) and Mike 'Bull' O'Hara (Tom O'Brien) is a bartender. The leading role of Jim Apperson went to John Gilbert, then the hottest star on MGM's payroll and second only to Valentino in Hollywood. Apperson is a rich playboy with no particular ambitions to be a hero; he is simply carried along with war-fever and enlists very much on the spur of the moment. Audiences of the day expected their heroes to become so through deliberate and conscious actions, not as the result of a casual whim.

Apperson leaves behind a fiancée, Justyn Reed (Claire Adams) but when in France takes up with a young peasant girl, Mélisande (Renée Adorée). His idyllic dalliance with Mélisande comes to an abrupt and somewhat melo-dramatic end when his regiment is ordered up to the front. The scene in which he leaves Mélisande is the first one in the film in which audiences are forced to confront reality in the form of a harsh separation. Desperately, Mélisande clings to her American lover, only to be wrenched away from him by the company sergeant. Then she clings to the truck carrying him towards the war; finally, she is dragged along behind the vehicle before being left prostrate in the roadway. He tosses keepsakes to her: his watch, his dogtags, then, lastly and with grim prophecy, a spare boot. Although extremely contrived by present-day standards, there is no doubt that this scene forced contemporary audiences to think more clearly than they had in the past about the real nature of war.

The ensuing battle scenes show a strange mixture of realism and stylized invention. Some of the sequences were shot by an assistant director at Fort Sam Houston, near San Antonio, Texas. They proved unsuitable to Vidor's conception because the assistant director allowed himself to be influenced by the army, who pointed out that in reality men and machines moved to the front in a manner designed to prevent them becoming an easy target for the enemy. Vidor wanted a stylized, straight-line approach to the front and the sequences had to be re-shot showing men marching in columns.

For many of the battle scenes Vidor developed a device to give the required rhythm to his actors' movements. By having a bass-drum beat time, he made it possible for the actors and extras to march through the woods in Los Angeles' Griffith Park to this rhythm. When the film was shown in theatres equipped with an orchestra capable of playing William Axt's score, these sequences were accompanied only by the same muffled drum beat.

During the battles the original trio of heroes is reduced when Slim is killed. In a well-conceived if somewhat theatrical scene, Apperson goes forward alone to avenge his friend's death, but when he has his bayonet at the throat of a wounded German soldier he cannot kill him. Instead, he lights a cigarette for the other man and when the German dies of his wounds, reflectively smokes the cigarette himself.

When the troops return from the front to the French village, Apperson has lost a leg (like author Stallings) as presaged by the solitary boot he left behind. But Mélisande is nowhere to be found and eventually Apperson is invalided home to America where his family and friends are forced to confront the inescapable truth of what the war has done to him.

Once again Vidor had broken with convention and compelled his audience to take stock of reality. Film audiences of the day were not accustomed to seeing their heroes, especially those with such romantic appeal as John Gilbert, suffer anything more than a few cuts and bruises. The loss of a limb had a notably dramatic effect.

With his family unable to accept the physical and psychological changes the war has wrought upon him and with his fiancée more interested in his stay-at-home brother, Apperson returns to France and is reunited with Mélisande. Once again convention, in this case the faithful woman at home, is avoided.

Many years later, Dalton Trumbo, having survived his blacklisting, wrote and directed a World War I film, *Johnny Got His Gun* (1971), which was based on his own 1939 anti-war novel. Trumbo's main character has lost both legs, both arms, and most of his face. Kept alive by the military, who will not let anyone, not even family, know he has survived the war, this grimly pathetic basket-case wants only one thing – to be allowed to die. Even in the 1970s audiences found this heavy-going; in the 1920s it would not have been tolerated. Jim Apperson's lost leg and faithless fiancée was as much as they could take.

Laurence Stallings' other story, *What Price Glory?*, came to the screen the following year in an excellent version starring Victor McLaglen and Edmund Lowe, and again in 1952 in an inferior re-make starring James Cagney and Dan Dailey. In this story, Stallings' uneasy blending of realism and patriotism is less jarring because the storyline concentrates upon the conflict between two Marines in love with the same girl rather than the war itself.

Attitudes towards the war changed as time passed. *The Big Parade*, while eschewing the heroics, had certainly fallen well short of being anti-war. A few years on, attitudes had shifted sufficiently for a truly anti-war film to be made. Generally regarded as the first such overt statement, Lewis Milestone's *All Quiet on the Western Front* (1930) also takes the unusual step of viewing the war not through American eyes but through those of the former enemy.

Based upon Erich Maria Remarque's best-selling novel, which was in turn based upon the author's own wartime experiences, the film traces the life of a young German soldier, Paul Baumer (Lew Ayres), from the moment he enters the army as an excited schoolboy who believes the tales of glory he is told, to his eventual death in the mud at Flanders. Between these moments comes Paul's gradual transition from innocence to cynicism as his comrades, many of whom are his former schoolfriends, are killed. Through these events he gains his manhood, but this is not the gung-ho variety of maturity that so often disfigured Hollywood's films of many wars. Paul's manhood comes about when he is forced to kill an enemy solder, a Frenchman, who could be a mirror-image of himself.

Wounded, Paul returns home for a while and finds only alienation; those left behind still harbour mistaken attitudes towards war, essaying jingoism and patriotic fervour which can only result in yet more young Pauls being sentenced to death in the trenches. By the time he returns to the front it is he who is the seasoned veteran, faced with inculcating into even younger men the means of survival in this war that none of them either wants or understands. Somehow, however, Paul has clung on to hopes and dreams of a better world which he may yet live to see.

In one of the film's two most memorable sequences he sees a butterfly settle on the mud behind the trench wall. Reaching through a loophole, he stretches out a hand – which is all that a French sniper needs. Moments later, Paul's hand falls limp. The other telling sequence shows columns of ghostly soldiers marching across fields massed with crosses. Paul is one of the shadowy figures and he pauses momentarily, turns and looks back. His eyes show the same bewilderment with which he has viewed so much of the war; but they also display something else. They accuse all the politicians who had allowed this war to happen, a war in which so many lives, German, French, British and American, were thrown away in what was eventually a useless struggle that few of the leaders, and almost none of the actual participants in the battles, understood.

A few years after the appearance of *All Quiet on the Western Front* another anti-war film was made, regarded by many as the best of its genre. Just as Remarque's novel served the purpose of cleansing from his mind the writer's own experiences in the war, Jean Renoir's *La Grande Illusion* (1937) served a similar need. Based upon Renoir's experiences and those of a French flying ace, this film covers a wider canvas than Milestone's in that it shows attitudes towards the war in both the French and the German armies.

Renoir elicits a customarily fine performance from Jean Gabin as Maréchal, a flier who is shot down and captured by the Germans, and a brilliant display from Erich Von Stroheim as the embittered German officer Colonel von Rauffenstein, whose war injuries reduce him to commanding a prison. It is from this prison that Maréchal and his friends de Boeldieu (Pierre Fresnay) and Rosenthal (Marcel Dalio) make their escape. Painting a vivid picture of the political changes which are sweeping through Europe, Renoir is able to develop empathy between the aristocratic Germany and the similarly upper-class de Boeldieu and enmity between Maréchal and Rosenthal which stems from the former's latent anti-Semitism. Eventually, von Rauffenstein is forced to kill de Boeldieu; Maréchal and Rosenthal bury their differences in a joint escape-bid. Their success, due in part to the reluctance of the pursuing Germans to shoot once the Frenchmen have crossed the Swiss border, might owe more to film-making convention than reality but the film most certainly carries enormous impact.

Deciding whether one film is better than another is beside the point. Here, in the 1930s, both America and France were prepared to take a view of war which was substantially realistic. The American film takes the German point of view while the French film takes both German and French views; on all sides merit is found. This, with their refutation of the old tradition of 'my country, right or wrong' shows a level of maturity very much missing from other films of the era.

By the middle of the decade, as Europe slipped towards another war, attitudes changed again. Nevertheless, publicity attending the reissue of *All Quiet on the Western Front* shows that some of the old, anti-war feeling had stuck: ' . . . it is a war against war itself . . . it is hell, not glory . . . war stripped of its glamour – war bared as the wrecker of humanity.' Theatre-owners were encouraged to organize essay contests in schools on such topics as 'Why, after seeing [the film], I think war should be abolished'.

Another message to theatre-owners contained a somewhat tasteless suggestion which inadvertently reveals much about movie-publicists of the day: 'Invite local disabled veterans to attend a special morning matinée as guests of the theatre. You can tie this stunt up with a local newspaper and the local bus company thereby getting additional publicity and ballyhoo. The bus company's share in the stunt will be to transport the veterans to your theatre.'

As for new films which appeared as war loomed in Europe, they reverted to earlier concepts, although some tried desperately to maintain a faintly anti-war ethos.

Sergeant York (1941) tells a version of the true story of Alvin York, a Tennessee farmer, who achieved folk-hero status after becoming America's most decorated soldier in World War I. York (Gary Cooper) is depicted as an extension of the quietly-spoken mythical cowboy who had developed out of the pioneers of the Old West. He starts out as a typical backwoods hell-raiser, but after running his poor old mother ragged, to say nothing of offending the local fundamentalist religious community, he falls in love with Gracie Williams

(Joan Leslie). To the mixed concern and delight of Mother York (Margaret Wycherly), young Alvin slaves away so that he can buy land suitable for his socially superior bride-to-be to live on. When the man who promised to sell him the land renegues on the deal, York sets out to kill him, but a providential bolt of lightning knocks him unconscious and destroys his rifle. York knows a message from God when he's struck by one and just in case there is any doubt a full symphony orchestra weighs in to underline the fact. He gets religion, much to the shiny-eyed delight of his mother, Gracie, and Pastor Pile (Walter Brennan) and all seems set for a rosy future. Then America enters the war and York's new religious beliefs force him to adopt a pacifist stance, but he fails to gain acceptance as a conscientious objector.

Once inducted into the army, York's natural ability with a rifle (he has previously been shown as capable of shooting the eyes out of a shoo-fly at a thousand paces) eases relations with those fellow soldiers and immediate superiors who mistrust his pacifism. The top brass view him very differently, almost paternally. They are like him, he is assured, they don't want to fight and kill, but if there's no choice . . .

Giving York a few days' leave and a book to read – a history of the United States – these highly improbable brass-hats sit back, secure in the knowledge that he will do what a man's gotta do.

He does, thanks once more to God, who arranges for the wind to blow York's Bible open at a page which takes him neatly off the horns of his particular moral dilemma: 'render unto God that which is God's, and unto Caesar that which is Caesar's.'

This, York concludes, means that so long as he keeps on a-praying he can kill as many Germans as he can set his sights on. It all works to such good effect that in the course of the second half of the film he achieves all the successes that brought the real Sergeant York his chestful of medals.

Among his feats are the killing of many Germans during the Argonne offensive, single-handedly wiping out a machine-gun post, and then assisting in the capture of 132 enemy soldiers.

Back home in Tennessee, by way of a New York tickertape parade, York marries Gracie and resumes the rural life from which he did not emerge until after World War II had begun in Europe. The reason for his return from obscurity was to sell his story to Warner's. Despite many offers during the previous two decades, York had steadfastly refused to capitalize on his fame by selling his story to the movies. The motivation behind his change of mind appears to have been primarily that of a concerned individual who had chosen his stance on the issue of whether or not America should enter this new war.

1941 was no time to have doubts about where to stand. Americans were much less equivocal than they had been at the outbreak of World War I, although there was much doubt as to whether or not the nation should be involved. Warner's, through the almost-true story of Sergeant York, left no doubt that their inclinations were aligned with those of the film's hero.

Despite its concern with pacifism, *Sergeant York* is essentially a return to the gung-ho tradition of American war movies. The rationalization of killing is bolstered by quasi-patriotic nonsense which allows characters foresight of events the film-makers know have happened. Thus Congressman Cordell Hull (Charles Trowbridge) can say, 'Some day, your people may ask you to serve them again. None of us can tell what we may be called on to do in years to come.'

By the mid-1950s, the mood had changed again and another powerfully realistic interpretation of World War I came to the screen. Using as its focus the mutinies in the French armies which had brought France close to abandoning the war just before America's intervention, Stanley Kubrick's *Paths of Glory* (1957) shows the real villains of the piece to be the military high command. There are none of the kindly staff officers that Sergeant York encountered in this army.

Based upon Humphrey Cobb's novel, which dealt with these grimly real events, the film traces the efforts of Colonel Dax (Kirk Douglas) to secure the release of three men who are to be court-martialled for cowardice. Unprepossessing and utterly unheroic, these three, Corporal Paris (Ralph Meeker), Private Arnaud (Joseph Turkel) and Private Ferol (Timothy Carey), have been selected at random from a battalion which failed to leave the trenches at Verdun when ordered forward on an impossible assault. Dax quickly finds himself in the middle of a conflict between General Mireau (George Macready) and General Broulard (Adolphe Menjou). Dax is helpless in this internecine battle and the three common soldiers are sentenced to death. One of these pathetic sacrificial victims is already at the point of death from wounds and another has gone insane.

Dax discovers that Mireau knew that the attack was doomed from the start and the court-martial is merely a device to get himself off the hook. Added to this, Mireau has also ordered his own artillery to shell French trenches in an effort to drive the men out and on to the offensive. But none of this helps Dax because he has missed the point of this bleakly cynical exercise. The three men have to die to encourage the others.

A General Broulard comments: 'Troops are like children, they need discipline. We must shoot a man now and then.'

A similar theme was developed in the British film *King and Country* (1964), in which the Dax-figure (portrayed by Dirk Bogarde) struggles vainly to save the life of Private Hamp (Tom Courtenay). Here, however, there was much less cynicism despite an ending in which the officer himself fires the final shot after the firing-squad has failed to kill Hamp.

The mood of *Paths of Glory* is one of deep cynicism. Kubrick goes beyond criticism of the military high command and becomes more concerned with the misuse of power and the corruption inherent in the class structure of old Europe. The old order should have collapsed with the end of World War I, but it survived. It was alive and well and controlling lives and deaths in Europe and also in America at the time the film was made. As to the 'land fit for heroes' for which so many fought and died, the old order controlled that too.

Regardless of Kubrick's main concerns in *Paths of Glory*, the overwhelming message of the film is that whatever might have happened in the world between Armistice Day, 1918, and the time this film was made, nothing has really changed. Wars go on; men are killed for many reasons, only a few of which have any relationship to the war in which they are fighting. The real enemy is seldom as clear-cut as just another ordinary man wearing a different uniform and holding another munitions manufacturer's rifle.

Paths of Glory, startlingly well-directed and photographed and with super-lative acting from everyone in its relatively small cast, stands in direct line with *All Quiet on the Western Front* and *La Grande Illusion* in its criticism of the war and the societies in which it was bred. In its realistic approach to events in World War I, *Paths of Glory* also aligns with *The Big Parade* while demon-strating clearly the essential down-home, cosy falsity at the core of *Sergeant York*.

There have been other anti-war films, of course, and some will be looked at in connection with other wars, but whatever its minor lapses, such as the somewhat sentimental ending as the captured German girl (Susanne Christ-ian) sings to the French troops before they return to battle, *Paths of Glory* stands today as one of the most powerful indictments of war ever made.

Yet none of these films, whether anti-heroic or anti-war, was as realistic as must have been hoped when they were planned. The overwhelming horror of the so-called Great War never comes through.

This was a war in which an estimated 13 million people died. On the battlefields alone, perhaps 3 million men were killed. They were machine-gunned in droves as they advanced slowly across impossible terrain or hung helplessly on barbed-wire entanglements; the bombardments which preceded such advances killed many more, not always the enemy, and in the process turned the rolling countryside into a lifeless, muddy moonscape. Barrages were so intense they could be heard as far away as England; the effect upon men only yards away was devastating. Men were deafened and driven mad by the noise, it mattered not at all that the barrage came from their own guns. Trenches, both the enemy's and those of the artillerymen's own comrades, were damaged and flooded as heavy rainstorms added to the chaos.

Men who were wounded fell into the mud and drowned. Even fit men who strayed off the wooden walkways sank out of sight before they could be rescued. More than sixty years on, the weapons of war and the bones of their victims still rise to the surface as farmers work the restored countryside.

The trenches shown in films often seem cosy, homes away from homes. True, some trenches were equipped with small comforts once it was realized that months, if not years, would be spent in the place, but the image remains false. Lice in men's clothing and hair and in the folds of their skin are not something which feature films could show very well even if they chose to do so. Had they chosen to, they could have shown the rats which gorged upon the bodies of men and horses and grew as big as cats and as aggressive as terriers – but they didn't.

And then there was gas. Suffocating, blinding, burning by gas caused innumerable casualties and left stark reminders upon survivors who could not see, or breathe properly, until the day they died.

The makers of feature films have stopped well short of depicting such things, with only Dalton Trumbo's *Johnny Got His Gun* venturing into this unspeakable territory.

Perhaps understandably, given the cost and difficulties of staging major battle scenes, to say nothing of the dangers of failing to recoup a multi-million-dollar budget, film-makers have chosen to concentrate their work on small groups or individuals. In so doing, however effective these films might be, the end result is invariably that audiences lose sight of the immensity of the slaughter.

One way of achieving an indication of the cost in human life comes at the end of *Oh! What a Lovely War* (1969). This film makes effective use of stylization in most of its sequences, whether dealing with the pompous jingoism of political and military leaders or by setting the popular songs of the day against the harsh reality of life in Flanders. At the end, the survivors of the Smith family, who have stood throughout as tokens for all those millions caught up in the war, are seen amidst rows of white crosses. The camera rises high into the sky and the white crosses are not just there in dozens, or even in hundreds but in tens of thousands. Higher still goes the camera and the rows of crosses go on and on and on . . .

But the manner in which *Oh! What a Lovely War* ridicules the military high command and the politicians falls well short of the treatment they deserved. Incompetence, criminal negligence, indifference to the fate of their helpless cannon-fodder were normal. Douglas Haig, pompous, stubborn, wilful, vain and opinionated, survived the war to receive the grateful thanks of the British government, a large sum of money and a bevy of awards and decorations. No one asked what the gassed, the maimed and the crippled, the blind and the shell-shocked, the deaf and the bereaved thought about Haig. Neither did anyone in government pay much heed to their fate. If they couldn't be hidden from sight in the way that Dalton Trumbo's basket-case was hidden, they could at least be conveniently forgotten. Film-makers could have done much more to lift the veil from the fate of these men, had they chosen to do so.

At the end of 1918, with the war finally over, British and American soldiers were anxious to leave alien Europe and return to their homes. But the nations to which they returned, and for which they had fought so courageously, had undergone many changes. Some of these would prevent former soldiers from ever again blending into normal social life.

In America, not least of the problems facing returning doughboys was the unexpected effect upon society of a new law which had been threatened for some time and finally hit home in 1919 – Prohibition.

CHAPTER FIVE

The world into which returning American soldiers marched was very different from the one they had left. They might have expected some changes, but few can have been prepared for the domestic conflict in which many were soon embroiled. Neither can they have anticipated that within a decade many would face ruin, despair and even starvation. When Johnny came marching home again it was with high hopes that if things were not the same, they would be better. He certainly did not expect them to be worse.

The plight of many ex-soldiers was well expressed in fictional form in Raoul Walsh's *The Roaring Twenties* (1939). The job Eddie Bartlett (James Cagney) confidently expects will still be his has been filled by a man who sneers at the uniformed and bemedalled hero, until laid out with typical Cagney expertise.

The realistic quality of the film is considerably aided by documentary passages inserted into the account of Eddie's post-war life. These effectively establish the era in which the fictitious events occur. These sections and the prologue by reporter Mark Hellinger, who would later produce many fine movies, give the film an honest touch although its central assumption is somewhat dubious.

The implication of the film is clear: Eddie Bartlett is any unfortunate doughboy who comes back from the war to find his job taken and is thus left with no alternative but a life of crime. Audiences quickly lost sight of this facile justification for life as an outlaw in the rapid flow of the exciting events depicted on the screen.

Despite this basic failing, the film takes a remarkably clear-sighted view of much of that period of American history which was, to the film's makers, only yesterday's news. After its opening moments, which hint at the approach of another worldwide conflict, the film flashes back to 1918 and shows three buddies in the trenches, living out the last days of the war to end all wars. The nature of the three characters is quickly spelled out: Eddie is tough but a dreamer, only interested in the pictures he carries of a girl back home whom he has never met but idolizes; Lloyd Hart (Jeffrey Lynn) is a sentimental good guy who cannot shoot a German soldier he has in his sights because he appears to be no more than fifteen years old; George Hally (Humphrey Bogart) is revealed as an out-and-out bad hat when he eliminates the same German youth and laconically remarks, 'He'll never be sixteen.'

Using a swift sequence of documentary montage, including newspaper headlines both visual and aural, the story whisks ahead to 1919 and the return of the soldiers to their homeland. After Eddie's scene in the garage, when he discovers the reality of what he has been fighting for, he joins forces with an old friend, Danny Green (Frank McHugh), and together they drive a cab, splitting shifts so that the vehicle is never off the road. So far, this could be the early stages of any young man's efforts to attain the American Dream.

But then more montage and newsreel inserts announce the passage of the Volstead Act and the beginnings of the hoodlum empires. Eddie is soon involved, but only as a delivery boy until he rumbles the fact that all it needs to become a supplier is a bathtub and a recipe for high-octane rotgut.

Rising swiftly upwards, and ignoring the advice of Lloyd, who is now a lawyer, Eddie soon shows all the outward signs of any American success story while avoiding the grosser manifestations of the bootleggers of reality.

A further montage sequence shows the Great Crash which wipes out Eddie's new riches just as though he were a legitimate businessman. This is perhaps the most significant shift from reality so far in the film. There may well have been some criminals who felt the pinch brought on by the Depression but after Black Tuesday most of them, especially those who had organized, were in a much stronger position than before.

More montage suggests that the Depression which has now hit America, and which the unshaven and ragged Eddie depicts, also put an end to the bootlegger and organized crime. Perhaps this was a legitimate view from the close vantage point of 1939 when the film was being made, but it was clearly mistaken. The profits from illicit alcohol did not fall appreciably in the Depression. Neither did the repeal of the Volstead Act in 1933 put a stop to organized criminals and their ability to make money.

Unlike Eddie Bartlett, the bigtime crooks had money in abundance and little if any of it was tied up in such insecure places as banks and Wall Street. With a steady flow of cash generated by almost a decade and a half of plying their trade in booze, together with illegal gambling, protection rackets and prostitution, the gangs pumped millions into any area of commerce that functioned in cash. Food, garments, restaurants, theatres, clubs and movies all became targets for this nebulous Mob. With no one else around with cash or muscle enough to compete, they quickly diversified into many fields that had hitherto been legitimate business. Even liquor continued as a mainstay of their trade following repeal of Prohibition. Profits could still be made by selling bootleg booze to customers who were reluctant to fork out double the price for the real thing, the result of the government's application of taxes.

Nothing of this entry into big business by the mobsters is indicated in *The Roaring Twenties*. Even the ending, a typical cleaning up of loose ends to prove that cime does not pay, ignores reality while rigorously applying the conventions of Hollywood's morality.

Most returning soldiers fared better than Eddie Bartlett, at least until the Depression, and those who did not seldom chose crime as their escape. Even the men who did transgress did so in a relatively minor fashion and the implication of *The Roaring Twenties*, that the gangland killings of the era were a direct result of society's failure to accommodate its war heroes, is greatly exaggerated.

Among the returning troops who found life bleak and unpromising were black soldiers who had learned in Europe that their colour was less of a handicap elsewhere than it was in their own homeland.

The opening sequences of the all-black musical *Stormy Weather* (1943) include some newsreel footage of black soldiers marching through New York. Any implication of joint participation in the war is undercut by the very fact they *are* all black. The US Army was as sharply segregated as any southern town and remained so until the 1950s. Even the separate-but-equal façade that featured in many areas of civilian life did not exist in the army; the officers commanding so-called all-black regiments were white.

Filmed sequences of Bill 'Bojangles' Robinson, the star of *Stormy Weather*, are intercut with the newsreel and show him carrying a bass drum in 'Jim Europe's 15th Infantry Band'. The band the real Jim Europe led was that of the 369th Infantry, the famous 'Hellfighters', who had acquitted themselves heroically in the war. Such a change is both trivial and unnecessary but then, the remainder of the film, despite brilliant musical performances by entertainers such as Fats Waller, Lena Horna, Ada Brown, Cab Calloway and Robinson himself, is also an exercise in faintly patronizing trivia.

Bill Robinson was a masterly performer who, had he been white, might have given Fred Astaire a dance for his money. Being black meant that most of his film career consisted of clicking interminably up and down conveniently-positioned flights of stairs in the company of a determinedly twinkling Shirley Temple.

The reality of what their return to America meant to black doughboys, who had experienced a brief taste of freedom at the expense of many lives, is not of interest to the film's makers – for this is not what *Stormy Weather* is about. Unfortunately, it seems to have been of little interest to any other maker of feature films since then.

One returning white American who ended up very much on the wrong side of the law was Robert E. Burns, whose post-war restlessness led him almost by accident into participation in a small-time robbery. As a result he was convicted and sentenced to hard labour on a chain gang at a Georgia prison. Eventually, he escaped and built a new life as a successful businessman in real estate and magazine publishing. When his secret was uncovered he was persuaded to return to prison on the promise of a nominal few days' incarceration before formal pardon and release. The authorities renegued on the deal they had struck with Burns and he found himself back on the chain gang, this time serving an indefinite sentence. He escaped again and wrote of his experiences in a book entitled *I Am a Fugitive From a Georgia Chain Gang!*

When Burns's story was filmed by Mervyn LeRoy, the public was outraged by depiction of the conditions in southern prisons and demanded changes in the law. *I Am a Fugitive From a Chain Gang* (1932) paints a picture of almost unrelieved grimness and even a half-century on its impact is powerful. As James Allen, the Robert E. Burns-figure, Paul Muni is compelling and believable. Many Americans must have seen the film and thought, 'There but for the grace of God . . .'

The re-arrest of Burns, three weeks after the film's release, served the dual purpose of bringing reality home with a bang and providing a dramatic boost to takings at the box-office.

Burns was eventually pardoned in 1945, ten years before his death. The changes made to the law had some effect but events in southern states as recently as the 1980s suggest that the mental processes which permitted the authorities to sanction such brutal penal institutions as those depicted in *I Am a Fugitive From a Chain Gang* have not changed very much at all.

The criminal element depicted in this film differs greatly from the fictional lawbreakers in *The Roaring Twenties*, yet for many people Cagney and Bogart and their contemporaries appeared as realistic impersonators of the hoodlums who were soiling the streets of many cities in America and of Chicago in particular. There was, however, little that was accurate even when these films purported to tell true stories about real people.

Hollywood quickly took up Al Capone as a suitable candidate for immortality but for many years failed to show him accurately. Not only that, the complex reality of organized crime in America might never have existed for all that Hollywood appeared to care.

In the late 1960s, when cued by Robert Kennedy's determined assault on organized crime, film-makers did take a serious crack at the problem but the results were mostly inadequate. Not until the early 1970s were true depictions of organized crime shown. Even then, the two best films on the subject, which Francis Ford Coppola based upon Mario Puzo's novel *The Godfather*, failed to stress the depths of the organized criminal's venality and depravity. However, *The Godfather Part II* contains many moments during its opening sequences which accurately depict the lot of the Italian immigrant.

In the half-century from 1875, Italians emigrated to America in ever-increasing numbers. Most came from the south of Italy and from Sicily, where custom and tradition had established a lifestyle very different from that prevailing anywhere else in Europe, different even from that of the north of Italy. Among these ways were the widespread corruption and extortion practised by those who lived outside what little law there was in Calabria and Sicily. The men from these regions, and to a lesser extent those from the city of Naples, had several important characteristics in common with one another.

Overwhelmingly of peasant stock, the *contadini* had strong family ties, both of blood and through a complex system of godparenthood. Outlaw bands flourished, engaging in many illegal activities including robbery, extortion, and smuggling. These bands became known as honoured societies – *onerate società*. Brutally opposed by the northern-based government, and spread thinly, these groups had little going for them except the code of manliness – *omertà* – and the immeasurably powerful bond exerted by the societies, the family, and their absolute refusal to reveal secrets. This final quality was underlined to no mean extent by each individual's awareness that to talk was to serve one's own death warrant.

The societies differed from region to region: in Naples there was the *Camorra* and *La Mano Nero*, the Black Hand Gang; in Sicily there was the Mafia. In America it was the Black Hand Gang which first claimed some attention, but their relatively unsophisticated, small-scale activities soon gave way to the much more organized, bigger-thinking *L'Unione Siciliana*. As early as the 1850s, there were links between criminals and the political bosses of those American cities which would soon play host to Italian immigrants. Understandably, the majority of Italian immigrants and their descendants who had no criminal connections whatsoever took, and still take, exception to being tarred forever with the same brush as the criminal minority. The criminal faction among Italians was probably no greater than that among any other immigrant group. The Irish and the Jews, for example, both featured extensively in early criminal activities in the New World, but the Italians, with their ready-made system of societies, were better organized.

The percentage of criminally-inclined Italians may have been small, but it is their nature that proved to be significant. As Kenneth Allsop has pointed out, the Sicilian community in Chicago was little more than a transplanted Sicilian village untouched by American life and customs. The nature of this transplanted community, now located in an alien land, is vividly realized in *The Godfather Part II*. This film also shows how smalltime Black Handers were ruthlessly removed by the Sicilians. Vito Corleone (Robert De Niro) eliminates an extortionist with almost casual ease as he begins his own rise to

The enthusiasm with which some Italians joined the ranks of organized crime and the relative passivity with which non-criminal Italians viewed the Mafia's activities can be partially understood by appreciation of the discrimination practised by other Americans. For example, the rates of pay for labourers working on Croton Reservoir in 1895 were listed as follows: White $1.30–1.50; Coloured $1.25–1.40; Italians $1.15–1.25.

American attitudes towards Italians in general were largely influenced by the prejudice of the Northern Italians who came to America in an earlier immigrant wave and who hated the Southern Italians and Sicilians. This prejudice undoubtedly alienated the new wave of Italians and strengthened their existing societal ties. Even if the origins of organized crime ante-date the arrival in America of the majority of Italians, these immigrants introduced a ruthless determination to succeed. This ruthlessness affected not just outsiders but also members of the family who betrayed or failed to lend aid when it was needed, and made the criminal organizations unstoppable.

Once again, *The Godfather Part II* contains the best portrayal of this element of *l'ordine della famiglia* as Michael Corleone (Al Pacino) orders the death of his weak-willed older brother Fredo (John Cazale), who has conspired against him. Unfortunately, due largely to the stress placed upon family loyalty, this vicious act appears logical and an almost acceptable form of punishment for breaking the rules of *onerate* and *omertà*. Nowhere is there a hint of awareness at the astonishing degree of religious hypocrisy displayed by any of the characters. There is also a permanent undertow relating the criminal family with the great business families of America. This is, of course, intentional as Coppola has confirmed that the Godfather films are a metaphorical critique of the American system.

Only rarely in *The Godfather Part II* and in its predecessor, *The Godfather* (1972), is any suggestion of the nature of the family's business activities allowed to break surface. At times the Corleones could almost be mistaken for the Rockefellers, or the Duponts, or, perish the thought, the Ewings. The house rules are the same, only the punishment for breaking them is rather more extreme – not to say, final.

The complexities of the criminal 'family' shown with such clarity in *The Godfather Part II* are strikingly absent from any previous Hollywood attempts to show the activities of organized criminals in America. In the earlier forays into the gangster's world, and especially those films which purported to deal with the life of Al Capone, the failing is understandable because in the 1930s and 1940s few, if any, outsiders knew what was really happening beneath the slimy stones of the underworld.

The underworld's Italian connection was well established by the early years of the twentieth century. A glance at the criminal roll-call shows a preponderance of Italian names – not that names alone are a reliable guide. Many names were changed, sometimes deliberately but as often as not by careless or overworked immigration officials at Ellis Island (wonderfully evoked in *The Godfather Part II*). This name-changing made some Italians sound un-Italian and certain non-Italians sound Italian. Thus, James Gebardi became Machine-Gun Jack McGurn and John T. Noland became Legs Diamond.

Unmistakably Italian was Calabrian-born Big Jim Colosimo, the head of Chicago's underworld when Prohibition began. Colosimo was bigtime, but that did not save him from threats from the Black Hand Gang who were notoriously freelance in their thinking and activities. For protection, Colosimo imported Naples-born Johnny Torrio from New York, who brought with him a deceptively soft-looking assistant named Alphonse Capone. This high-powered protection did not work out the way Colosimo expected. Torrio, quick to assess Chicago's possibilities, hired Frankie Yale (Uale), at the time the national head of *L'Unione Siciliana*, to kill Colosimo.

This was in 1920, and although Colosimo was followed by Tony D'Andrea and Mike Merlo, Torrio was soon the leading figure. His nerves were not up to the job, however, and when he was shot and wounded in 1925 he opted for an early retirement. Torrio's successor was Al Capone and he was made of sterner stuff. Because Capone was not a Sicilian (he was probably born near Rome) he could not hold outright leadership. To compensate for this accident of birth Capone quickly had Frankie Yale murdered and brought Torrio out of retirement as nominal leader of the national Mafia.

Capone's greatest gift was his ability to adapt the techniques of the Old Country's rural outlaws to suit the sophisticated setting and urban needs of the New World. He did it with such consummate skill that his organization remains to the present day. The extent to which American life has been infiltrated is a matter of speculation. There are those who choose to pretend that organized crime does not exist, as J. Edgar Hoover so chose for many years. Others choose to think it will go away, as did Ramsey Clark, former Attorney-General of the United States. Contrary views are held by some who think the extent to which organized crime has burrowed into American life is so deep that it may control political bodies and individuals who might one day hold the highest offices in the land, if they have not done so already. As J. Garth observed in an article in *SunDance* magazine, 'Organized crime will put a man in the White House someday, and he won't even know it until they hand him the bill.'

As early as 1912 D. W. Griffith had tinkered with urban criminals in his film *The Musketeers of Pig Alley*, but it was not until the close of the silent era that a film was made which established public interest in gangsters as a staple part of their movie-going entertainment. *Underworld* (1927) drew the crowds and showed Hollywood's moneymen that it was not necessary to hold up banks to make millions, just show such events on the screen. The film was made at a time when the average citizen need only open a daily newspaper to learn what was happening on the streets of the nation's cities. Al Capone was already ruling Cicero County, Chicago, with a rod of blued steel, but had yet to perpetrate the St Valentine's Day Massacre.

With sound coming to the movies and the ensuing surge of enthusiasm for the new gangster-genre, many films followed. *Little Caesar* (1930) traces the career of an individual gangster in much the same way as did *Underworld*, but immediately proved that the squeal of rubber on rain-slicked streets and the crash of gunfire were not the only benefits sound brought to the gangster-movie. The dialogue spoken by the actors portraying gunmen, cops, molls and the rest of the rich panoply of characters who swept across the screen is just as vital. Laced with slang, the words are spat out with the speed and ferocity of bullets. Whether or not real-life gangsters spoke like this was immaterial. If they did not, then it mattered little because this was the way audiences expected them to speak; and, anyway, before long the gangsters would pick up the requirements of their larger-than-life role in society and make sure that they spoke like the movie actors.

The results were so persuasive that a few years later many young men and women, caught up in the acute poverty of the mid-West, would use these movies as blueprints for their own forays into crime which would, in their turn, generate still more movies.

The concept of automatically equating Italians and Sicilians with crime was underlined by many films of the era. The principal character in *Doorway to Hell* (1930) is called Louis Ricarno, while Caesar Enrico Bandello is the central figure in *Little Caesar*.

In many respects – complexity and depth of characterization, interestingly multi-layered storyline, production values and overall quality of acting among them – *Doorway to Hell* is the best of these early entries to the genre, but it was Edward G. Robinson's portrayal of Rico Bandello which set in motion the massive audience enthusiasm for and, perhaps surprisingly, identification with the mobsters who were making the streets of American cities unsafe for law-abiding citizens.

Or is it so surprising? The establishment of Prohibition had made the wholly law-abiding citizen something of a rare bird. Very ordinary people broke the law; some were caught and punished viciously, unlike the gangsters who quite literally got away with murder.

There was also a pervading view that none of it mattered too much. Encouraged by official comments which suggested that the internecine gang wars were a good thing because the criminals were busily killing themselves off, the people stepped back a pace and saw only the surface gloss provided by the movies.

The successes of the screen gangster were something to applaud and enthuse over. What did it matter if the Hays Office forced tag-on endings which showed the criminal getting his comeuppance? To many Americans, who were broke, ragged and hungry and saw no promise of change in their circumstances, being shot to death at the end of a rampage through champagne, cigars, silk shirts, fast cars and even faster women was not so much a punishment as a reasonable price to pay for the fun to be had along the way.

Robinson's Little Caesar was clearly modelled upon Al Capone, despite the movie being set in New York, yet the similarities were few. Rico is a smalltime criminal and gathers about him relatively few hoodlums to do his dirty work. There is no indication of the massive army of soldiers with which Capone controlled Cicero County.

Much closer to the reality of Al Capone's fiefdom was the background to *Scarface: The Shame of the Nation* (1932), which took the risk of giving its central character the same nickname while only just disguising his real name as Tony Camonte (Paul Muni). By this time the malevolent mobster was on his way out. Sentenced in October, 1931 to eleven years' imprisonment on income tax evasion charges, Capone managed to put off the evil day until early summer, 1932 when he was incarcerated in Atlanta penitentiary.

It was while he was there, cutting trousers in the prison tailoring shop, that he learned that Howard Hawks was making a movie to be entitled *Scarface*. He sent word that he expected to be consulted and allowed to comment on the manner in which the central character was depicted. Hawks declined this unwanted offer.

Much has been made of the incestuous relationship clearly indicated by the Camonte character in his attitude towards his sister. The origins of this lay in the overall concept for the film, which Hawks described in an interview with Peter Bogdanovich. The director had wanted to treat Capone and his immediate family and associates as if they were the Borgias updated and set down in Chicago. The incestuous element in the story of the Borgias was also carried over for its undoubted dramatic effect.

If Capone managed to see the film in one or another of his prison homes, it is unlikely that he took offence since even such a hawk-eyed body as the Hays Office missed the incest, objecting instead that the gangster's relationship with his sister was too beautiful for such a villainous individual. They did, however, press for lengthening the title *Scarface* to indicate how people should feel about it all.

The censor's needs were also accommodated in the ending and Tony Camonte, unlike the real-life Scarface, is gunned down in the street. The final scene, in which what looks mightily like half of Chicago's police force gather around to look at the body, undercuts the desired effect: Scarface Tony Camonte must have been quite a man if it needed all that firepower to cut him down.

Scarface, which was based upon a novel by Armitage Traill, floats reasonably close to reality. Given the proximity in both time and distance to the real people being depicted, such accuracy, however limited it might appear by later standards, is more than merely surprising. It also suggests the film's makers might have had a collective death-wish. The names given to the principal characters are only barely changed from those of real criminals in the hierarchy of Cicero County. Apart from Camonte/Capone there are Big Louis Costillo/Big Jim Colosimo, Johnny Lovo/Johnny Torrio and an Irishman named O'Hara representing Dion O'Banion, whose heroic declaration 'To hell with them Sicilians' proved to be a fatally unwise remark. Two major events of Capone's career are shown: the machine-gunning at the Hawthorne Hotel in which he almost lost his life, and the St Valentine's Day Massacre in which his men, dressed as police officers, machine-gunned Bugs Moran's acolytes in a garage.

These same events have appeared in most of the Capone films. The early *Bad Company* (1931) was the first to show the St Valentine's Day Massacre while Roger Corman's *The St Valentine's Day Massacre* (1967), which stars Jason Robards Jr., has this event as its main concern.

For *Party Girl* (1958) film-makers were still using a made-up name for Capone, hence Lee J. Cobb, in lip-curling form, as a character named Rico Angelo. In *Capone* (1975), starring Ben Gazzara in the title role, a serious attempt is made to cleave to reality in appearances and setting, but the storyline takes a few liberties with events.

In the earlier *Al Capone* (1959), in which Rod Steiger plays the gang boss, the need still existed for an evil-doer to pay for his actions, and an entirely fictitious sequence is added during Capone's term of imprisonment. A group of other convicts attack and beat up the Big Fellow. This was wishful thinking, for even in the pokey Capone had power and influence. The warders, let alone the other cons, would have been reluctant to test their heroism by giving him anything other than kid-glove treatment. The real-life stabbing of Capone in 1936 while in Alcatraz was an impulsive attack by a mentally-disturbed inmate who felt he had a personal grievance against the crime czar from Chicago. Either that or he had decided that death was preferable to life on the Rock.

Al Capone juggles a few facts around to create a better-balanced structure. Johnny Torrio (Nehemiah Persoff) is merely a night-club owner (which, technically, he was, because between them the Mob owned just about every booze-outlet in town) and the nephew of Big Jim Colosimo (Joe de Santis).

Al Capone also indulges in some heavy-breathing over the widow of one of his victims and arranges the killing of Kelly (Martin Balsam), a corrupt journalist who has double-crossed him. This element of the fiction touches upon the demise of Jake Lingle, a bottom-rung newspaperman. When Lingle was shot in the back of the head one summer's day in 1930, his bank account was found to contain considerably more money than his meagre salary should

Lingle appears to have been many things – most of them unsavoury, to many people, all of them dangerous. Obviously someone had decided that enough was enough. It probably was not Capone but by 1959, when *Al Capone* was made, no one cared.

A much earlier film, *The Finger Points* (1931), deals circumspectly with the Lingle case. The central character's name is changed to Breckenridge Lee (Richard Barthelmess) and the screenplay necessarily resorts to invention to conceal the fact that few people at that time knew the truth. Certainly Lingle/Lee was in someone's pocket; certainly he was uncomfortably cosy both with criminals and with the federal authorities who were patiently digging into Capone's financial affairs. The connections made by the film may have been legitimate but it was not especially successful, despite the fact that by the time of its release Capone had been indicted for tax frauds.

Of the later Capone films only *The St Valentine's Day Massacre* makes any attempt at explaining the complexities of the criminal corporate structure he was building. The others are just gangster movies, out of their time and with nothing new to say.

The massacre on St Valentine's Day, 1929, did of course provide a moment of high drama in a masterly film which was concerned neither with organized crime nor with reality. *Some Like It Hot* (1959) did not have much to do with American history, even if it has taken a permanent and deservedly honoured place in the history of American film.

The 1936 stabbing of Capone, allied to partial paralysis and the mental deterioration brought about by syphilis transmitted from one or more of the girls who helped provide his income, reduced him to a state where he could no longer be regarded as a threat. He was taken to San Pedro prison, later moved to Terminal Island Correctional Institution, finally to Lewisburg prison in Pennsylvania. Towards the end of 1939 he was released and went to live on his estate in Miami where he died in January 1947 at the age of fifty-two.

It is Miami which provides the setting for the re-make of *Scarface*, although by this time there is little of the Capone figure left. In *Scarface* (1984) Al Pacino plays Tony Montana, a Cuban thrown out of his own country along with many other criminals when Fidel Castro took advantage of a moment of weakness on the part of the American government. Montana's building of a criminal enterprise based upon narcotics is a harsh indictment of contemporary America but owes little other than its storyline to the era of the Big Fellow. There is one link with that earlier reality, however. Just as Al Capone made the grave error of sampling his own wares and contracting syphilis, so Montana takes his own medicine and becomes a cocaine addict. If Scarface Al Capone had been around when the criminal empire he had built went into drugs, he would not have been dumb enough to make a mistake like that.

Rarely in the gangster movie is there a distinctive moral tag, whatever the Hays Office and successive censors may have tried to impose. Crime is not shown to be bad of itself. It is almost as if that most illogical of clichés – that a gun is as good or as bad as the man who holds it – has been expanded into the wider world of criminal activities in general. Criminals, even the real ones brought to the screen by Hollywood, are seldom seen to be thoroughly immoral. There is usually a hint that matters could be worse. If men impersonated by such deep-down nice guys as Cagney, Bogart or Robinson were not there to control the booze and the drugs or the women and the political machine, then someone else, someone even less accountable and more venal, might move in. It is a fallacy Hollywood has not done enough to discredit.

The other side of the political and social thought which marked the era, that of the people who supported and believed in Prohibition, was shown in the film version of a novel by Upton Sinclair. *The Wet Parade* (1932) falls far short, however, of Sinclair's anti-alcohol polemic. Primarily the reason lay in the changing times. The novel was written and published in 1931, by which year the national mood had already shifted. The public wanted the Eighteenth Amendment to the Constitution repealed and so too did Franklin D. Roosevelt, the Democratic candidate for the forthcoming presidential election. MGM, the makers of the film, altered the balance of the novel, which showed that alcoholism was something that could afflict anyone in any class. In the film version, booze becomes instead the curse of the lower orders for whom moderation is a meaningless word.

There seems little doubt that the changes made by MGM, then ruled by Louis B. Mayer and Irving Thalberg, were partially a result of personal responses towards a story which openly attacked the class of Americans to which they themselves belonged. For one thing, this class believed it could hold its liquor; for another, even if it was engaged in mild bootlegging activities, this was done with a view to providing a social need and not to support, or to be linked with in any way, the Al Capones of the world. In any event the film's director, Victor Fleming, was partial to a taste and could not have found the novel's theme too close to his heart.

For a while, Mayer was the California State Chairman of the Republican Party and had actively supported Herbert Hoover in the 1928 election, hoping to be rewarded by being appointed Ambassador to the Court of St James. Hoover had other ideas, but Mayer remained politically active, garnering party funds by means of a compulsory deduction from the wage packets of his employees. This was an action which endeared him to neither the labour unions nor to the Democrats on MGM's payroll.

His political activities placed him in the opposite camp to Upton Sinclair and by 1934 any vestiges of cordiality which might have remained were shattered when MGM, under instruction from Mayer and Thalberg, produced a series of fake newsreels. These showed hordes of unwashed unemployed descending on California to take advantage of proposals from Sinclair who was then running for state governor under the EPIC banner (End Poverty in California). The use of film in this way, while commonplace at the time in Hitler's Germany and in Stalinist Russia, marks a sad moment in Hollywood's history.

Politically, this period of American history, running from the end of World War I to the beginning of the Depression, was one of considerable dissension, with extremes of thought emanating from both ends of the spectrum.

Reactionaries were at work on such matters as the teaching of Darwin's theory of evolution, and when John T. Scopes, a schoolmaster in Dayton, Tennessee, was charged with the heresy of teaching something other than the biblical version of the Creation to his pupils, two heavy guns of the legal profession turned the trial into big news.

William Jennings Bryan, by now bereft of any chance of achieving his ambitions for the Presidency, was brought along for the prosecution while one of the most famous men of this or any other period in American legal history, Clarence Darrow, led the defence. The events of the trial formed the basis of a mid-1950s stage play written by Jerome E. Lawrence and Robert Edwin Lee. First presented in Dallas in January 1955, the New York production later that same year starred Paul Muni and Ed Begley. The screen version of *Inherit the Wind* (1960) stars Spencer Tracy as Henry Drummond (the Darrow-figure) and Fredric March as Matthew Harrison Brady (Bryan).

In the film, as in real-life, Brady/Bryan agrees to testify as an expert on the Bible and is reduced to a hesitant, stumbling wreck by Drummond/Darrow. Soon after the trial Bryan died, a pathetic relic of past times and forgotten beliefs. At least, they were forgotten until the 1980s when, under the impetus created by Born-again Christians in the highest offices in the land, the teaching of evolution was once more banned in some American schools.

Contrasting with such reactionary thought as that which prompted the Scopes 'Monkey Trial', the 1920s saw the flourishing of radicalism in America. Although of great importance to the political and social history of the nation, stories of radicals have seldom been tackled by film-makers, perhaps out of the fear that to do so might be thought as catering to the communist threat. Certainly many film-makers of the 1930s and 1940s who touched upon anything that was even faintly left-of-centre later found themselves having to defend these lapses of Americanism. Some of the more notable examples, made when the USSR was a wartime ally, will be dealt with in Chapter 7.

Radicalism in the first quarter of the twentieth century was barely touched upon at any time. Anyone depending upon films as the sole means of discovering what went on in America in this period could be excused for thinking that Sacco and Vanzetti were the only radicals in the country. Even these two were usually classed as bomb-throwing, foreign-born anarchists who stood well outside the mainstream of American life. Such alienation was a necessary adjunct of developing the mental state required to tolerate their appalling treatment, the rigged trial and their eventual execution after seven years on Death Row. *Winterset* (1936) touches upon the case in a filmed version of Maxwell Anderson's stage play but concerns itself more with the character of a young man (well played by Burgess Meredith in his screen début) seeking the real perpetrators of a crime for which his father was executed. An accurate version of the case appears in *Sacco and Vanzetti* (1970), an Italian film which leaves no doubt that its makers believe the two immigrants were railroaded.

The leading figures of the radical movement of this era include Eugene Debs, who ran for President in 1900, 1904 and 1912 (attracting 6 per cent of the popular vote in the latter) and Big Bill Haywood, the leader of the International Workers of the World (the Wobblies). Along with several others both men were imprisoned in 1918 following trial for sedition. In reality, Debs had publicly opposed American intervention in the war in Europe and had vilified the new Sedition Act, part of which forbade, for example, behaving disloyally to the government and vilifying the Sedition Act. He thus fell foul of an early version of Catch-22.

As in most radical movements, the working-class activists were joined, whether they liked it or not, by left-wing intellectuals. Among those who became associated with the movement were Max Eastman, Emma Goldman, Eugene O'Neill and John (Jack) Reed.

Jack Reed's story had to wait until more than a half-century after his death before a major film brought it to the screen. Reed came from a wealthy family in Portland, Oregon and was educated at Harvard. These places might seem strange breeding grounds for radicalism, but some understanding of his attitude towards the privileged world into which he was born can be gained by examining the political atmosphere in the north-western states of America at the time.

This part of the country was home to people who belonged to the opposite extremes of American political thought. Inevitably there were confrontations which often resulted in acts of physical violence.

Wesley Everest, a doughboy who had served his country with distinction in World War I, was one of a number of radicals who planned to attend a meeting and parade organized in Centralia by the Wobblies in celebration of an event which meant a great deal to the ex-soldier. A mob led by local businessmen and American Legionnaires attacked the meeting hall and Everest was one of several men pursued by a crowd obviously intent on violence. Cornered, he shot at the mob and fatally injured one of their number. When his gun was empty he was captured and beaten up, but remained defiant. He was also confident the mob would go no further; after all, it was broad daylight and the parade he and his comrades were attending was in celebration of the first anniversary of Armistice Day, for this was 11 November 1919.

Everest's confidence proved to be fatally ill-judged. That night the mob re-formed and broke into the jail where he was held. He was dragged outside and into a car where he was beaten up and castrated with a knife; then a rope was put around his neck and he was thrown from a bridge, not once but three times. Finally, just in case Wesley Everest's friends had not got the message, the mob spent the rest of the night shooting bullets into his body. Before dawn, the body was taken back to the jail and dumped in a cell, no doubt to encourage the others.

At a subsequent hearing the local coroner made his position clear when he brought in a verdict of suicide. Some years later this same coroner was appointed superintendent at the notorious insane asylum at Steilacoom. This was the institution where another north-western radical would later be illegally incarcerated and lobotomized. She was the beautiful Hollywood actress Frances Farmer, whose appalling story was told in *Frances* (1983) – a film which presented almost the whole truth.

This, then, was the region and atmosphere in which Jack Reed's political ideology was formed. *Reds* (1980) tells his story from 1915 when Reed (Warren Beatty) returns to Portland and meets Louise Bryant (Diane Keaton). He is already involved deeply in left-wing activities and is writing for *The Masses*, the most radical journal of its day. He is constantly fighting against the social injustice which he sees at every turn.

Reds traces the burgeoning relationship between Jack and Louise (thus somewhat over-inflating her role in real events) and their involvement with other noted radicals of the day, among them Emma Goldman (Maureen Stapleton), Max Eastman (Edward Herrman), editor of *The Masses*, and playwright Eugene O'Neill (Jack Nicholson). After America's entry into World War I, something which Reed has struggled to prevent, both Jack and Louise leave America. She goes to Europe to report on the war; he follows and persuades her to accompany him to Russia to report on the Revolution. Their experiences in Petrograd bring their already fiery enthusiasm for change in America to white heat.

Returning to America, they fling themselves into radicalization of the American Socialist Party. When this fails, Jack forms the breakaway Communist Labor Party of America. By now other factions have formed the American Communist Party, and much of the potential power of the movement is dissipated through internecine squabbling. Added to this, the Red Scare is on and neither Jack nor Louise can escape the resulting crack-down by the authorities.

By now Louise has become concerned at Jack's involvement in factional politics and strenuously urges him to continue with his writing, which reached its apogee with the publication of his book *Ten Days That Shook the World*, an account of the Russian revolution.

Jack decides to return to Russia to seek recognition for his party from the Communist International. *En route* he is imprisoned in Finland, where his already suspect health deteriorates badly. Eventually he reaches Russia and is appointed to the Executive Committee of the Comintern, but his support for the Wobblies and his opposition to the American Federation of Labor lead to conflict with Grigory Zinoviev (Jerzy Kosinski). Discovering that an important speech he has written for the Congress of the Eastern Peoples has been altered in translation, Reed quarrels with Zinoviev.

On his return to Moscow Jack is joined by Louise, who has finally reached Russia after an arduous journey through Finland. But Jack's health finally gives way and he dies.

After his death Jack Reed was buried in the Kremlin wall, a Russian honour never afforded any other American.

When first conceived, the film was very faithful to the life of Jack Reed and was also strongly politically committed. The screenplay was written by Trevor Griffiths, perhaps the most highly political of British television writers. His first draft screenplay was subjected to many changes, mostly by Warren Beatty, who, in addition to starring in the film, was also producer and director. These changes weakened some of the political content in favour of the personal relationship between Jack and Louise. As Jack Reed's life was totally committed to his political beliefs this dilution weakened the whole film.

Nevertheless, given the role of Jack Reed in American politics, it is a measure of the growing maturity of American film-makers that his story was made at all. For several decades after Reed's death, Hollywood would not even have considered making such a film. Even in the diluted and romanticized form in which it eventually reached the screen, *Reds* is an important milestone in Hollywood's treatment of America's history.

Much more appealing to film-makers and their audiences than tales of radicals were the exciting events close to home, such as the gangster stories already discussed. There were other topics of course: the growing threat of fascism abroad; demagoguery bordering on fascism at home; above all, the deepening Depression which many hoped might be countered by newly-elected President Franklin D. Roosevelt and his much-vaunted New Deal. But legal government measures would take time and some otherwise ordinary Americans decided not to wait. Instead, they took matters into their own hands and turned to crime.

While some of this new generation of criminals eagerly modelled themselves upon individual screen gangsters, all eschewed the organized criminal fraternity. Perhaps the nearest thing to a blueprint for many of these law-breakers was the image of the outlaws of the Old West, who were also regularly shown on movie-theatre screens in the act of robbing banks and shooting up posses.

With the appearance of these latterday outlaws, the mid-West became linked with names which were soon as well-known as that of Chicago's Scarface Al, and far better known than political activists like Jack Reed and his successors. Among this new breed of outlaws-cum-idols were an amiable bank-robber named John Dillinger and a pair of narcissistic, gun-happy psychotics, Bonnie Parker and Clyde Barrow.

CHAPTER SIX

'I'm for Roosevelt all the way, and
for the NRA – particularly for banks.'
(John Dillinger)

Few areas of American life escaped completely the effects of the Depression, although the motion-picture industry certainly capitalized on the era by providing cheap entertainment for millions. The movies and radio were all that brightened many existences.

The Depression's impact upon one small but significant group of men was forced home to the nation in 1932, when veterans from World War I marched on Washington demanding relief. The Bonus Marchers, as they were dubbed, were not seeking anything that was not rightfully theirs. They wanted payment *now* of bonuses granted at the end of the war to compensate for loss of pay suffered through serving in the army. The bonus was due to be paid in 1945, by which time they and their families stood a fair chance of starving to death.

Beginning in Portland, Oregon (once again the source of action that irritated the national government), a few hundred men began an eastward journey. By the time they reached Washington D.C. they were 10,000 strong. Most were genuine veterans, more than half had served in Europe and many had suffered disabling injuries. They camped out in the capital, their dirty, hastily-made tar-paper shacks an unpleasant blot on the nation's seat of government.

President Hoover wanted this eyesore removed. First the police, then Federal agents and finally the army were called in. For the first time since the Civil War two armies confronted one another on American soil. One army was made up of ex-soldiers who were now starving, ragged and without hope; the new army was younger and stronger, well-fed and armed. This army was commanded by the Army Chief of Staff General Douglas MacArthur.

The raggle-taggle band was dispersed with rifles, tear gas and tanks. Some men died, as did two babies who were unable to withstand the gas, the shabby camp was burned and peace was restored. The disfiguring blot was removed from the nation's capital although, somewhat surprisingly, no corresponding blot appeared on the records of either General MacArthur or any of his junior officers, who included George S. Patton and Dwight D. Eisenhower.

The Bonus March slipped into the nation's consciousness, even if it failed to stir its conscience. First there was a popular song of 1932, 'Brother, Can You

Spare a Dime?', then there was the finale of a film released the following year. When the chorus sang 'Remember My Forgotten Man' at the end of *Gold-diggers of 1933* it was the Bonus Marchers they sang about.

President Hoover's response to the heroes of World War I served only to reduce his standing still further in the nation's eyes. His defeat at the 1932 election was practically guaranteed; the fact that he had not personally created the Depression counted for nothing. The nation needed the hope offered by Hoover's successor, Franklin D. Roosevelt, and nowhere was that hope more desperate than in rural communities.

Initially, the effects of the Depression on farming areas were probably little worse than its effect upon urban-dwellers, but matters deteriorated when the elements conspired to destroy the very land from which the barest subsistence was being scratched.

Forced farm sales struck at some communities, especially in Iowa and the Dakotas. By May of 1933 the Tennessee Valley Authority was established, bringing some measure of hope along with lasting benefits as the great system of dams provided irrigation and hydro-electric power on a hitherto unimagined scale. There was benefit, too, from the Agricultural Adjustment Act of 1933 which granted benefits to farmers who were prepared to limit production on certain crops. The Act also encouraged farmers into using specific planning and merchandising methods designed to prevent the over-production which had so drastically depressed prices.

Yet despite such efforts rural communities in the mid-West, the south-west and the South were all adversely affected, and many previously affluent farmers were reduced to subsistence-level while those who were already merely scraping by fell far below the poverty line. Inevitably, small farmers suffered more than their bigger brothers.

As for the poor whites and the blacks in the Deep South, in some respects the effect of the Depression upon them was only marginal. For them, abject poverty and near-starvation had always been a way of life. The Depression was nothing new, except that now it was a word spelled with a capital letter and many who had previously ignored their plight now shared their destitution.

Times were hard, and despite the efforts of the New Dealers in Washington they would grow worse before they got better. Even communities in normally affluent New England suffered from such diseases as pellagra.

Just as earlier depressions had spawned criminals, so too did these new hard times. The rural criminal, and those who operated in urban centres but for whom the country was home, attracted just as much attention from the public as did the big-city hoodlums. But there was a marked difference in the public's attitude towards them. Just as in the late nineteenth century, when those who chose to live outside the law found themselves legends in their lifetimes and enjoyed the status of contemporary Robin Hoods, so too did these new outlaws quickly become idolized and idealized.

Many small farmers lost their all to the banks, who thus became the enemy. It was only logical that anyone who opposed the banks should be regarded as a friend. It was with this surface smear of justification, enjoyed in earlier times by Jesse James and his contemporaries, that the actions of several smalltime gangsters were coated. This quick-drying gloss effectively concealed from public gaze the reality of squalid lives and behaviour and allowed the myth-makers to take over. In some cases, the myth-makers were the criminals themselves.

The careers of these country cousins to Al Capone and his growing city Syndicate have been explored by journalists and film-makers since the times in which they lived and operated. Few of these explorations paid much heed to reality, preferring instead to build myth upon myth. The most noted exception to this was the work of John Toland, whose book *The Dillinger Days* is a painstakingly researched account of all the 'stars' of this strange period in the history of American crime.

Characters of the time whose lives have been subjected to the Hollywood bio-pic treatment include George Nelson, who came to the screen in *Baby Face Nelson* (1957), George Kelly, who surfaced as *Machine Gun Kelly* (1958), and Charles Arthur Floyd who was *Pretty Boy Floyd* (1960) and also featured in *The Story of Pretty Boy Floyd* (1974). Only the last of these four films came reasonably close to the truth about the individuals concerned; the film also benefited from a fine central performance by Martin Sheen.

The distaff side of the outlaw world was examined in *Machine Gun Mama* (1944), *Ma Barker's Killer Brood* (1960) and *Bloody Mama* (1970), all of which traced an approximate course through the lives of Ma Barker, her son Dock, Alvin Karpis and their various unsavoury hangers-on. 'Creepy' Karpis also managed top billing in *The FBI Story: The FBI Versus Alvin Karpis, Public Enemy Number One* (1974), a film which had the marginal merit of being much less clumsy than its title.

Of all the outlaws of this period, undoubtedly most attention has been paid to an insipid pair of petty thieves who killed indiscriminately and usually for very little financial gain. The story of Clyde Barrow and Bonnie Parker has attracted the attention of many film-makers, with predictably variable results according to the needs of the industry at the time of their making.

Fritz Lang made *You Only Live Once* (1937) with Henry Fonda and Sylvia Sidney; *Persons in Hiding* (1939), which was one of several films loosely based upon a book ghost-written for J. Edgar Hoover; *They Live By Night* (1948) was directed by Nicholas Ray and starred Farley Granger and Cathy O'Donnell; *Gun Crazy* (1949) featured John Dall and Peggy Cummings; a cheapie, *The Bonnie Parker Story* (1958), starred Dorothy Provine in the title role; *Bonnie and Clyde* (1967) co-starred Warren Beatty and Faye Dunaway; and in *Thieves Like Us* (1974) Keith Carradine and Shelley Duvall, who looked most like the real criminals, were directed by Robert Altman. This film, and *They Live By Night*, were both based upon the 1937 novel by Edward Anderson.

98

The real couple who had attracted so much attention and adulation were decidedly unlike the almost uniformly attractive actors called upon to portray them in these films. Bonnie was plain and angular, Clyde weak-chinned and slouching; their morals, both sexual and otherwise, were highly dubious.

After their original meeting in Dallas in the spring of 1933, the couple launched a miniature crime wave in East Texas and nearby states. They were aided at first by a boyfriend of Bonnie's named Raymond Hamilton (Bonnie, though married, appears to have had a sexual appetite voracious enough to keep several men at exhaustion point at any one time – frequently in the same bed). The gang wound its way northwards, committing a series of violent crimes for peanuts, and eventually losing the boyfriend to the police. Later they added a young car-thief-cum-stud who helped out with the robberies and with keeping Bonnie relaxed between hold-ups.

Joined by Clyde's brother Buck and his wife Blanche, the gang ran foul of the law but escaped in a frantic, tyre-squealing chase leaving behind a sample of Bonnie's semi-literate verse. The ensuing publicity given to this doggerel encouraged her, and soon she was sending verses directly to newspapers along with copies of the endless photographs the gang took of themselves.

Despite having sworn to stick together at all costs, the Barrow brothers parted company during an ambush in which Buck was mortally wounded and his wife captured. Bonnie and Clyde escaped with young Henry Jones, the car thief, whose duties were now so onerous that he had to be chained to a tree overnight to prevent his desertion. Eventually, Jones managed to escape the deadly duo and was evidently relieved when he was captured by the police. Prison, it seemed, was a desirable alternative to being forced to rob banks, kill people and service the insatiable Bonnie.

Needing help, in more ways than one, Bonnie and Clyde now shot up a prison work-detail freeing several convicts including Raymond Hamilton, Bonnie's boyfriend, who had been their original partner in crime. They also gathered in Henry Methven, another young lad for whom the gang, especially Bonnie, had plans. The gang soon fell out and Hamilton went his own way. That left Bonnie and Clyde with young Methven, who was to prove a fatally unfortunate member of their *ménage à trois*.

Learning that the gang occasionally visited Henry's father, a farmer in Louisiana, the FBI worked closely with local law-enforcement officers to set up a deal: Henry would be treated lightly if his father betrayed the gang.

Eventually ambushed by six law officers near Arcadia in East Texas in May, 1934, Bonnie and Clyde died in a massive fusillade of bullets when they stopped to talk with old man Methven, who was faking a flat tyre on his truck. Bonnie was twenty-two years old, Clyde was twenty-four. Directly or indirectly, they had been responsible for the deaths of more than a dozen people.

Given the time they had in the last year of their lives, and the fact that both courted publicity, revelling in the attention paid to them by the press, it is not at all surprising that Hollywood took an interest in the pair. In earlier years the romantic angle was accentuated, as it seems unlikely that many people knew of Bonnie's sexual proclivities or that Clyde was probably homosexual. By the time of *Bonnie and Clyde*, Toland's book had been published and the full truth was known. Nevertheless, the film not only perpetuates the glamorous image but actually enhances it.

Bonnie and Clyde has become one of the most written-about films, with the screenwriters, David Newman and Robert Betton, contributing in various ways including publication of their screenplay. As they have indicated, to circumvent some of the problems of filming the story coherently, it proved necessary to condense events drastically.

Although Clyde's brother Buck (Gene Hackman) and Blanche (Estelle Parsons, who won an Oscar as Best Supporting Actress) appear much as they did in real life, they do tend to form a jokey pair with Blanche's regular bouts of hysteria, triggered by the numerous gun battles, being played largely for rather shrill laughs. The various gang members are concentrated into one man, a fictitious C. W. Moss (Michael J. Pollard) whose character was changed somewhat after the role was cast to accommodate the actor's quirky screen presence.

Bonnie's sexual aberrations were completely removed while Clyde's homosexuality was changed to impotence (something of which he is 'cured' before the film ends). Bonnie and Clyde also underwent changes wrought by the casting of Dunaway and Beatty, neither of whom looked remotely like the scrawny, unattractive individuals they portrayed.

More significant in the overall concept of the film is the broad glamorization of the activities of a pair who showed an appalling lack of moral scruples when it came to killing people. True, the film, directed by Arthur Penn, does highlight the violence in such a manner that the killings come as a shock; as in the moment when Clyde shoots a bank teller in the face when the unfortunate man makes the grave error of trying to hang on to the escaping gangster's car. The sound and the effect of the shot are startling but the impact is short-lived because the audience is immediately caught up in the excitement of the getaway and, as elsewhere in the film, is thus prompted into identifying with the killers, not their victims.

From the moment of the film's release, almost as much excitement appeared in print as had appeared thirty-odd years earlier over the real-life protagonists. Bosley Crowther, writing in *The New York Times*, panned it unmercifully. Other critics, especially Andrew Sarris in *The Village Voice* and Pauline Kael in *The New Yorker*, for once on the same side of a battle, rebutted Crowther, who soon afterwards hung up his pen and recapped his bottle of vitriol.

Kael's review of *Bonnie and Clyde* raised many points including the issue of the degree to which historical accuracy should be observed in films which deal with historical figures or events. She suggests that a movie which shows new versions of a legend can be justified for being historically inaccurate because it may well shake people up a little. Kael's analysis of the film, and the attitudes of its makers and audience, is long, detailed and highly perceptive. It is therefore unfair and possibly misleading to pick up one short passage for comment but there certainly seems to be a degree of misapprehension at work here.

As time passes and knowledge increases, as awareness of society's needs deepens, as understanding of what motivates people broadens, is it not time to look beyond legend and see what the truth has to offer?

Bonnie and Clyde, as seen in *Bonnie and Clyde*, are clearly children of the 1960s. The 1930s were an irrelevance. Audiences responded to these new heroes because they cast a little light upon contemporary times. In the movie, Bonnie and Clyde were bucking against a system that had contributed to the nation's farthest-reaching depression; American audiences in the 1960s were unhappily aware of another system towards which they had undergone an emotional sea-change a few years earlier. Following the death of John F. Kennedy, Americans were beginning to question the attitude of government towards the people in a manner which would eventually lead the Establishment towards a complete *volte face* in its handling of the war in Vietnam.

Bonnie and Clyde may have had its glossy side, accentuated by the fashions and hairstyles which came in its wake, but it also caught the nation in a raw moment when its mood was midway between post-Dallas apathy, which had hit liberal Americans, and pre-Watergate bitterness, which affected just about everyone. Americans were beginning to understand the mechanics of violence and to recognize the psychological needs which government manipulated so shamelessly in its desire to stop people thinking too much about what really happened when triggers were pulled.

Bonnie and Clyde undoubtedly gave a legend an extra coat of gloss, but was only marginally successful in making audiences think again about the violence with which they were surrounded. Even that marginal success was something which might have given the lily-gilding some small degree of justification had it not countered it with a facile glamorization of petty depravity and cynical disregard for human life.

The fact remains that Bonnie and Clyde were a pair of rather dumb two-bit thieves who became heroes at a time when no heroes existed other than the people themselves. They broke out of a trap by killing others of their own kind, and were fêted for it.

They also openly acknowledged a debt to the movies, which were showing them every week how to get rich quick. These very movies, with their inevitable dénouements in which the bad guys paid with their lives, also showed them repeatedly how it would end. A blueprint, the movies might have been; a deterrent they were not.

As later films would demonstrate, other young people would learn in their turn from the lesson of Bonnie and Clyde.

Badlands (1974), a much better film in almost every respect than *Bonnie and Clyde*, traces the homicidal path of real-life killers Charlie Starkweather and Caril Ann Fugate, who committed ten murders in Nebraska and Wyoming in

Blanche Barrow is restrained from reaching her
mortally wounded husband Buck . . .

Associated Press

. . . but the movie allowed them one last contact.
(*Bonnie and Clyde*)

Dillinger's attitude towards the law angered
Americans . . .

. . . but made a good scene for movie-makers to
repeat. *(Dillinger)*

1957–8. Despite the mindlessness, akin to that of Bonnie and Clyde, displayed by this pair, audiences for the film were able to understand rather than empathize with the central characters, largely aided by excellent performances from Martin Sheen and Sissy Spacek. This response is, on balance, infinitely more satisfactory than the response to Bonnie and Clyde, which was usually empathy coupled with a complete lack of understanding.

If any future film-maker wishing to re-make the story of Bonnie and Clyde were to build upon *Badlands*, the result could expose those 1930s heroes and their associates as the unglamorous, sick, wrong-headed and gun-crazy morons they really were. Unfortunately, such a film would probably not make money; nor, incidentally, would it bring in its wake a rebirth of 1930s style and fashions.

Although John Dillinger was the most famous of the outlaws of the mid-West in the early 1930s, he has been overshadowed in Hollywood by his contemporaries, Bonnie and Clyde. Rightly, John Toland used Dillinger's name in the title of his book. These were not the Bonnie and Clyde Days, they really were the Dillinger Days. Yet this amiable bank robber has come a very poor second in Hollywood's pantheon of rural bandits. A few films have been made about him, including *Let 'Em Have It* (1935), starring Bruce Cabot, and two which purported to tell the whole truth, one in 1945, the other in 1973, and both entitled simply *Dillinger*.

The original version was a relatively straightforward entry in the post-gangster movie genre which linked gangsters with G-Men. This *Dillinger*, which stars Lawrence Tierney in the title role, suffers from being ordinary in all departments while the re-make, although a much better film all round, fails to grasp the reality of the individual whose story it tries to tell. Indeed, along the way, it is not Dillinger so much as his hunter who becomes central to the plot.

John Dillinger was a rather genial man who endeared himself to jaded newspaper reporters early in his lawless career by leaping over bank counters as if he were a latter-day Douglas Fairbanks. Dillinger's casual charm and easy-going attitude towards everything and everyone made his local idolization much more understandable than that which was lavished upon Bonnie and Clyde. Indeed, it is easy to believe that Dillinger really was popular with ordinary people, while the popularity of the other two was largely fabricated either at the time or in the immediate aftermath of their bloody deaths.

Sentenced to a short prison term for robbing a grocery store, Dillinger's cavalier attitude towards authority and his frequent attempts to escape, often successful if only temporarily so, caused his prison term to stretch and stretch. Eventually, he served a total of nine years for his relatively trivial offence.

By the time of his release, finding work was out of the question. With millions already jobless and the army of unemployed growing bigger every day, anyone with a record was bound to come pretty low on any prospective employer's list. Indiana-born and -bred, Dillinger did not stray very far from

104

his home state and the adjoining state of Illinois during the rest of his life. Most of his criminal exploits took place in rural communities and small towns, although he was naturally attracted towards Chicago on those occasions when things became too hot in the sticks.

Between his release from prison in May 1933 and his eventual death in July 1934, Dillinger managed to become a household name thanks to several bank robberies (although not as many as were attributed to him). He also had more than his fair share of prison escapes, most of which made the law-enforcement officers who pursued and occasionally held him look very silly. Yet, while they may not have liked this, not many of them seemed to develop feelings of bitterness or anger towards him. One government official was even moved to admit it was the penal system which had made Dillinger what he was.

The people of his home town were similarly amiably disposed towards their most famous son and even at the height of his brief tenure as Public Enemy No. 1 he was able to visit friends and relatives who later, once Dillinger was safely hidden away in another part of the state, had no hesitation in boasting of the fact to newspapermen. This irritated the police and especially angered the FBI, who had got into the act when the outlaw took a stolen car across the state line. Unfortunately for their reputation, the federal officers proved no more skilful than anyone else in tracking him down.

Among the FBI agents on Dillinger's trail was a small, light-voiced, dapper man named Melvin Purvis. Apart from any other qualities he might have possessed, Purvis had a flair for publicizing his own activities in a manner which can hardly have endeared him to the publicity-hungry FBI boss, J. Edgar Hoover.

Purvis eventually caught up with Dillinger at Little Bohemia Lodge on the shores of Little Star Lake in northern Wisconsin, where the outlaw and his gang, which at that time included Baby Face Nelson, were holed up with some lady friends.

When the G-Men reached the Lodge they were just in time to see a group of men leaving. Thinking this was the gang, they opened fire. In fact, the men, one of whom died in the fusillade, were local workers who had the misfortune to use the Lodge as their watering-hole. The gunfire alerted Dillinger and the gang, who fired on the government agents before escaping along the lake shore.

The response from the press was predictably massive and, given the operation's failure, cannot have pleased the usually publicity-conscious Purvis. This interest was not confined to America; the press in Britain and Europe were just as fascinated: Germany recommended that America should follow its example and sterilize gangsters as a means of eliminating this threat to law and order.

After their escape from Little Bohemia, Dillinger and his gang, except for Nelson, who had gone his own way, accidentally happened upon the Barker-Karpis gang, with whom they had not previously been associated. Public concern grew. One government agency which took advantage of this was the FBI. Several measures were taken which broadened the scope of their activities. The range of offences in which the FBI was permitted to intervene was increased. However inadvertently, John Dillinger was helping J. Edgar Hoover tighten his grip upon American law-enforcement.

Although it was only a year since his release from prison, Dillinger had made such a name for himself that many usually slow-moving government agencies were prodded into action. Even President Roosevelt was moved to comment, and in an appeal to the nation asked for co-operation in securing the arrest of the folk-hero bandits whose actions were making everyone except the criminals themselves appear foolish and incompetent.

Dillinger allegedly underwent cosmetic surgery in an attempt to change the face that now grinned cockily from every news-stand, but time had run out for the man who somehow never lost the quality that had endeared him to the people of his hometown. He remained unassuming and likeable in his amiably unconcerned manner all through the fourteen months of his criminal super-stardom.

His casual, jokey style brought about the swift fall from grace of at least one public official. During one of his occasional brief moments spent in custody, Dillinger casually draped an arm across the shoulders of Prosecutor Robert Estill just as photographers snapped this convivial scene. The result brought cries of anger from the public, who did not take kindly to seeing an elected official on such apparently good terms with America's most wanted man.

The end came in July on a Chicago street, where Dillinger was shot to death by federal agents under the command of Melvin Purvis. Not far away was the garage where Capone's men had carried out the St Valentine's Day Massacre. Dillinger had just come out of the Biograph movie theatre, where he had watched William Powell and Clark Gable in the 1934 gangster film *Manhattan Melodrama*. A scriptwriter could not have created such an appropriate setting for the death of America's most wanted man.

In the 1973 version of Dillinger's life, the structure of the film allows most of the real events of his short time at the top of the criminal heap to be used but shifts them around in a somewhat haphazard manner.

Warren Oates' portrayal of the bank robber effectively captures his wry jokiness but makes him more violently disposed than was the real man. Indeed, despite his notoriety and the intense manhunt, Dillinger was wanted for remarkably little 'federal crime' when the FBI finally nailed him. It was what he was doing to their image that put him so high on their list.

Unfortunately, that fine actor Ben Johnson unbalances the film with his interpretation of Melvin Purvis. Johnson's personal characteristics, those of solid, good-natured charm, gleam through every one of his screen appearances, and this is no exception. The problem here is that Purvis simply was not as nice as this, neither was he especially active in the field. Like the big boss, Hoover, he directed most operations in his area from behind a desk.

Here, Purvis is intent on cleaning up the men who perpetrated the Kansas City Massacre in which Pretty Boy Floyd (Steve Kanaly) helps gun down four agents while attempting to free a prisoner being transferred to another jail. In an excess of enthusiasm and bullets, the prisoner dies as well, but that is small consolation either to the FBI or to the outraged public.

Purvis's trail of vengeance leads him to Machine Gun Kelly (Terry Leonard), who had entered mythology when, on his capture, he allegedly called the government agents 'G-Men' for the first time. Whatever Kelly said or did not say, Purvis probably saw nothing of this action in real life.

True to known fact, the film has Purvis lead the disastrous assault on the lodge at Little Bohemia, but instead of allowing all the gang to escape as did the real G-Men, here all the members of the gang, bar Dillinger, are killed.

Dillinger's end, as he leaves the movie theatre with his long-time girlfriend Billie Frechette (Michelle Phillips) and Anna Sage (Cloris Leachman), marginally romanticizes the truth. It was not Billie who was with Dillinger that night but Polly Hamilton. Anna Sage, his betrayer, who *was* there was, in fact, a madam and Polly one of her hookers. Purvis, although present at the death of John Dillinger, did not fire the fatal shots.

For the most part these changes are trivial, although they do perpetuate the fictions of Dillinger's importance, which thus upgrades the status of the FBI in general and Melvin Purvis in particular. They also tend to make Dillinger much more murderous than in reality, and certainly much less pleasant than most people, on both sides of the law, believed him to be. This film did not, however, thrust him into the same depths of depravity as the 1945 version, which had the amiable bandit gunning down an old couple in cold blood and settling a disagreement over a woman by killing a rival in love with an axe. In fact, Dillinger probably killed only one man, a police officer named O'Malley. While one murder is no less deplorable than two or more, the nature of the man is thus changed. Maybe Hollywood thought he needed to kill a few more people to justify its interest in him.

As suggested, the changes made to the status of Purvis reflects the behaviour of the real lawman for whom publicity meant almost as much as it did to other self-aggrandizing law-enforcement officers of the era such as Eliot Ness and Hoover himself, who contrived to avoid ever mentioning Purvis by name in any official record.

Eliot Ness came to the screen in *The Scarface Mob* (1962), starring Robert Stack as the intrepid gangster. Originally a two-part TV programme, this was the forerunner of an interminable TV series, *The Untouchables*, at the beginning of which, week after week, Walter Winchell hollered praise for Hoover's G-Men.

As for the FBI's Director himself, for many years he ruled his personal task force with unbending enthusiasm for the elimination of criminals, perverts and radicals (which in his lexicon amounted to pretty much the same thing) with all the zeal of a religious crusader. In the movies, the Bureau mostly came in for straightforward, slightly noble, gun-blazing treatment, as in *G-Men* (1935), which starred James Cagney in an early role on the legal end of a machine-gun. Also noble, and much more stiff-backed, was *The FBI Story* (1959), which was made with Hoover's approval and co-operation. Through its quasi-documentary style, this film contrived simultaneously to be dull and to create an impression that this was how the FBI really was. No one could be quite as unswervingly decent as James Stewart's central character, but the impression took a lot of shaking loose despite the revelations which followed Hoover's death in 1972.

In his later years, Hoover succeeded in putting himself beyond the reach of Presidents. This was partly through having his tenure of office extended to his lifetime and partly through digging up any dirt he could find on any current incumbent at the White House, not least John Kennedy.

Once Hoover was dead and gone, the truth about this self-appointed guardian of the public virtue who was also, supposedly, an impartial representative of the law came out, and he was revealed in all his sordidly unpleasant detail.

The Private Files of J. Edgar Hoover (1977) laid out all the dirty linen for public view but managed to do so in an unsensational manner. Produced, written and directed by Larry Cohen, and starring Broderick Crawford as Hoover (with James Wainwright playing him as a young man), the film sticks close to the truth which had emerged about the man whom Walter Winchell had dubbed America's Top Cop. Hoover's sexual proclivities are rightly shown but, also rightly, are not held up for ridicule or condemnation. It is enough for a present-day audience to know that this man, who used what he knew about the sexual practices of others to their detriment, should himself have suppressed inclinations which he affected to despise in others.

Hoover's role in the affairs of the Kennedy brothers is something which will be dealt with in a later chapter. In the present context, there can be no doubt that like Purvis, Ness and others Hoover benefited from the upgrading of the outlaws of the mid-West and south-west in the early 1930s. As a direct result of making them appear better than they were, the FBI was thus similarly enhanced. Generally speaking, film-makers have tended towards maintaining or even embellishing the fictions which surrounded these cheapjack criminals and the men who hunted them down.

The eagerness with which both contemporary and subsequent audiences have accepted Bonnie and Clyde, Dillinger and their kind as folk-heroes undoubtedly stems from the fact that these men and women appeared to be ordinary people who became criminals through their condition. That this was a condition over which they had no control is offered, perhaps subconsciously, as an excuse for criminality. It is not a view which will withstand much careful thought and analysis, yet it remains disturbingly understandable.

For those who faced starvation and the utter hopelessness of the chronically unemployable but would not or could not turn to crime, there were occasional bizarre alternatives.

They Shoot Horses, Don't They? (1969) demonstrates one such way out. The marathon dances of the early 1930s displayed the exploitation of the weak by the strong for the titillation of . . . whom?

In Horace McCoy's 1935 novel upon which the film is based, the marathon dance is set in Los Angeles, and among the crowds who came to watch the pathetic efforts of the dancers are criminals, movie stars and ordinary people who differ from the contestants only in that they still have jobs.

McCoy names the stars, which is not to say that they actually attended such affairs, and they include Ruby Keeler, William 'Stage' Boyd, Alice Faye and Ken Murray. As many of the contestants hope to be 'discovered', fact and fiction intertwine persuasively.

The film's protagonists, Gloria Beatty and Robert Syverton (Jane Fonda and Michael Sarrazin), although attractive, manage not to look like their more glamorous selves and thus heighten the essential truth of the occasion, which is turned into a humiliating spectacle by the egregious MC (brilliantly played by Gig Young).

Whatever liberties were taken with reality by novel and film in the interests of dramatization, the hopeless desperation of the contestants casts an unpleasant sidelight on showbiz excesses in 1930s America.

In political terms this was a time when increasing efforts were being made to lift the country up off its knees. President Roosevelt was actively pursuing all manner of policies which he hoped might have some beneficial effect. For a while Congress went along for the ride, before digging in its heels. Then, with the aid of the Supreme Court, it succeeded in severely restricting many of the President's moves on the grounds of unconstitutionality. Initially, however, Roosevelt's personality and popularity held the day. He had won in 1932 with a massive majority, claiming 89 per cent of the electoral vote and 57 per cent of the popular vote; only six states went to Hoover. As the 1936 election approached, there were some fears that unexpected opposition might make a dent in the incumbent's apparent impregnability.

This opposition came from Huey P. Long, the former governor of Louisiana. Elected to the Senate in 1930, Long was a Roosevelt supporter who became quickly disaffected due to the President's refusal to back his proposals for radical changes in the distribution of wealth. With the slogan 'Share Our Wealth', Long built up a substantial following in the South, where his downhome oratory roused rabbles and sent the rich into fits of depression. The champion of Louisiana's poor whites, Long's policies in his home state built many roads, schools and hospitals funded by taxes levied against the oil companies and the income and inheritances of the wealthy.

Long believed he could cure the ills which beset the nation in much the same way as he had done in Louisiana. He calculated that every family in America could enjoy an annual income of $2000 by the simple expedient of taking money away from all those who earned over $1 million and who inherited more than $5 million.

When Long broke away from Roosevelt, Democratic party workers feared that he might prove to be an attractive vote-catcher for the 'third party', but any such fears vanished when, in the fall of 1935, Long was assassinated in the State House at Baton Rouge by a man allegedly concerned with the alarming resemblances between Long's demagoguery and the rise of fascism in Europe.

With Long out of the race, Roosevelt had no problems in the 1936 election and even managed to increase his previous massive majority, taking 98½ per cent of the electoral vote and 61 per cent of the popular vote, with only two states going to the Republican candidate, Alfred Landon.

The life and career, and of course the dramatic death, of Huey P. Long appealed to film-makers. *A Lion is in the Streets* (1953), based upon a novel by Adria Locke Langley, stars James Cagney in the role of a Long-figure. In *All the King's Men* (1949) it was Broderick Crawford who portrayed the Long character with such power and intensity that he won one of the three Academy Awards which went to the film. That this should happen at a time when the motion-picture industry was keeping a low profile for fear of attack from politicians is rather surprising.

All the King's Men makes no claim to be realistic, taking as its basis the novel by Robert Penn Warren. The central character of Willie Stark cannot be regarded as anything other than a facsimile of Huey Long; if anyone had any doubts, they were dispelled by the novel's title, which played upon another of Long's slogans, 'Every Man a King', which he also used as the title of his autobiography.

Willie Stark aids his rise to power by means of any tactic he thinks necessary, legal or otherwise. As long as he appears to be striving towards general benefits for the community at large he takes the electorate with him, just as Huey Long had. Later, as Willie Stark is corrupted by power and riches, the film's audience is expected to make a corresponding shift in its view of him. It does not happen in quite the way the film's makers intended. In part this may be due to the performance of Crawford who, Oscar or not, blasts his way through the film without too much regard for the character he is supposed to be building. If Willie Stark is not especially likeable at the outset, it is difficult to be too upset by his later appearance as a downright bad-hat. Another factor which alienates audiences, other than those with experience of the South in the 1930s, is the problem of understanding why Huey Long did not lose his following in real life.

In the South of his times his blatant corruption and misuse of power were not seen as a betrayal of trust, nor even as especially criminal. Reared on generations of corrupt politicians, the people who voted Long into office with such regularity and enthusiasm did not really care if he too was corrupt. If corruption had to exist, and many truly believed it to be a fact of life, then it was better that one of their own kind should be the beneficiary.

The corruption of the political machine built by Long in real life and by Willie Stark in the movie is made to appear justifiable because nothing else

110

could defeat those other machines which syphoned money off to the already-rich. Above all, the demagogue retains his grip because he contrives always to be a man of the people.

Missing from both film versions of Long's life is his latent fascism, although his cavalier attitude towards right of property and of individuals is well shown. Even *The Life and Assassination of the Kingfish* (1977), a far more accurate version of his life in which Long is played by Edward Asner, fails to depict him as a potential dictator, a role in which Long's many political enemies frequently cast him, if only in their nightmares.

While not rife, fears about dictatorships taking over America were of sufficient general concern to prompt films like *Gabriel Over the White House* (1939), in which Walter Huston stars as President Jud Hammond, a benevolent dictator. Among his measures are the ending of Prohibition, thus matching Roosevelt's similar plan on coming to office. The broad similarity between many of Hammond's measures and those of the real-life President stem from the fact that the film was financed by William Randolph Hearst, who was, at that point, backing F.D.R.

Another film of the period, *The President Vanishes* (1934), has President Stanley (Arthur Byron) frame his own kidnapping in order to expose fascists who plan to subvert the Constitution.

Apart from Huey Long, and Roosevelt of course, few real political figures of the 1930s attracted the attention of film-makers, although one man, Anton Cermak, became the subject of *The Man Who Dared* (1933). The film was probably made more because of Cermak's public death than because of his hard-working, socially-conscious life. At least, that is how the film portrays Cermak, here disguised as Jan Novak (Preston Foster), a mayor of Chicago in the 1920s who struggles to clear the town of gangsters and corrupt politicians.

The corrupt politician on which the real-life Cermak had his sights was Big Bill Thompson, mayor of Chicago immediately before he took over. Thompson certainly was corrupt, in an overt, flashy manner. Cermak was more circumspect, and much better organized. He had sizable interests in gambling and booze and was believed to have sided against the Capone mob during the Big Fellow's confrontation with Terrible Roger Touhy.

In Miami with President-elect Roosevelt, Cermak was shot during what appeared to be an assassination attempt upon F.D.R. Subsequent revelations suggest that the assassin was a loner out to get Roosevelt and that a Capone hit-man took advantage of the uproar to eliminate Cermak, whose activities back in Chicago were proving detrimental to Scarface Al's ambitions.

Roosevelt appeared as the central figure in a number of films, with one of the better efforts, *Sunrise at Campobello* (1960), concentrating upon his earlier life and his struggle to continue in politics after being stricken with polio. This film allowed Ralph Bellamy to continue his stage interpretation of the President and can scarcely be faulted. For the most part, even in the more revealing *Eleanor and Franklin* (1976) and its sequel, *Eleanor and Franklin:*

111

the White House Years (1977), in which some of the President's peccadilloes are allowed to surface, Roosevelt has been treated reverentially by film-makers. They have not given him the mystical aura with which Lincoln is surrounded, but they have always stopped well short of debunking him.

Roosevelt also appears in a number of films dealing with the immediate pre-war years and with World War II itself, discussed in Chapters 7 and 8.

In the first half of the 1930s, America had too much to worry about at home to pay close attention to events overseas, and for the most part Hollywood followed suit. One exception at the mid-point in the decade was the Spanish Civil War, which caught at the imagination of a generation of liberal-minded Americans. The naming of a brigade after Abraham Lincoln was not a casual decision; this conflict between two extremes of political thought was seen by many as a matter of moral choice, decision and action. Morality in political matters was something Americans automatically associated with Lincoln.

It is surprising, and somehow uplifting, that so many Americans, Britons and uninvolved Europeans should have voluntarily elected to become involved in such a war. Fired by moral and/or political beliefs, their response was startlingly unlike the reactions of men to earlier wars. It is difficult, if not impossible, to call to mind any subsequent war which drew men for similar reasons.

Sadly, the response of film-makers in Hollywood was not as unequivocal as that of the men who actually went to Spain to fight or to serve as ambulance drivers. The first step taken by anyone planning to make a movie about this conflict seems to have been a hasty and usually thorough de-politicization of the storyline.

Best known of the Spanish Civil War films is the screen version of Hemingway's *For Whom the Bell Tolls* (1943), which contrives with great skill to eliminate the political content of the novel. Anyone seeing the film without having first read the book would learn as much about fascism in Europe as one would gather about the workings of the Space Shuttle from watching an old Flash Gordon serial.

The central issue of the film is the love story between Robert Jordan (Gary Cooper) and Pilar (Ingrid Bergman). The ideals for which they fight are only vaguely observed and appear to be only marginally superior to the great American tradition of a man doing what a man's gotta do. In the light of the events in Spain in 1936, this is one of Hollywood's grosser trivializations. The communists fade completely from sight and so, too, for all practical purposes, do the fascists. Given the removal of the two main opposing forces from the screenplay, any member of the audience who cannot fill in the gaps from knowledge gained elsewhere is left with no understanding of who is fighting whom, or why. As Constance Pohl has pointed out, such changes to the novel as were made are largely attributable to the actions of producer-director Sam Wood, who possessed acute anti-communist feelings, and to direct intervention in the making of the film by representatives of General Franco's régime.

112

Allowing itself to be dictated to by its own government was something at which Hollywood kicked feebly at many times in the 1930s and 1940s, usually without much effect; letting itself be so treated by a foreign government, especially one like Franco's, was a grave abdication of responsibility.

Blockade (1938), which stars Henry Fonda, was clearly set in Spain in 1936 but the two sides of the conflict are not delineated. The de-politicizing of this story must have caused screenwriter John Howard Lawson a few sleepless nights since the source material was Ilya Ehrenburg's story of expatriate Russians, *The Love of Jeanne Ney*. Not only did Lawson succeed in ridding the story of matters Russian and/or political but he also managed to remove any element which made *Blockade* especially Spanish. What remains is a facile spy thriller – which is most surprising, given the fact that Lawson held left-wing views extreme enough to have him blacklisted in 1948.

The Last Train from Madrid (1937) is little more than a routine Hollywood melodrama in which a cast of oddballs is gathered together and vaguely threatened with unspecified off-screen violence.

Although America's internal problems were far from over in the second half of the 1930s, Hollywood began paying much more attention to overseas events than had previously been the case. Given the mounting tension in Europe, of which the Spanish Civil War was the most obvious expression, it would have been difficult for it not to have paid some heed.

The complexities of the war in Spain, problematical for film-makers who did not want to commit themselves on the subject of communism, were generally brushed aside. Fascism in Central Europe appeared to be a much simpler subject to handle, and it was this area of fascist growth and particularly the Nazis in Germany which offered subject-matter for films. Hollywood turned to this area with enthusiasm, although often with some caution.

But the Depression was still a fact of life for millions of Americans and could not be ignored. Neither could Hollywood continue to treat it merely as a background for tales of rural gangsters. It was a serious matter demanding serious attention. Perhaps surprisingly, given the gross changes to known fact made in the rural criminal films, some of the results gave a remarkably truthful account. Nevertheless, given the inaccuracies and omissions of the Spanish Civil War films, it was correspondingly unsurprising that Hollywood managed to avoid going all the way and telling a wholly true story.

CHAPTER SEVEN

'There is no man in the world I
would trust more fully than Joe Stalin.'
(Joseph E. Davies, US Ambassador
to the Soviet Union)

Despite all the efforts of the New Dealers, when Franklin D. Roosevelt began his second term in office the nation was still in bad shape. 'I see one-third of a nation ill-housed, ill-clad, ill-nourished,' he had declared during his Inaugural Address.

Many Americans who fully matched this description lived in the mid-western and south-western states of Oklahoma, Kansas, Texas, New Mexico and Colorado, where they scratched a subsistence-level existence from the soil. Not all their problems were a direct result of the Depression; some owed their origins to traditional farming methods which did more than merely take away the land's goodness.

Over the years this vast region had been overgrazed and its relatively few trees felled. Low annual rainfall and frequent high winds caused soil erosion on a massive scale. Dust storms were constant, and the farmers were helpless against them. The severe drought of 1934 led to vast quantities of any remaining topsoil being swept up and carried thousands of miles to be dumped in the oceans. The affected region became one enormous dust bowl. The farmers were left with a simple choice: starve, or get out. For the great majority only one place offered any hope of work – California.

Tens of thousands of poor and hungry Okies and Arkies trekked westwards in hope of finding work in the fruit-rich lands on the Pacific Coast. Their hopes were seldom fulfilled and most dragged their squalor and desperation with them to what had hitherto beckoned as a new, golden Promised Land.

The conditions and fate of these migrant would-be workers was movingly captured in John Steinbeck's novel *The Grapes of Wrath*, and the images of the region were recorded vividly by many photographers, especially Dorothea Lange, Ben Shahn and Walker Evans. Steinbeck's words and the visual imagery of these masterly photographers were eloquently blended by John Ford in his film based upon the novel, yet something was missing.

The Grapes of Wrath (1940) traces the ill-fortunes of the Joad family from their derelict farm to what they hope will be a new beginning. Although the film, which stars Henry Fonda as Tom Joad, effectively captures the look of the period, much of the novel's political content is gone. However, its social conscience remains largely undiluted. In place of Steinbeck's suggestion that socialism will offer a cure to the specific ills afflicting this section of the population, Ford offers a brand of religious populism. There is also an air of optimism about the film that is missing from Steinbeck's novel. This is most noticeable in the upbeat ending to the film, which contrasts starkly with the essential pessimism of the novel's final pages. This imposed element of hope owes much to the conventions of film-making at the time and to Ford's often-stated belief in the importance of the family. The harsh reality facing migrant workers in their struggle to survive did not fit prevailing ideas of what audiences wanted.

Even Tom Joad becomes a vaguely defined threat to the family and must leave. It is Ma Joad (Jane Darwell) who prevails and represents the nation's dispossessed in her stirring declaration that the people will go on.

Nevertheless, much of the grim detail of life for the Okies appears constantly throughout the film and nowhere with greater impact than when the Joads first enter a Hooverville.

These shabby collections of huts and tents made from tar-paper, packing cases, rusting metal and the like had grown up around the cities to which the rural homeless flocked in the hope of jobs at the beginning of the Depression. Giving the name of the President of the United States to these pathetic testimonies to the failure of the nation's economy had been a strained effort at making light of this enormous tragedy. Although the Hooverville into which the Joads drive post-dated Hoover the old name clung on, as did dreams that happy days really were here again.

The fate of rural people who moved to the cities, often succeeding only in transferring their squalor and hopelessness along with their few worthless possessions, is depicted in *The Dollmaker* (1984). Here Jane Fonda, inevitably evoking echoes of her father in *The Grapes of Wrath*, plays the indomitable young mother of an Appalachian family.

In another Steinbeck story brought to the screen at about the same time as the story of the Joads, the true hopelessness of the dreams of the migrants was shown for what it really was with even greater clarity. *Of Mice and Men* (1939) is in many ways a more sharply perceptive analysis of the fate of the migrant worker than is the better-known film. Lacking the artificial optimism of Ford's film, *Of Mice and Men* underlines the false promise of the dreams which its central characters, George and Lenny (Burgess Meredith and Lon Chaney Jr.), use to help them through the days. No films before *Of Mice and Men*, and remarkably few since, have been so bleakly dismissive of that staple of the American subconscious, the dream of success. Directed by Lewis Milestone and superlatively well-acted, *Of Mice and Men* also remains the best film adaptation of a literary work ever made.

It is a measure of the maturity of Milestone's work in this film that the role of the solitary black worker is neither softened nor patronized. Crooks (Leigh Whipper) is segregated and oppressed in exactly the same manner as his real-life counterparts. Although not directly concerned with racism, the film's matter-of-fact treatment of Crooks' life gives a lesson few film-makers have taken the trouble to learn.

Yet, despite the abject poverty displayed in these films of Steinbeck's works, and the difficulties and hardships which permeated almost every home across the land, this era showed a rapid expansion in two major areas of popular entertainment: the radio and the movies. Both brought into lives of drab desperation a little laughter and, especially so in the case of the movies, glimmers of hope that there might be a better future if only the people could hold on just a while longer.

The films of the period showed a remarkably wide range of subjects, only a few of which relate directly to what was happening in real life. Occasionally, as in *It Happened One Night* (1934), some images of the Depression flit across the screen but optimism and enthusiasm abound, giving audiences a double shot of hope and happiness. In some cases, however, films appear to have had a different effect from what their makers expected. If *Bonnie and Clyde* is to be believed, the song 'We're in the Money' from *Golddiggers of 1933* was the spur which set the lethal pair on the road that was to lead to the ambush at Arcadia.

Towards the end of the decade the rise of European fascism became a subject of endless fascination for film-makers. At first, the films of the period steered cautiously around the subject, setting their stories in unnamed countries wherein people speak with vaguely Germanic accents and wear uniforms that look more than a mite Teutonic, but no one actually makes a positive connection.

Mortal Storm (1939) was the first film to mention Adolf Hitler by name; also mentioned are concentration camps and Jews. Set in Germany between the wars, this fictional tale follows the fortunes of a family split into warring camps: those who support the Nazis and those who oppose them. All this was bold for the era but the film's impact is weakened through a combination of low production values and inappropriate casting of the leads.

The same three leading actors turned up the following year in *The Shop Around the Corner*. Margaret Sullavan, James Stewart and Frank Morgan fit much better into this fine, light-comedy about young love, which is also set in Central Europe. This time, the presence of Stewart and Morgan, two very 'Hollywood' performers, does not intrude because audiences can readily equate the Prague of the film with practically any American city untroubled by political matters. In *Mortal Storm* it is impossible to think of Stewart as a German, not even a 'good' one.

Margaret Sullavan, who was quite unlike the standard Hollywood beauty, fitted into this kind of film so well that for a while she risked becoming typecast. *Little Man, What Now?* (1934) and *Three Comrades* (1938) also find her in between-wars Germany with the former qualifying as probably the first Hollywood film to adopt a positively anti-Nazi stance.

116

Confessions of a Nazi Spy (1939) was a much sharper effort all round. Based upon a real case, the story drew upon the memoirs of the FBI agent responsible for smashing a spy-ring in New York in 1938. The agent, Leon G. Turrou, published his story in the *New York Post* (thus earning a swift dismissal from J. Edgar Hoover, who probably saw him as another Melvin Purvis) and the rights were picked up by Warner's. The studio found itself under some pressure from the German-American Bund and there were also threats that the film would not be screened in Germany, which would lose the studio valuable revenue. As relatively poor business had been done by other fascist-spy movies, such pressures cast doubt over the film's viability, but the studio persisted and, aided by an excellent performance from Edward G. Robinson in the Turrou role, the film made money. It was doubtless helped by the fact that its release coincided with the beginning of Germany's march through Europe.

The film's success may have eased some of the distress caused to Warner's when Joe Kauffman, their man in Germany, was beaten to death by Nazi thugs for a reason that was already becoming grimly predictable – his race.

Hitchcock's *Foreign Correspondent* (1940) takes a fairly sharp look at fascism but contrives to do so within the faintly 'clubby' atmosphere of the kind of between-wars novel in which the villain is an individual out for personal power and gain rather than a nation bent on submitting another nation to its will.

Based upon *Personal History*, the memoirs of real-life foreign correspondent Vincent Sheean, the property had hung around Walter Wanger's office for quite a while. The impending war gave the story an added urgency and a central theme for the film. Despite this, there is a marked element of fudging with reality, doubtless caused by script changes made when war, real war, broke out.

Initially, the villains are not too clearly defined apart from being vaguely fascist. As historian John Rossi has shown, dated copies of the screenplay reveal that important changes were made after Germany had taken Poland and launched attacks on Denmark and Norway. Once these changes were made the shadowy fascists become clearly German Nazis.

Although not especially Hitchcockian (apart from fine dramatic set-pieces in a Dutch windmill and atop London's Westminster Cathedral) the film's sense of topicality was greatly enhanced by some on-location sequences shot by the second unit in Holland and England after the outbreak of war. These moments (and a marvellous mid-Atlantic airliner crash which proves that Hitchcock could have shown latterday makers of disaster movies a thing or two) helped add urgency to a film which suffered from stagey sets and sub-standard model work.

Good acting from the principals, especialy Albert Basserman as Van Meer, the Dutch Premier, and the action sequences kept the film merrily rolling along, although newspaperman Johnny Jones (Joel McCrea) does not seem to take anything very seriously, not even an impending world war. The ending of the film, however, makes its overriding message very clear when Jones broadcasts to America from London in the middle of an air-raid. America had already heard the broadcasts of Edward R. Murrow which took place in mid-1940 and could relate what they heard from him to what Jones says in the film: '. . . it's too late to do anything here now except stand in the dark and let them come. It's as if all the lights were out everywhere except in America. Keep those lights burning, cover them with steel, ring them with guns. Build a canopy of battleships and bomber planes around them. Hello, America! Hang on to your lights – they're the only lights left in the world.'

Once the war in Europe had begun in earnest, American attitudes took a much sharper and more readily definable turn. Although many Americans still hoped that their country would not be drawn into the conflict, the divisions upon lines of ethnic origins which had been relatively clearly defined in the early years of World War I were less apparent. The great choice was to fight or not to fight; the question of which side to fight on, should the need arise, was one that was asked by only a few.

Mrs Miniver (1940) is strongly pro-British, even if it does portray a chintzily-cosy Home Counties England that owes more to American preconceptions than to the reality of late-1930s Britain. Setting aside the hopelessly inept interpretation of the British class system, the film is a genuinely caring response to the fate of the British and undoubtedly did much to bring home to Americans the dangers of the war in terms of the havoc it could wreak upon their homeland. In 1940, the fear that an aggressor might invade the American continent was very real in many minds.

But there was still room for comedy, and just as he had taken a fling at World War I in *Shoulder Arms*, Charlie Chaplin took a strongly satirical look at the Nazis in *The Great Dictator* (1940). Chaplin subsequently declared that had he known of the horrors of the concentration camps at the time he would not have made the film. On reflection he might have reversed this view. It would be facile to suggest that a man like Hitler could have been diverted had more people laughed at him. Nevertheless, it is tempting to speculate upon the degree of influence a few more, but earlier, pinpricks like Chaplin's Adenoid Hynkel might have had inside Germany before the dictator's grip was immovable. The globe with which Hynkel dances in one of the best scenes in the movie is suddenly deflated; perhaps . . . perhaps . . .

Similarly dismissive of Hitler is Ernest Lubitsch's hard-black comedy *To Be Or Not To Be* (1942), which stars Jack Benny and Carole Lombard. Although greeted less than enthusiastically at the time of its release, on the grounds that jokes about Hitler and concentration camps were not in good taste, the film can now be seen as one of the best comedies ever to come out of Hollywood. The 1984 remake by Mel Brooks, while brilliantly funny, excellently performed, and just as committedly anti-Nazi, misses the incisive bleakness of the original. This is, perhaps, a quality of the times in which it was made rather than any reflection upon the quality of the film itself. Nevertheless, hanging over it is the question that almost always draws the wrong answer: to re-make or not to re-make?

Comedies are exceptions, however, and most films set in the late 1930s, and particularly in the early war years before America's entry, usually take a serious view of events: serious but not particularly accurate.

Although made after America's declaration of war on Japan and then on Germany, *Mission to Moscow* (1943) deals with a period immediately prior to this and takes as its text the book written by America's former Ambassador to the Soviet Union, Joseph E. Davies. With Davies himself appearing on-screen to speak a prologue, a credibility is implied that the film does not fulfil.

Davies secured extensive rights when he signed his contract with Warner's. Among other conditions he had script approval, something which proved to be a permanent irritant to the screenwriter Howard Koch and the director Michael Curtiz. The prologue was one of Davies' ideas, and any subsequent doubts about the motives of the studio (and they were many) should have been dissipated by the ex-Ambassador's words.

Speaking of his motives in writing the book, Davies says: ' . . . nothing as I saw it was more important than that the fighting nations should understand and trust each other. There was so much prejudice and misunderstanding of the Soviet Union in which I partly shared, that I felt it was my duty to tell the truth about the Soviet Union, as I saw it, for such value as it might have.'

Davies then talks at length about himself, his background, his religion and his view of American society: 'I came up the hard way, and I am glad of it. I had a deep conviction and firm faith that that system and our form of government is the best the world has yet produced for the common man, such as you and me. I went to Russia with that conviction, and I returned from Russia with that conviction. But while I was in Russia, I came to have a very high respect for the honesty of the Soviet leaders. They respected the honesty of my conviction, and I respected theirs. I also came back with a firm conviction that these people were sincerely devoted to peace, and that what they and their leaders most desired was to live as good neighbours in a world at peace.'

There is more of the same before the real Davies fades from the screen to be replaced by his surrogate, the actor Walter Huston, who came to the role fresh from his success in *Abraham Lincoln*. This juxtaposition doubtless influenced audiences even more than the sight of Ambassador Davies.

All this, allied to look-alike actors playing the roles of Stalin and Churchill, among other political figures, prompted many of the audiences of the day to accept what they saw as a truthful depiction of life in the Soviet Union in the immediate pre-war years. Added to the impressions created by the film was the fact that the book had been serialized in *Reader's Digest*, a reasonable guarantee to many that it was not only true but also highly unlikely to be a fiendish commie plot.

After the war, Warner's claimed to have acted on a specific request from the President of the United States in deciding to make the film. Certainly, by 1943, Roosevelt was aware of the need for a powerful ally on Hitler's eastern front. He wanted to aid Russia and therefore needed backing from Congress and from the people for this delicate and politically dangerous move. Sending aid, especially in the form of munitions, to the Russians might appear tantamount to treason or, at best, a sign of advanced insanity.

When, in 1947, the Committee on Un-American Activities of the US House of Representatives began digging into Hollywood's affairs, Warner's were badly beaten about the head with the club they had fashioned for themselves. Howard Koch, although not himself a radical, was blacklisted; his work on the film was clearly a factor which weighed heavily against him.

The film's variance with facts is endless. In order to justify alliance with Russia, and to encourage granting aid which it was hoped would deter Stalin from further collaboration with Hitler, the Nazi-Soviet Pact of 1939 needed explaining away – this despite the fact that the pact post-dated Davies' tenure as Ambassador. Thus, with a little piece of convoluted logic, the film set out to justify something of which Davies had never been aware.

Part of Stalin's ruthless cleaning-up activities within the Soviet Union occurs in the film's depiction of the 1936, 1937 and 1938 Moscow trials of high-ranking Bolsheviks. It was through these that Stalin rid himself of some of his opponents. He also eliminated some important military figures by the much less showy method of having them shot without trial. As for the rank and file, the true numbers of dead can never be known but probably ran into eight figures. Stalin once made the hideously glib remark that a million deaths were merely a statistic; presumably ten million deaths did not even register on either his consciousness or his conscience – if he had one.

The Moscow trials in the film are condensed into one show trial in which a star performer, who busily recants his previous unspeakable acts against the state, turns out to be a certain Marshal Tukhachevsky (Ivan Trisault), which is a mite surprising as he was one of the senior army officers Stalin arranged to have shot without trial in 1937. The decision to condense several trials into one is difficult to argue against, given the exigencies of film-making; to depict as one of the people on trial a man who had been denied that right seems dubious in the extreme. Maybe Davies did not know what had happened to Tukhachevsky but neither could he have witnessed his trial.

The trial is justified as a necessary action by Stalin when confronted with a massive plot led by Trotsky, who is in the pay of Japan and Germany. That the plot never existed was not something which Warner's could have been expected to know at the time the film was made, but it is not unreasonable to expect the United States Ambassador to have been somewhat more perceptive – to say nothing of being rather less naive.

Although Davies' book shows too much naivety and not enough perception, the overall view of actions taken by Stalin in Russia at the time suggests that

Davies was not completely misled. This leads to the conclusions that certainly he, and probably the makers of *Mission to Moscow*, quite deliberately bent reality to suit the purpose of the day.

The purges are not merely laundered into something quite innocuous and even justifiable; they also become a kind of Slavic version of *Gangbusters*. Stalin himself, in Mannart Kippen's portrayal, becomes suitably avuncular. For this disturbingly simplistic view of Stalin, Warner's had the equally short-sighted support of Ambassador Davies. At a function which helped launch the movie, he remarked: 'There is no man in the world I would trust more fully than Joe Stalin . . .'

If Warner's had known the post-war problems they would have over this particular example of historical adjustment they might at least have given Stalin a worse case of acne.

Apart from acting as Roosevelt's eyes and ears, in addition to his overt role as America's Ambassador to the Soviet Union, Davies takes what later visitors to the country would recognize as the standard Intourist trip around cosmetically-improved factories where he meets the ordinary people. Surprise, surprise, they are just like ordinary working-stiffs back home.

Returning to America via London, Davies meets Churchill (Dudley Field Malone, a lawyer who took part in the Scopes Monkey Trial and had never acted before), who is doing what American audiences doubtless expected of him – he is laying bricks in his garden.

Back in America, Davies tries to convince his fellow-countrymen that war is coming and that preparations must be made. Contrasting startlingly with the clean-limbed intrigues in the Praesidium, the antics of members of Congress are positively venal. Profiteering is the order of the day, even if it means dealing with Hitler.

With the war eventually a reality, Davies again visits Russia and does his bit towards cementing relations between the two countries, finally returning to America to press for intervention.

Davies becomes irritatingly prescient about most things that take place, and extensively knowledgeable about Soviet affairs. As David Culbert has indicated in his perceptive analysis of *Mission to Moscow* and Davies' real-life role, the Ambassador actually spent no more than a total of nine months in Russia, partly in 1937 and partly in 1938, and most of that time he was searching for works of art for his personal collection.

Aggression against Finland and the USSR's relationship with Nazi Germany, which led to the signing of the Pact in August 1939, are made to appear as matters of great statesmanship – which clearly they were not. The Pact was designed to give the Soviet Union a large slice of Poland, not to give Stalin influence over Hitler's subsequent actions. Neither was the fact that Germany later turned on the Soviet Union expected by Stalin, as the film implies; rather, it was a result of one power-crazed megalomaniac failing to understand the underlying motivation and inherent capacity for duplicity of another.

After a while it was hard to tell the real Franklin
D. Roosevelt from . . .

UPI/Bettmann Archive

. . . Ralph Bellamy. (*Winds of War*)

Davies' book, which was a best-seller, contained many errors, some of which were corrected by the insertion of postscripts which benefited from hindsight, although in 1941, when the book was published, it must be conceded that much of the truth about Stalin's Russia was still well-hidden. As indicated earlier, the deal Davies struck with Warner's gave him script approval and therefore any errors of fact, or, more importantly, of interpretation, must be laid at his door.

The combination of Davies' total commitment to the film being made the way he wanted it, and his close working relationship with Roosevelt, point towards a measure of collusion in ensuring that the finished film told a story which suited Roosevelt's needs. Added to this is the fact that, as Culbert has reported, the Soviet Ambassador to the United States, Maxim Litvinov (played in the film by Oscar Homolka), was close to Davies and the two men had a number of meetings while the film was in production. Although the Russians subsequently expressed some displeasure at the finished film, it was regularly screened in the Soviet Union. Quite clearly, just as it was expedient for Roosevelt to convey an image of Russia which met his needs at a time of national crisis, the film did no harm to Stalin either at home or abroad, albeit for much less idealistic reasons.

The use of a central figure who has presidential authority to talk to British and Russian leaders, and to visit and report personally upon events in Germany, also appears in *Winds of War* (1983). Made for television at enormous expense, this 16-hour epic drama uses as its source material Herman Wouk's excellent novel. The story traces the events of the years immediately prior to America's entry into the war through the career of an entirely fictitious naval officer, Victor 'Pug' Henry (Robert Mitchum), who is sent on a series of missions by President Roosevelt (Ralph Bellamy) on which, like Davies, he is to look, listen and report.

The film's depictions of real people are a mixed bag. Hitler, in the 1930s, cut a dangerous figure not least because of the frightening degree of control he displayed even when launched into one of his tirades against Jews, capitalists, communists or any other group he felt like offering up as sacrificial victims. Film taken of Hitler during his pre-war rabble-rousing public orations shows a man who knows exactly what he is doing and why. Gunter Meisner's Hitler in *Winds of War* appears as a man whose driving demons are already in the front seat. Also, thanks to cartoon-comic appearance, mannerisms and voice, he appears as little more than a suitable opponent for Batman.

In *Mission to Moscow* Davies took great care to point out how unusual it was for a foreign visitor to meet Stalin. Pug Henry has no such problems. He merely turns up at a party being held inside a building big enough to house the battleship *Potemkin* and there is Uncle Joe (Anatoly Shaginyan), who, naturally, makes a point of trading speeches and drinks with the American.

Clearly it would be wrong of latterday film-makers to exploit hindsight in depicting the past, but too much has been learned about Stalin in the forty years between the two films to allow another avuncular performance to slip by unnoticed. Shaginyan makes this man no more alarming than did Mannart Kippen, except that this time Stalin appears to be suffering from a severe over-application of panstick – doubtless an attempt to cover up acute, if not terminal, acne.

In much the same way as Davies, Pug Henry is remarkably accurate in the forecasts he sends to President Roosevelt and his perception of the situation in Hitler's Germany, Stalin's Russia and Mussolini's Italy (he certainly gets around more than Davies did) benefits more than somewhat from hindsight. Pug Henry also meets Churchill (Howard Lang) and does a reprise of Ed Murrow in his report on the London blitz.

Although often over-inflated and too dependent upon its manifold sub-plot love-affairs (required to make the package acceptable to TV audiences lulled into critical stupor by endless *Dallas*-like sagas), most of the military and political background of *Winds of War* is infinitely superior to that shown in *Mission to Moscow*. The main reason for this is that *Winds of War* has no political axe to grind.

For its main sub-plot *Winds of War* enters an area which was omitted from *Mission to Moscow*, Hitler's attempted genocide of the Jews. Although some information was at hand in the war years regarding what was really happening, little was in the hands of Hollywood's film-makers. Nevertheless, they were not entirely ignorant, otherwise a movie such as *Address Unknown* (1944) could not have been made. This bleak study of the ease with which men can allow themselves to be led into inhuman treatment of their fellows is remarkable for its day, and set a standard which few films of later decades have matched. Certainly *Winds of War* makes no attempt to duck the issue, although the manner in which the treatment of the Jews is depicted falls well short of the brutal reality either of the facts or even of Wouk's novel.

As Wouk also wrote the screenplay for *Winds of War*, the implication is that any failings lie elsewhere. It is almost as if, having invested many millions of dollars in their package, the makers were unwilling to risk alienating the mass audience they needed, which presumably prefers its holocausts to be covered with the thin gloss of a thousand other sagas of love and war. Wouk himself returned movingly to this theme for his novel's sequel, *War and Remembrance*, which centres upon the fate of Natalie Jastrow Henry (played in *Winds of War* by Ali McGraw).

Those films which have concentrated upon the treatment of the Jews will be examined in Chapter 8, although it should be mentioned here that in the 1930s America (and much of the rest of the world) knew more about what was happening than was ever admitted.

As historian Annette Insdorf has observed, American newsreels showed the authorities refusing admission to refugees. The documentary film *Who Shall Live and Who Shall Die?* (1981) indicates clearly that the American government not only knew about the extermination at the time it happened but chose to follow political expediency rather than show simply humanitarian consideration.

There was an attempt to do something practical: a special government agency was set up in 1944 which sought ways and means of rescuing the Jews from their fate. By then, however, such action was too little and too late. The American government's slow and limited response was not necessarily anti-Semitic; American Jews were also remarkably inactive and in some cases actually encouraged a policy which would not rock the boat.

This turning of a politically blind eye towards millions of deaths was not something uniquely American in the 1930s. Recent disclosures have shown that the British government deliberately chose to ignore information received about famine in the Ukraine in 1932 and 1933. The failure of the grain harvest, allied to impractical application of Stalin's directives on collective farming in the region, brought death from starvation to an unknown number of people, perhaps as many as ten million. Undoubtedly Britain could not have done much to alleviate the situation but political expediency dictated that they did not even try.

As *Winds of War* draws to a close, Japan attacks Pearl Harbor and thus precipitates America's entry into the war. The Pearl Harbor attack has been touched upon in many fictitious films. *From Here to Eternity* (1953), while not directly concerned with either the war or the political events leading up to it, does paint an accurate picture of the lives of bored soldiers in peace time and effectively establishes the atmosphere within the lower levels of America's armed forces which allowed them to fall victim to a sneak attack.

A blow-by-blow account of these events was screened in *Tora! Tora! Tora!* (1970), which examines the story from both sides. Filmed jointly by American and Japanese units, directors and actors (who speak their own languages, with sub-titles where necessary), the film goes a long way to establishing what actually happened while never fully explaining how such a massive Japanese attack could have been mounted without someone, somewhere, getting wind of it. A popular theory, never proved, is that Roosevelt knew and kept quiet because he also knew this would jolt America into war. The sheer scale of the attack devastated the American fleet and cost many lives, both at the time and in the months which followed, when America was bereft of sea and air power in the Pacific. This fact alone makes nonsense of such claims. A Stalin or a Hitler might have been capable of such an action, or even the World War I generals who had their own trenches bombarded, but not Roosevelt. Nevertheless, there were those who might have gained from casting such aspersions.

The villains of the piece in *Tora! Tora! Tora!* are the bureaucrats, on both sides, who show monumental incompetence and inefficiency at all levels. Indeed, the higher the position, the worse the idiocies perpetrated by the individuals involved.

No attempt is made to conceal the catalogue of blunders and misjudgements which allowed America to present such an open target to the Japanese.

If anything, the Japanese come out of *Tora! Tora! Tora!* fairly well. The surprise attack resulting in this day of infamy would have been much less of a surprise had their embassy in Washington been able to find a more efficient typist, thus allowing them to transcribe and deliver a written ultimatum before the attack took place.

The final moments of this film, the attack itself, make up for the staginess of the rest of it which, coupled with less than effective performances from a cast of normally competent actors, reduces events to a dreary catalogue.

For Americans who relied upon the movies for their understanding of world events and the war in which their nation was now suddenly embroiled, everything must have appeared rather hazy. Pre-war anti-fascist films all too often showed the Nazis as a variation upon the bad guys hunted down in countless cops-and-robbers melodramas. The political, economic and social conditions which had moved the world slowly but inevitably towards the war seldom if ever appeared in films. The Nazis were villains not because of what they represented but because they were double-dyed Hollywood bad-hats who persistently tried to commit unspeakable acts upon all-American heroines and otherwise sought to jeopardize the American Way. The deeper philosophical background was ignored in favour of simple, clear-cut responses: if the likes of Gary Cooper, Clark Gable, Joel McCrea and Jimmy Stewart were against them, then what else need be known?

Once the die was cast, Americans went at the task of fighting the war with commendable enthusiasm and efficiency. Hollywood was a few jumps ahead and already making movies about the war but had so far stayed clear of films which depicted battles and bombings and all the awful panoply of total war. Now that the nation was directly involved in the fighting, it was a marvellous opportunity for film-makers to get into the act in a big way and with the kind of movie they made so well.

Real war may be hell, but war movies are great box-office.

CHAPTER EIGHT

'No bastard ever won a war by dying
for his country . . .'
(General George S. Patton)

The attack on Pearl Harbor had an effect upon the American people much like that which came in the wake of the Alamo: shock, outrage and anger.

Any overt qualms Americans still had about involvement in a foreign war were dispelled by the surprise attack on the Hawaiian Islands. Isolationists who retained their principles, and they were many, kept quiet about them. The mood of the nation called for vengeance, and woe betide any politician who resists grass-roots opinion when a substantial portion of the nation is caught up in war-fever.

The dangers to America in the Pacific had been hinted at several years earlier by General Billy Mitchell, who had predicted the need for air power as protection for any future offensive against Japan. The die-hards refused to take cognizance of the need and Mitchell went public and was court-martialled, found guilty and dismissed from the service. His story was told in *The Court Martial of Billy Mitchell* (1955), which starred Gary Cooper in the title role. The film spelled out the uncomfortable truth that not only was Pearl Harbor predictable, but American air power was less than adequate before it was smashed to pieces on the ground.

With America committed to war against Japan, and soon against Germany too, Hollywood was free to begin a new wave of films. No longer obliged to tell tales of British and European resistance to fascism, or to rake up tales of old wars, film-makers now buckled down to generating accounts of home-grown American heroism. They did so with such gusto that some of the Allies, especially the British, were understandably irritated when it appeared that America was fighting the war on its own.

The first rush of war movies were mostly plain, straightforward, gung-ho adventure yarns in which every (American) man was a hero and every enemy soldier a double-dyed villain who richly deserved to be blown apart. Some of the titles are a clear indication of a simplistic approach to the complexities and horrors of total war: *We've Never Been Licked* and *Gung Ho!* (both 1943) leave no doubt that their intentions, even if the former spent most if its running time in boot camp and the latter was a true-ish record of the US Marines' assault on Mackin Island in 1942.

128

Clearly Hollywood considered it was its public duty to persuade the home audience of the need for sacrifice and hardship, just as British audiences were being similarly exhorted by their own film industry. True, there were differences in approach. The American movie soldier was likely to be a hard-nosed, back-talking iconoclast who shared mess-tent and foxhole with a carefully constructed cross-section of ethnic types, an inexperienced junior officer who looked barely old enough to shave, or a gruff, tough sergeant who had fought in World War I and knew all the answers.

The GI sergeant's British counterpart was self-effacing and professional even if he had never held a gun before. If working-class he came from the North and knew his place; if middle-class he worked in a London bank and was politely heroic. The officers were the epitome of an elegant aristocracy with upper lips stiff enough to hack through Hitler's Siegfried Line unaided. Those who died did so with dignity and not too much blood.

Neither the American nor the British army had any real cowards, although in British war movies Richard Attenborough and Bryan Forbes were often cast as decidedly shaky types who usually managed to do the right thing before the final fade-out, even if it meant getting themselves blown to bloodless bits in the process.

Both countries were happy to have their war efforts aided by amiably un-warlike types. Britain allowed Will Hay, George Formby, radio comedian Tommy Handley and music hall's Old Mother Riley to have a go at Adolf in various films of variable quality. Similarly uneven were some light-hearted American efforts in which comedians Abbott and Costello, Bob Hope and Eddie Bracken took a fling at the Nazis and the Japs in and out of uniform. Even the Red Shadow and Tarzan of the Apes got into the act; probably the only factor holding Dracula back was that strange shortage of spilled blood.

For the most part, however, war movies were taken seriously, if over-heroically, and no one questioned the rights and wrongs of it all – at least, not until the war was over, when questions, sometimes disturbing ones, were asked in films set during the conflict.

Few early American war films were especially realistic. The lessons of *All Quiet on the Western Front* were forgotten. Attempts at injecting realism usually stopped at a smear of dirt on the forehead of the leading man, who would often hand in his dogtags in the final reel. When this happened, a survivor from quite low in the cast list would then deliver a shiny-eyed declamation which owed more to Shakespeare than to the linguistic gifts of the average GI – especially one under fire.

Soon, changes began to occur. Newsreels shot on the battlefields of Europe and the Pacific showed audiences what was really happening and feature film-makers took note, sometimes including newsreel footage in their own efforts.

In Hollywood, as in Britain, the film community temporarily, and occasionally permanently, lost several well-known faces to the war effort: Clark Gable, James Stewart, Victor Mature, Tyrone Power and Henry Fonda all put on uniform, and South African-born Louis Hayward, who had bounded through a variety of swashbuckling roles including those of the Man in the Iron Mask, the Count of Monte Cristo and the Saint, became a war photographer. Directors William Wyler, Frank Capra and John Ford also served, the last two making documentary films about the war, and screenwriter Dalton Trumbo became a war correspondent in the Pacific.

Just as in World War I, the value of films for propaganda purposes was not overlooked. All belligerent nations turned out such films, often using a historical setting to underline the significance of this new crisis in their country's affairs.

As mentioned earlier, America weighed in with *Wilson*, which drew unjustified parallels with Roosevelt, while Britain waved the flag with *The Young Mr Pitt* (1942), which also drew a parallel, this time with Winston Churchill. In *Lady Hamilton* (1941) Horatio Nelson's opponent was Napoleon, who also served as the villain in the Russian film *General Suvorov* (1941) and in a German entry in the propaganda stakes, *Kolberg* (1945). That this film should have been made so near to the end of the Third Reich is a measure of the desperation felt by the nation's leaders. The message imparted to the German people was clear: just as Generals Gneisenau and Nettlebeck had defended the village of Kolberg against Napoleon, so too must the remaining corners of Germany be defended against the advancing armies – regardless of the cost to human life. Just where German audiences were supposed to find the time, or the place, to go to the movies is open to speculation.

Italy had entered the propaganda war before the real war began by making its own historical film, *Scipio Africanus* (1937), which feebly attempted to defend Italy's indefensible attack upon Ethiopia. By the standards of the conflict to come, the war in Ethiopia was a small affair in which the heavy armaments, bombers and poison gas of the invader proved to be rather more than a match for the spears and swords of the defenders. Not surprisingly, the film, which set out to justify Italian claims in Africa, impressed no one but the Italians.

As the American war effort began its forward surge, the main thrust was in the Pacific. Although help was desperately needed in Europe and was forthcoming, it was understandable that the Japanese should be seen as the principal enemy of America. It was, after all, the Japanese, not the Germans, who had attacked Pearl Harbor.

The war in the Pacific has been depicted in innumerable films, most of which followed the new tradition of the ethnically-mixed platoon commanded by a tough sergeant. The Marines took a substantial slice of the credit, and also provided a string of film titles which played variations upon the words of their battle hymn: *The Halls of Montezuma* (1951), which stars Richard Widmark as the grizzled veteran, and *To the Shores of Tripoli* (1942), which set leathery Randolph Scott the task of whipping former playboy and now recalcitrant rookie John Payne into shape for the ensuing conflict.

The Sands of Iwo Jima (1949) finds John Wayne tackling a similar problem with John Agar, whose main problem is that he is an officer's son (for some reason a perpetual hazard in the life of Hollywood's soldiers). This film has excellent battle scenes, some apparently genuine, others seemingly shot during peacetime manoeuvres. Against these were set the actors, sometimes photographed on location (not in the Pacific), often in the studio. The process work is not always as good as it might have been and most of the studio-shot scenes stand out glaringly against the realistic backgrounds.

The film has a traditional ending, with Wayne getting it in the back from a dastardly Nip sniper, thus allowing Agar to read an unfinished letter to Wayne's son which reveals what a big softie he had been all along. Agar, now a worthy successor to Wayne and to Dad, then clenches his jaw muscles and leads the rest of the platoon into the smoke of battle while the Marine band plays on.

The full sweep of the American effort in the Pacific is set out in a film which traces part of the life of Douglas MacArthur, the American general many thought to be god-like. MacArthur undoubtedly agreed with such idolators, except that he would probably have spelled the adjective with a capital G.

MacArthur the Rebel General (1977) begins in 1942, which at once unbalances the film. A decade before, MacArthur had taken tanks and rifles to rout the Bonus Marchers in the nation's capital; omission of this event makes his subsequent career appear almost routinely Hollywood and distinctly two-dimensional.

In fact, MacArthur's story, which has been thoroughly recounted by William Manchester in his book *American Caesar* (also the title of a major TV documentary about the General), begins much earlier than his 1932 Washington adventure. By then he was already the Army's Chief of Staff. Curiously enough, MacArthur's life and career touches upon most of the principal areas of American history dealt with in this book.

His father, Arthur MacArthur, fought with distinction in the Civil War and later fought the Indians; he also numbered Buffalo Bill among his friends.

In 1893, when Douglas was 13, he was with his father at Fort Sam Houston in Texas; this was where sequences of *The Big Parade* were shot in 1925. As a junior officer, Douglas was in Mexico during the difficulties America had with the revolutionaries; he was press relations officer at the War Department when General Pershing went after Pancho Villa.

He was instrumental in establishing the efficient operation of the draft which facilitated the swift mobilization of men at the start of American involvement in World War I; he also served in France where he met George C. Marshall and George S. Patton (who commanded the tanks used against the Bonus Marchers).

Gassed in 1918, MacArthur returned home and became Superintendent at West Point. In 1925 he served on Billy Mitchell's court-martial, apparently casting the only 'not guilty' vote.

His connection with the Orient, and with the Philippines in particular, began in 1898, when he went on a tour of China (and during the next few years visited many of the Pacific islands where he would later fight) and Japan. He took command of American forces in the Philippines in 1929 and remained closely associated with the region either as an officer in the American army or with the Philippine army until Pearl Harbor.

MacArthur even had a tenuous connection with the movies: his first wife, Louise, later married film actor Lionel Atwill. MacArthur himself, and Jean Faircloth, who became his second wife, were avid moviegoers.

Despite a World War I record of swift decision-making, MacArthur was caught uncharacteristically flat-footed the day after Pearl Harbor when his aircraft were destroyed on the ground. In February 1942, the overwhelming might of the Japanese forced President Roosevelt to order the General's personal withdrawal from Corregidor in the Philippines. Uttering his theatrical declaration ' . . . I shall return,' MacArthur left for Australia and soon afterwards the American forces in the Philippines, now commanded by General Wainwright, surrendered to the Japanese.

MacArthur took command of the allied forces in the south-west Pacific, rebuilt the shattered morale of the army, and also enjoyed appreciable successes in a war that was part-traditional, part guerilla-orientated. In 1944 he redeemed his pledge to return to the Philippines when he landed on Leyte. There, impatient at being held up, he jumped into the surf and strode ashore knee-deep in the ocean. An alert news photographer snapped the moment and MacArthur, whose self-awareness included an acute nose for publicity, repeated the move the next day on arrival at another island in the group.

Everyone back home was impressed. The residents of the town of Mikado in Michigan, smarting under the misfortune of having named their town after something positively Japanese-sounding, promptly renamed it MacArthur.

The men who served under the General were much less adulatory, yet MacArthur had a remarkably good record of losses. Wherever he was in command, the death toll of American soldiers was always lower than that of any comparable unit in less efficient hands.

The battles fought in crossing the Pacific were regularly successful both on MacArthur's part of a two-pronged attack and on that commanded by his great rival, Admiral Chester Nimitz. But these battles were no Bonus March pushovers.

The tiny island of Tarawa was taken after a three-day battle, after which only 17 Japanese surrendered. They left 3,000 dead; the Americans lost 1,000 men. In an eight-hour air battle for Guam the Japanese threw in 430 aircraft and lost all but 100. At Saipan the Americans lost 3,000 men with more than 13,000 wounded. More than 10,000 men were either killed or wounded on Peleliu in the Palaus.

The statistics go on, becoming steadily more meaningless when viewed from a distance of both time and space. American veterans who fought in the battle

MacArthur's theatricality made life easy for
movie-makers . . .

UPI-Popperfoto

. . . all they had to do was copy the great stage
manager's design. *(MacArthur the Rebel General)*

for Iwo Jima were interviewed for the superb television documentary *The World at War* (1975), and were unanimous in their impressions: 'If there's ever been hell, this was it.' 'If there is a hell, I'm living through it now so I don't have to worry about going to hell any time in the future. I've been there.'

Eventually, the Stars and Stripes was raised on the summit of Mount Suribachi, a moment used graphically as a set-piece of many movies. One of the men who raised the flag was Ira Hayes, the Indian, whose life story has been told twice on the screen.

Of 20,000 Japanese who had defended Iwo Jima, 200 were taken prisoner. This was due in part to their steadfast refusal to surrender, and in part to the fact that by this stage of the war in the Pacific the Americans had learned some hard lessons. Often, prisoners were taken who were found to be holding primed grenades which they let off as soon as they were among a group of GIs. As one veteran declared in *The World at War*, 'You're a little bit leery about taking prisoners when they're fighting to the death and so are you.'

Okinawa, the first Japanese island to be reached by the Americans, was massively defended by 100,000 men, although by this time some were growing less certain about the logic of dying for a country whose leaders were beginning to bend from their previously rigid path. Conversely, Okinawa also saw the emergence of a last-ditch band of young Japanese fliers, the Kami-kazes, who flew their explosives-packed aircraft into American ships. The degree of determination of these men has subsequently been questioned, with revelations that in many instances the canopies of their aircraft were bolted from the outside to deter the pilot from abandoning his mission before impact.

It was a brutal, bloody campaign and knowledge of it goes some way towards explaining, if not justifying, the decision to drop the atomic bomb.

The immensity of the Pacific War, the huge death toll on both sides, never emerges in any film set in this place and time. Faced with the same problems confronting film-makers who sought to show the reality of World War I, most settled for the small unit which represented all the other small units which made up the whole. Additionally, once again, the scope of the war was beyond the imaginations of many, and for those who experienced it first-hand before coming to film-making there was the added fear that maybe audiences would not be able to take it if the reality were shown.

By the time General MacArthur came aboard the *USS Missouri* to accept the Japanese surrender on 2 September 1945, he was not only deified in the American consciousness, he was also presidential material, something which had not escaped Roosevelt's attention while the war was still in progress. By now, however, Roosevelt was dead and his successor, Harry S. Truman, must have seemed like pretty small beer to the General.

In the event, Truman turned out to be rather more than he appeared, as MacArthur discovered to his cost at another time and during yet another war.

MacArthur the Rebel General follows most of the events recounted above with a fair degree of accuracy. MacArthur (Gregory Peck) looks the part, complete with putty nose and corncob pipe, and most of the set-pieces are staged effectively. Indeed, MacArthur had stage-managed many of them in the first place. The leap from the landing-craft when he strides ashore at Leyte is uncannily like the real thing. Similarly accurate in its reconstruction is the surrender ceremony on board the *USS Missouri*.

MacArthur's role in the determination of a new way of life for Japan is rightly given great importance. In real life his role was far more significant than that granted to any other army officer in the affairs of a nation conquered by American forces.

Overall, the film sticks to known facts about the public man but there is very little reference to his private life; as William Manchester has shown, with two wives and at least one mistress, he certainly found time for life outside the army. As for the man of war, here much of the film's running time is taken up with meetings between MacArthur and Roosevelt (Dan O'Herlihy), MacArthur and Truman (Ed Flanders), and MacArthur and more top brass than are featured in the cast list of any half dozen other war movies put together.

The imbalance of the film stems from its failure to reveal what drove the man; yet again in dealing with an American historical figure, the film-makers banged their heads against the wall of divine intervention, however imaginary, and failed to come up with a credible view.

Then there is the matter of the Bonus March; what did MacArthur really think and feel about the actions he took in Washington which led to the deaths of some of the men with whom he had fought in France?

If *MacArthur the Rebel General* fails to dig into what makes a senior army officer tick, another film about another American general, this time in the European theatre of war, at least makes the effort.

Patton (1969) takes as its subject a man who commanded almost as much attention and respect as MacArthur. One thing George S. Patton did not command was reverence: he was too earthy for that. No one could ever imagine MacArthur remarking, 'No bastard ever won a war by dying for his country; he won it by making the other poor dumb bastard die for *his* country.'

Like MacArthur, Patton was flamboyant in his personal behaviour and dress. MacArthur usually wore a gaily-coloured scarf, a threadbare but immaculately laundered uniform, and a carefully remodelled cap; Patton favoured pearl-handled pistols.

Also like MacArthur, Patton restored battered spirits, raised hopes and enthusiasm, and drove himself harder than he ever drove his men in his attempts to win swift, and hence less damaging, victories.

Unlike MacArthur's implacable public face, Patton frequently displayed acute concern for the fate of his men, often openly weeping over and even kissing wounded men in army hospitals. Such moments, depicted with care and no sense of embarrassment in the film, contrast vividly with the better-known instances of his volatile behaviour such as the incident when he slapped soldiers he believed to be malingering.

In the film, Patton (George C. Scott in brilliant form for which he won, but rejected, the Academy Award for Best Actor) is almost as much at war with his fellow officers as he is with the Germans. His deputy, later his superior, General Omar N. Bradley (Karl Malden), is the only close acquaintance he has (even he could not be called a friend) but they seldom agree on tactics. Bradley was technical consultant on the movie, which might account for some slight imbalances in those areas of the story where the two men disagree over how to conduct their part of the war.

Patton's brilliance and the speed with which he tries to move often finds his colleagues just as much on the wrong foot as the enemy. He clashes with Montgomery (Michael Bates) in Sicily and again, much more critically to the course of the war, in France. Historian Alan Landau has suggested that when Patton's 3rd Army literally ran out of gas, the much-needed fuel having gone to Montgomery, it might well have added almost a year to the war. Instead of being able to sweep the enemy before him and with Montgomery failing to cut off their retreat, Patton had to sit and watch the Germans redeploy and mount a counter-attack which led to the Battle of the Bulge.

The slapping incident had prompted many to call for Patton's dismissal but Eisenhower knew that the fiery officer was needed, and events in France proved him right. But Eisenhower did insist that the General should apologize publicly for his intemperate action. This scene in the film, with Patton standing before the stiffly silent ranks of soldiers, is surprisingly moving and goes a long way towards making this complex man understandable.

The role of the ordinary American infantryman in the North African, Sicilian and Italian campaigns through which Patton strode was also traced in the usual gung-ho movies. Among the exceptions was one of the best films ever made about World War II; an accolade all the more surprising because it was made while the war was still in progress, long before the later rush of soul-searching movies began.

The Story of GI Joe (1945) is understated, laconic and honest. Based upon the book *Here Is Your War* by Ernie Pyle, which was in turn based upon the author's experiences as a war correspondent, the film is largely anecdotal as it follows the men of Company C from North Africa to Italy. Although the men are the usual cross-section they manage somehow to avoid cliché and maintain a convincing reality. In some measure this is due to all the actors concerned being virtually unknown at the time the movie was made. Indeed, most of them would remain that way, although the actor playing the role of the company commander went on to superstardom.

Lieutenant (later Captain) Walker is played by Robert Mitchum at a time when he was barely out of the string of bit parts he had played in a score of B-Westerns, yet his weary efforts to hold his men together are portrayed with assurance and dignity. His conversations with Ernie Pyle (Burgess Meredith) have neither the flag-waving rhetoric associated with Hollywood's war movies, nor the mindless platitudes of those other, later films which sought, but usually failed, to restore some balance to the image of war created by the rah-rah brigade.

A particularly telling scene, and one which was usually conveniently overlooked, has a bone-weary Lieutenant Walker striving to write letters home to the parents of those of his men who have been killed. In a dispassionate yet moving moment, he sets aside his pen and tells Pyle in simple, unaffected words the thoughts that are in his mind. They are not especially heroic; he is not repeating the mindless pap which Hollywood has led audiences to believe army officers speak. He is speaking the bleak, uncompromising truth about what war really means to the ordinary soldier. More than any other scene in the film it is probably this one which contributed to the decision to withhold release until the war was ended.

The film does not show very much in the way of fighting. The main battle is always just a little farther down the road. Men are not killed on-screen in gory detail, they simply fail to reappear and no one mentions their passing. This casual, almost indifferent acceptance of death has a surprising impact.

The manner of Walker's death is an example of this. Pyle catches up with Company C after being away for some weeks. The men await Walker's return from reconnaissance. Slowly, a line of mules comes down the hillside, each bearing a body. The body on the last mule is Walker's. His men look at the body in silence, then turn and quietly move off up the line to fight the next battle. Pyle too looks down at the body; a line of crosses marking many graves is silhouetted against the skyline, and the movie ends without fanfare.

One event in particular added a further touch of sombre realism to *The Story of GI Joe*. While the film was still in production, Ernie Pyle went off to report on the war in the Pacific and was killed.

One young American soldier who became a national hero was eventually depicted on film in a manner which linked the real war with the make-believe war of the movies in a strangely inextricable fashion. The young soldier was a slightly-built Texan named Audie Murphy. He ended the war as its most decorated hero, thus suggesting comparisons with World War I's Sergeant York. Unlike York, who buried himself in the backwoods until World War II prompted him to allow his story to be filmed, Murphy took advantage of his post-war fame and became a movie star.

Most of his forty-odd films were forgettable westerns (in one of them he played Billy the Kid), but he acted well in the Civil War drama *The Red Badge of Courage* (1951). In 1955 he achieved something few American heroes have succeeded in doing – he played himself in a screen adaptation of his book about his wartime experiences, *To Hell and Back*.

The Pacific and Europe were not the only battle fronts Hollywood explored. There was also that most important of all places where wars are fought, the Home Front. Predictably, one of the best-known of these went over the top not in heroics but in three-handkerchief sentimentality.

Since You Went Away (1944) shows that if the stiff upper-lip so beloved by makers of British war movies had no place in the American counterpart, there was plenty of scope on Main Street, USA.

The mood of the film is established with an opening caption stating: 'This is the story of the Unconquerable Fortress: the American Home – 1943.' Just in case any member of the audience came in late and missed this, Max Steiner's score proceeds to milk every opportunity for nostalgic tear-jerking. Among the numerous themes wound in by Steiner, most prominent is 'America the Beautiful', which gave everyone the message.

Excellently photographed by two of Hollywood's pastmasters, Stanley Cortez and Lee Garmes, the film never fully gets to grips with the problems created by the producer. David O. Selznick wanted the entire movie to follow the theme established by both opening caption and music; it should have been the other way round.

Anne Hilton (Claudette Colbert) is bravely holding the fortress because an inconsiderate government has drafted her husband. She clearly thinks she is badly done by, but in the eyes of non-Americans (and probably many less well-heeled Americans, too), things could be a whole lot worse. The Hiltons live in a house big enough to accommodate half a dozen blitzed London families and they even have a black maid, named Fidelia (Hattie McDaniel). Anne decides she has to economize, which means ditching the maid (who, living up to her name, returns faithfully at a later date and weighs in for free), selling the car and, horror of horrors, renting a room to a lodger. This last act is frowned upon rather severely by the eldest of the Hilton girls, Jane (Jennifer Jones), who equates having a lodger in the house with communism! The local storekeeper, aware that the maid has been fired, delivers the groceries himself, probably because he thinks Anne Hilton has led such a sheltered life that she doesn't know the way to the store.

The distance between America and the war which was currently devastating Britain and other European countries was so great in miles and atmosphere that anyone who did not have personal experience could not hope to capture effectively the spirit of people caught up in such situations. With fear of bombing raids and invasion set aside, all Selznick could do was to project into war time the standard crisis-situation of countless Hollywood dramas. The resulting crises are often laughable when set against the real-life experience of, for example, the British.

In one scene Anne goes out to dinner with Tony Willett (Joseph Cotten); at the restaurant they settle for a hamburger-steak, having been told that real steaks are no longer available. Since they have just passed up the chance of ordering lobster from what appears to be a pretty comprehensive menu, this touch of austerity fails to create the intended impression.

Despite her sudden comparative poverty, Anne can still raise enough loot to buy railroad tickets for herself, Jane and her other daughter, Brig (Shirley Temple), so that they can travel to New York where they hope to see Dad. Unfortunately, they miss him through the kind of logistical error with which all such films abound. The entire exercise seems to have been slotted into the movie so that they can meet an old lady on the train who shows them what courage is all about by recounting how her daughter has not been heard from since Corregidor was taken by the Japanese.

Eventually, however improbably, Anne takes herself off to the shipyards and becomes a welder, doubtless having heard about her working-class sisters, Swing Shift Maisie and Rosie the Riveter. The glimpse of Claudette Colbert in well-laundered and possibly custom-made overalls doing her impression of Rosie is fortunately fleeting.

Deaths occur but only off-screen and they are engineered to provide dramatic effect rather than an atmosphere of reality. An aircraft crashes at a nearby base killing the storekeeper's son; another young man, Bill Smollett (Robert Walker), dies in action, thus proving his bravery to his grandfather, old Colonel Smollett (Monty Woolley, giving a reprise of his Sheridan Whiteside character), who is the Hiltons' lodger.

Anne's husband never appears in the film, although his photograph is very much in evidence and is wept over copiously. He goes missing in action but miraculously survives, the news coming through exactly when it is most needed – on Christmas Eve.

The predictability of the script takes the edge off what might have been a movie of some merit. As it stands, while it undoubtedly served an important need at the time, it is as soft-centred and ultimately as false as any bullet-strewn epic which sought to show war as an experience which made men out of boys rather than as something which turned men into corpses. Anne Hilton's war merely deprives her of material comforts.

In *Rosie the Riveter* (1944) Rosalind Warren (Jane Frazee) nobly delays her wedding because it is more important to help win the war. She then plunges headlong into factory work with considerably more zest than Claudette Colbert showed in *Since You Went Away* and earns the doubtful accolade (from a man, naturally) that she typifies the Miss America of today.

A more accurate portrayal of the life of women workers in war time appears in a 1980 documentary entitled *The Life and Times of Rosie the Riveter*. Here those wartime factory-workers talk for themselves without benefit of Hollywood screenwriters. These women are not Anne Hiltons and Rosalind Warrens, who left comfortable middle-class homes to labour on production lines, but ordinary working-class women who were encouraged to take on men's work when their husbands were drafted. Just as enthusiastically, they were exhorted to return to dead-end jobs, or no jobs at all, at the end of the war, and to accept a commensurate fall in the standard of living they had briefly enjoyed. Reality for Rosie and her companion, Swing Shift Maisie, was not quite the way Hollywood had depicted.

Other American Home Front events were simply overlooked by film-makers during the war and immediately thereafter. The internment of the Issei and Nisei Japanese on the West Coast was one such occurrence that passed virtually unnoticed by Hollywood.

When Japan attacked Pearl Harbor many Americans suddenly woke up to the fact that among the mass of immigrants their nation had attracted over the years were large numbers of Orientals. About one-third of a million Chinese and Japanese had entered the country; the majority of the latter had taken up residence on the West Coast, where they turned their hands to fruit farming and fishing. Their success in both business and assimilation was profound, and by the time of Pearl Harbor they were as dehyphenated as their Italian and German fellow-Americans in other parts of the country. Unlike them, however, the Japanese were subjected to deplorable treatment. Mass internment and deprivation of both property and Civil Rights were commonplace. These Japanese-Americans (the Issei were first generation, the Nisei their children) were designated as aliens and subjected to arrest warrants and transportation to internment camps.

No comparable action was taken at either official or street level against those of Italian and German descent. This difference stemmed from three main causes: the fear and anger generated by the attack on Pearl Harbor, especially in California, which appeared to be the logical place for a Japanese invasion; the fact that unlike Americans of Italian and German descent the Japanese-Americans were readily identifiable on sight; thirdly, although more than one hundred thousand were rounded up, had the authorities gone after the Italians and Germans they would have been faced with interning many millions. The whole sorry affair was a triumphant mixture of panic and pragmatism.

A side issue, that of the removal from the local business scene of some highly successful competitors, is another factor which should not be overlooked.

A TV movie, *Farewell to Manzanar* (1976), made considerable amends for earlier neglect by film-makers and also helped restore to their proper status in American eyes the Issei and Nisei who were so badly treated in California. Based upon the book by Jeanne Wakatsuki and her husband James D. Houston, the film traces the events leading up to the Wakatsuki family's incarceration in a camp at Manzanar in California when Jeanne herself was a little girl. Understated, neither hectoring nor apportioning blame, this film must have caused many Americans to pause and think about what had been done to yet another minority – if anyone needed proof, as late as 1976, that being a hyphenated American was no big deal.

Two earlier feature films had touched upon the same subject. *Go For Broke* (1951) is about the Nisei soldiers who were eventually allowed to enter the US Army in World War II. Naturally they were sent to Europe where, as the 442nd Regimental Combat Team, they acquitted themselves well, albeit under the command of all-American noncoms and officers. Unlike *Farewell to Manzanar*, there is no mention of the ultimate irony which befell many of these soldiers: that they were away fighting for America while their parents languished in American internment camps.

Bad Day at Black Rock (1955) uses the form of a suspense thriller to tell the story of the fate of one Japanese-American. When John J. Macreedy (Spencer Tracy) steps off the train at Black Rock he wants to talk with an old Japanese who lives nearby. The town's residents close ranks in resentful silence and this one-armed veteran from the war has to fight for his safety and eventually for his life. Then he declares his motives: one of the men he served with in the army was awarded a posthumous medal for gallantry. This man was a Japanese-American, the son of the old man he is seeking. All Macreedy wants is to hand the medal to the hero's father.

The townspeople's motives for their obstructive behaviour is now revealed. In a fit of drunken rage at the presence in their midst of a Japanese, one of their number has killed the old man, his body has been burned, and the rest of the town has decided to protect their own kind.

The use of the atomic bomb to bring about the end of the war with Japan does not surface very often in American feature films about World War II. *The Beginning or the End* (1947) takes a half-hearted swing at the story of the Bomb's development. Unfortunately, it manages to lose the magnitude of the Manhattan Project in both explosive and moral terms, thanks largely to a scientifically hazy script and an entirely unnecessary and fictional sub-plot.

Using a semi-documentary style and with lots of earnest scientists delivering incomprehensible monologues over the heads of the audience, the film dodges most of the issues. Only one man, the film's fictional central character (played by Tom Drake), is allowed to question the morality of what is happening. No one else, from J. Robert Oppenheimer (Hume Cronyn) to Albert Einstein (Ludwig Stossel) or from Franklin D. Roosevelt (Godfrey Tearle) to Harry S. Truman (Roman Bohnen and Art Baker), appears to have any doubts about it all. In fact, the alacrity with which the film's Truman gives the order to bomb Japan caused the President's advisers to complain to the film's makers. Not only did they want Truman to be seen to think a little longer before ordering the annihilation of many thousands of men, women and children, but they also felt that the actor originally cast in the role, Roman Bohnen, was too militaristic; hence another actor was called in to make some additional scenes.

Nowhere in the film is there a hint that many scientists urged the government to give the Japanese a warning and a demonstration before the Bomb was dropped on Hiroshima.

Similarly unconsidered here (necessarily so, given the secrecy at the time of the film's making) are the political considerations which pushed Truman and Secretary of State James Byrnes ahead with the decision to drop the Bomb. Paramount among these was the knowledge that if the USSR came into the war against Japan her post-war claims might unbalance the power struggle which everyone knew was inevitable. Although the Soviet Union nipped in sharply and declared war, it did not, thanks to the Bomb, have a large-scale military involvement, and hence had less influence in post-war affairs in the Pacific.

The special effects in *The Beginning or the End*, for which A. Arnold Gillespie won an Academy Award, stop short of reality in the laboratory sequences. Despite the tension and drama of the experiments which led to the

Bomb's development, there was not much to see. Filmgoers, accustomed to the flashing lights and crackling electricity needed to give life to Franken-stein's monster, got what they expected.

Above and Beyond (1952) also took a fling at the story, on this occasion from the point of view of the man who flew *Enola Gay*, the aircraft which carried the Bomb to Japan. The film stars Robert Taylor, whose widow's peak proves a near-perfect match for that of Colonel Paul Tibbetts, the real-life pilot. While treating the events surrounding the dropping of the Bomb with a mixture of awe and misunderstanding, this film also ducks the moral issues raised by President Truman's decision to bomb Hiroshima and Nagasaki.

Given the cost in American lives of the Pacific campaign, much of the pro-Bomb thinking can be understood, even if it cannot be endorsed. Neverthe-less, a modern audience requires to know rather more of what went through the President's mind, especially in respect of Russian involvement in the Pacific. Similarly, the pressure from the military needs explaining. All other considerations aside, Truman appears to have been unequivocal, whatever his advisers might have inferred to the contrary in their complaint against *The Beginning or the End*. 'Let there be no mistake,' he declared shortly before the Bomb was dropped, 'we shall completely destroy Japan's power to make war.'

Destroy it the Americans most certainly did.

The real effect upon the two Japanese cities chosen as targets has been seen in recently released archive film long hidden in US Army vaults. Some of these films were shot by Japanese, some by an American film unit within days of the blasts. A number of Hollywood technicians were among these men and they helped produce a moving and frightening record of something not since seen anywhere on earth. That some of these American film-makers subse-quently fell prey to cancer, almost certainly induced by their visit to the sites, adds a further element of grim truth to the documentary film.

These men were obviously subject at the time to official rulings on secrecy, yet in the light of the development of the hydrogen bomb, the ICBMs, and the arms race in general, it is unfortunate that they were unable to bring their first-hand knowledge to a mass audience by way of a major feature film.

For the most part, until nuclear weapons had proliferated to the point where there were enough for every American to have his name on his own personal bomb, they were treated by film-makers merely as a commodity. In much the same way that in later films drugs were something to be stolen by the bad guys and chased after by the good guys, rather than a serious problem for millions of citizens, so too did atomic secrets become the subject for thrillers. Rarely did film-makers offer any comment upon the morality of the matter. At times the Bomb was merely a *deus ex machina* which popped up to create problems of a rather final nature in what were otherwise routine melodramas.

Equally little has been done by American film-makers, although their Japanese counterparts have considered it, to show the effect of the Bomb upon individual victims and the often astonishing humility with which they view their limited world.

Sodako Sasaki, the little Japanese girl, knowing that she was dying of radiation sickness, set herself the task of spreading peace by adopting an ancient tradition. She began making paper cranes, intending, but tragically failing, to complete 1,000 before she died. Each of the 964 she did complete was inscribed: 'Paper crane, I shall write "peace" on your wing and you shall fly all over the world.'

Film-makers could spread the word so much more easily and effectively – if only they cared to.

World War II received considerable attention from British film-makers both during and after events. As indicated earlier, a strong inclination towards stiff upper lips sometimes prevents audiences understanding what motivates characters in these films. Nevertheless, many of them stayed reasonably close to events and individuals.

Among the more notable films is *A Bridge Too Far* (1977), which tells the truly heroic tale of the British paratroopers at Arnhem. By the time the film was made the British film industry needed American funds and hence had to accept Americans in the cast. Fortunately, they are well and correctly integrated and the film brought forth none of the complaints which had surrounded some earlier American movies which, while understandably concentrating upon American soldiers, inadvertently created the impression that America alone had fought the Second World War. *Objective, Burma!* (1945) brought forth most bile in this category, but even *The Story of GI Joe* was subjected to complaints and restricted screenings in Britain.

A Bridge Too Far was based upon a book by Cornelius Ryan, as was *The Longest Day* (1972), which traces the events of D-Day in 1944. Again American money, stars and director were used but so too were British money, stars and director, together with similar involvement from Germany. This splitting of roles and responsibility meant that the film ended up as a series of not too well linked anecdotes which fail to generate the excitement worthy of the occasion.

Much better, if the literal reverse of an invasion, was *Dunkirk* (1958), which tells in sharp detail the story of the rescue of the men of the British Expeditionary Force in 1940 who were thrown back on to the beaches by overwhelming German forces. This, more than any other war story, including those set in prison camps, is a fitting place for the firm top lip. Heroism in defeat, especially when the audience knows that defeat is only temporary, is somehow more acceptable than over-the-top bravura.

With the fighting over, there was still work to be done – especially in Europe, where the last remnants of Hitler's gang were being tried in Nuremberg. This was made the subject of a major feature film which was in turn based upon a TV play by Abby Mann. Entirely fictitious though it is, *Judgement at Nuremberg* (1961) is serious and well-meaning, if somewhat heavy-handed in its treatment of an admittedly grim subject. The film is studded with stars, all of whom worked for next to nothing in order to appear and thus make a public statement of personal beliefs.

Among the more impressive performances are those of Judy Garland as a German girl who had associated with an elderly Jew; Montgomery Clift as a Jew who was sterilized; Burt Lancaster as a self-deluding former senior member of the judiciary who allowed his idealism to be subverted by nationalistic and racist fervour; Maximilian Schell as a defending counsel in whose fervent efforts to secure the release of his clients it is possible to discern something of the neo-Nazism yet to come; and Spencer Tracy as an ordinary American judge attempting to bring simple down-home principles of justice to bear upon matters which are beyond belief, let alone beyond the rule of law.

A line in the script, although written with the benefit of hindsight, remarks upon the fact that none of the men found guilty at the trial will serve more than a small fraction of their sentences. That much was all too depressingly true.

Part of the background to the trials, by then known to everyone, was the fate of the Jews at the hands of the Nazis. For film-makers, the Holocaust has proved to be something of a problem. The manner in which a subject of such horrifying proportions should be dealt with is a puzzle few feature film-makers have succeeded in solving. Often the wholesale slaughter is relegated to the background, which sometimes serves merely to undervalue, even to trivialize, what happened. In her thorough and perceptive analysis of all such cinema and TV films and documentaries, Annette Insdorf rightly comments that any film tackling the subject with visibly good intentions has to be commended.

Good intentions abounded in the 1978 American TV series *Holocaust*. Despite an inevitable amount of trivialization created by the need to construct a story which could be screened at peak viewing times and withstand the death of a thousand cuts imposed on any film which has to fit into television schedules built around advertising revenue, *Holocaust* emerges with most of its principles intact. (*Judgement at Nuremberg*'s original television version was subject to problems when one of the advertisers, a gas company, threatened to withdraw).

Once again, the sheer size and scale of the depradations caused most of the problems for film-makers. The cheap remark made by Stalin, that a million deaths is merely a statistic, carries an uncomfortable truth beneath its glib surface. How can a film-maker depict six million deaths? And at what point does the exercise so de-sensitize an audience that it ceases to have any further effect?

One solution, attempted with varying degrees of success by some film-makers, has been to set the story in later times and to touch fleetingly upon the Holocaust through momentary flashbacks which give weight and purpose to present-day actions. Thus *The Pawnbroker* (1965) and *Sophie's Choice* (1983) frequently succeed more than did *Holocaust* in making their point. An

144

audience can identify more readily with an individual or with a small group. Taking this solution to its logical extreme would be to show nothing at all of the reality of the death camps; astonishingly enough, a documentary which adopted precisely this method succeeded where other much more ambitious efforts failed.

Kitty: Return to Auschwitz (1980) was made by Peter Morley for Yorkshire Television in England, and took as its central theme a young woman who as a child had been taken to Auschwitz with her mother. After establishing her as she is now, living and working in Birmingham, England, the film follows Kitty Hart as she returns to Poland with her adult son, David. No one else is seen, no newsreel is intercut, not even a still photograph is shown of Auschwitz as it was then. All that the audience sees is Auschwitz now; and walking among the rows and rows of empty, silent huts is Kitty, followed by her occasionally awkward and slightly embarrassed son. The only sounds are Kitty's words and even they are few as memories flood back into her mind. Surprisingly, Kitty holds up for most of the time and her breakdown, as she describes her work of loading the corpses of friends and relatives on to carts for transportation to the site where they will later be burnt is unbearably moving.

Even more moving, and startlingly dramatic, is the moment when Kitty and her son stand on a marshy patch of ground and she explains that this was where the bodies burned. Among them were her relatives; they were his relatives too. David looks down, as does the camera. He digs into the ground with his shoe and ashes are visible. It is a moment of astonishing revelation. For the first time the son understands his mother; for the first time an audience, the majority of whom are not Jewish, and many of whom were not born at the time being described, understand the horror of it all. It is a moment which no feature film has ever captured, and probably never will. It needed no dramatization, no exposition, no external imposition or another's notion of interpretation. Kitty Hart says all that needs saying, all that can be said.

The problems facing many returning Americans at the end of World War II bore marked resemblances to those confronting their fathers and grandfathers at the end of the Great War. They did not fit in; times had changed and, more to the point, so had they.

A long string of films traced the manner in which some GIs confronted these problems: some were good, some bad, most were indifferent. The better ones included *Crossfire* (1947), which showed the awkwardness of returning GIs in the setting of a tough and gritty murder story which also looked at anti-Semitism more openly than had any previous Hollywood film. *Till the End of Time* (1946) was also very good and deserves more attention than it has had. Unfortunately, it was overwhelmed at the time of its release by a blockbuster from Sam Goldwyn which was not only big, expensive and star-studded but also happened to be the best of the bunch.

Critically and commercially successful, *The Best Years of Our Lives* (1946) follows the fortunes of three veterans returning to their home town, which was precisely the kind of town in which most ex-GIs were trying to re-establish themselves. The three are former soda-jerk turned bombardier Fred Derry (Dana Andrews), Homer Parrish (Harold Russell) and banker Al Stephenson (Fredric March), all of whom bring back to Boone City a problem rooted in the recently ended conflict.

Fred's wife Marie (Virginia Mayo) has been playing around in his absence and clearly has no further interest in her Air Force husband. Homer has a fiancée who loves him still but the problem he has brought back to Boone City is one which can never go away. Homer has lost both hands and has convinced himself that Wilma (Cathy O'Donnell) feels pity and duty rather than love. The casting of Harold Russell, a veteran who really had lost both hands in the war but was remarkably well-adjusted, in the role of Homer added a dimension of reality to the film.

Al's problems are less simply defined since they are those of a philosophical nature which even the character himself does not fully understand. At the bank where he works, Al can no longer apply the tenets required by his employers. Times without number he has seen evidence that what makes a man a good risk has nothing to do with what he owns but with what he is inside. Eventually, aided by his wife Milly (Myrna Loy), Al figures out a compromise which will allow him to help get America back on its feet again without turning his back on the men he knows are needed to build the future.

Despite its all-ends-happily gloss, *The Best Years of Our Lives* stands out sharp and clear against other films of its time as a coherent statement of the problems facing returning veterans and of the nature of American society in the immediate aftermath of the war.

Having emerged from the war, and with the immediate post-war problems being faced up to and tackled with enthusiasm, if not always effectively, the nation could look forward to a gleaming future. Hollywood too, saw the future with complacency.

Peace time and prosperity were hand-in-hand; the enemy was defeated, America was free and powerful – so powerful, in fact, that it could take on the mantle of a great international power without embarrassment from within or argument from outside. It was the beginning of an era which must surely go on forever. But it did not.

Not only was America's role soon to be challenged on the world's stage but Hollywood, too, faced trouble.

The nation's problems came from far across the sea, in a country long thought of as the true enemy but temporarily overshadowed by the fascist posturings of the Hitler gang. The USSR had never seemed a fit ally for America, whatever *Mission to Moscow* might have suggested. Very soon there was ample evidence that the threats from communism were all too justified.

The film world's problems came from both without and within. From outside there was a shift in what the public wanted in the way of entertainment, and film-makers were not fast enough to react to these new needs. There was also the alternative screen, television. Inside Hollywood there was a resurgence of anti-communist hysteria and investigations were initiated that were to shatter many careers. There had been this kind of trouble before, back in the 1930s, when Martin Dies had made a name for himself and in the process proved that he was a joke who could be laughed away.

Dies' successors, J. Parnell Thomas and Richard M. Nixon, could not be laughed at quite so readily, if at all. In the end they helped split Hollywood's sides not with laughter but with self-inflicted wounds that would take decades to heal.

CHAPTER NINE

'We believe in fair play and all that sort of thing.'
(from *Big Jim McLain*)

America fought two wars in the late 1940s and 1950s. One, a cold war, was fought chiefly at home, and if blood was not spilt, honour was certainly lost; the other war was overseas and so hot it threatened to engulf the world. The cost of this hot war, fought in Korea, was the loss of many thousands of lives: American, British, Australian, Korean, Chinese; yet, on balance, the Cold War, bloodless though it might have been, proved to be the most damaging to the nation's morale. Its repercussions can still be heard, however faintly, in many places, not least in Hollywood.

The first shock waves felt in Hollywood in 1945 had as their epicentre investigations into alleged communist infiltration into the motion-picture industry. In 1947 hearings began before the House UnAmerican Activities Committee, where J. Parnell Thomas had replaced Shirley Temple's nemesis, Martin Dies. Any hopes that Thomas would prove as ineffectual as Dies, who had set himself up as a butt of jokes by attacking the diminutive moppet as a communist dupe, were swiftly dispelled. This was to be a much tougher time, even if Thomas was not the brightest of men: he once asked, 'Which WPA payroll is Christopher Marlowe on, New York or Chicago?' Someone kindly pointed out that Marlowe had died in 1593, but the joke swiftly died.

Thomas and his Committee knew they were on to a good thing; investigating communism in the film capital of the world guaranteed headlines and in retrospect it seems that this was what the Committee was after, although some, like John Rankin, were little more than uncloaked Ku Kluxers. Among the smartest when it came to grabbing headlines was the Representative for the State of California, Richard M. Nixon. The methods he adopted in order to advance his career were sufficiently reprehensible to have hoisted warning signals for the future, but few took heed.

By the early 1950s, Hollywood was 'clean' but hearings dragged on while some of HUAC's earlier victims languished in prison for contempt of Congress having refused to answer questions. Investigations into communism continued unabated, however, and no corner of the nation was safe from the rheumy eye and lying tongue of a red-baiter who made HUAC's members seem like raw beginners. He was Senator Joseph R. McCarthy.

There was much more to America in these years, although, even in retrospect, it is hard to believe so. For what seemed like unending aeons the nation was transfixed by images of this scowling, hypocritical, dishonest bully until he took on the trappings of a national deity. By the time he was seen as he truly was, too many things had happened to permit an easy return to past attitudes and responses.

Undoubtedly the McCarthy Era witnessed other events of equal or greater signficance, but every facet of American life was affected by the damage inflicted by the junior senator from Wisconsin and his unscrupulous acolytes and supporters.

Certainly, Hollywood suffered wounds, many of which were self-inflicted, that reflected badly upon both the industry and the individuals. Like the nation, Hollywood eventually recovered its equilibrium, but it took time and effort.

HUAC's Hollywood victims were many. The attention paid to the Hollywood Ten, ten persons who were subpoenaed, refused to answer questions and were cited for contempt of Congress, occasionally overshadows the fact that hundreds of men and women – actors, directors, writers, technicians – were put out of work. Add in their opposite numbers in television, then predominantly centred in New York City, and the numbers ran into thousands. The reasons why these people lost their jobs was sometimes because they were communists; often merely friends or colleagues of communists; too often it was enough that someone merely accused them of being a communist. Proof was neither important nor necessary; the fact that, at the time, membership of the Communist Party was not illegal mattered not at all.

The effect upon individuals, and the measures many took to solve the problems of blacklisting, were dealt with effectively in *The Front* (1976), one of few films to tackle the subject head-on. Although a comedy, the film has some incisive comments to make about a subject uncomfortably close to some of the people involved in its making.

In *The Front* Howard Prince (Woody Allen) is a cashier at a restaurant who doubles as bet-collector for the local bookmaker. An old friend of Howard's, Alfred Miller (Michael Murphy), is a recently blacklisted television writer. Miller asks Howard to submit his teleplays to the networks under his own name. Howard agrees, for a fee, takes on a couple of Miller's similarly blacklisted friends and is soon the hottest writer in TV-land.

A sub-plot has the network's leading comic actor, Hecky Brown (Zero Mostel), also ousted as a result of his unacceptable political sympathies. Unlike the writers, Hecky cannot have a front. Unable to give the investigators what they want – names – Hecky throws himself from a hotel window.

Although set exclusively in the troubled air of the TV networks, *The Front* has many parallels with Hollywood. There, blacklisted writers such as Dalton Trumbo, Ned Young and John Howard Lawson worked under pseudonyms, if at all, or left the country. Trumbo's rate under these conditions dropped from $75,000 to $3,000 per script.

Actors and directors in Hollywood were similarly hit; among them were Larry Parks, Gale Sondergaard, Howard da Silva, Lionel Stander, Joseph Losey, Carl Foreman and Jules Dassin.

The farcical element just below the surface of *The Front*, highlighted when Howard Prince criticizes the quality of the work to which he supplies only his name, afflicted Hollywood too. Using the pseudonym Robert Rich, Dalton Trumbo won an Academy Award for *The Brave One* (1956) while Ned Young, under the pseudonym Nathan E. Douglas, was co-winner of the 1958 Academy Award for *The Defiant Ones*. Everyone knew who hid behind these false fronts, but the deception was played out with straight faces.

The inherent unreality of blacklisting makes serious depiction of these events difficult, which is why *The Front* scores. The scene in which Howard Prince, who is barely literate, is shut in a room in the television studio so that he can rewrite part of one of 'his' scripts almost falls apart because a contemporary audience may see only the farcical angle. But it could have happened that way; it probably did.

One thing that certainly did happen was the blacklisting of Zero Mostel, whose performance in *The Front* therefore gains added texture. Unlike the character he portrays, Mostel, of course, survived. Less fortunate was the successful stage and television actress Mady Christians, who really did commit suicide. Unfortunately, the almost imperceptible impression she had made in the wider world of politics proved to be more important than her work in the theatre. Artistic ability mattered not at all to the narrow-minded few who, for a while, told the American people what to think.

The efforts made by HUAC in bringing to book imagined infiltrators in Hollywood certainly made headlines. Especially successful was Richard Nixon, who took on Helen Gahagan Douglas, then Representative for California, in the 1950 election for the Senate. As Helen Gahagan she had enjoyed a successful stage career before turning to politics. Married to screen actor Melvyn Douglas, she was smarter than her attacker in all respects but one. When it came to manipulating reality in order to gain political advantage, Tricky Dick was a pastmaster. He dubbed her the Pink Lady, and after that she never stood a chance.

Nixon later moved on to fry bigger fish. His most famous victim was Alger Hiss, an ex-employee of the State Department. Maybe no one had heard of Hiss beforehand but they certainly knew about him later; they also knew about his nemesis, Whittaker Chambers, whose testimony had become increasingly suspect as the years have gone by. Most important of all to Richard Nixon was the fact that when he had finished with Hiss, everyone knew about *him*.

Like others before him, Nixon had discovered the advantages to be gained from making an opponent seem more important than he was. Pat Garrett had done it with Billy the Kid; Melvin Purvis had done it with John Dillinger; J. Edgar Hoover did it with just about everyone. Richard Nixon had significant precedents. For all his efforts, however, Nixon was still a tyro at the time of his membership of HUAC, as was his chairman, J. Parnell Thomas, whose own integrity was sufficiently suspect to land him in jail for misappropriation of funds. The king-pin was Joe McCarthy, Congress's self-appointed tail-gunner, who had more important targets in his sights than a handful of Hollywood figures, be they hacks or stars.

McCarthy took on a bigger threat – world-wide communism – but his aim was so wilfully erratic that all manner of individuals and organizations were hit: the Senate, not one but two Presidents, the US Army and above all the American people.

But it would be wrong to imply that McCarthyism was a phenomenon deriving solely from the actions of one man. He alone could not have achieved the deep schisms of the era which bears his name. There were many other people involved; especially, there were those Americans who encouraged him and his kind either directly or by the simple act of not resisting him.

The people were afraid and paranoid and responded in a variety of ways. Some lashed out at friends, neighbours and even at relatives; some cut and ran; a tiny few stayed and fought back, and usually lost; most, and this included an alarming number of film-makers, accommodated McCarthyism and tried to prove their honesty and patriotism through their work.

Viewed today, the films of the era, often of appallingly inferior quality, evoke discomfort and embarrassment. Too many show overt signs of the alacrity with which film-makers ducked issues and sought to placate McCarthy, HUAC, and all the other red-baiters.

I Was a Communist for the FBI (1951), *The Red Menace* (1949) and even *Red Planet Mars* (1952) let their titles state their intentions. These were deliberate attempts to show communism in the worst possible light, but not in order to show Americans what threatened the nation; their aim was to show HUAC that the makers of these tatty wares were good boys at heart and could be trusted.

In some respects the cheapjack *I Was a Communist for the FBI* is inter-changeable with comparable tales of J. Edgar Hoover's destruction of criminal gangs of earlier times. Although Hoover was still asserting that there was no such thing as organized crime, he had no such doubts about the existence of a communist conspiracy.

The film is based loosely upon a book by a former federal agent. By this time, Hoover must have been growing weary of the eagerness with which his agents burst into print. The agent concerned with this epic appears to have made up most of his testimony as he went along and, indeed, his erratic behaviour eventually degenerated into alcoholism and insanity.

As Norah Sayre has pointed out, the film appears to have been designed to make amends for Warner's *Mission to Moscow*. That earlier venture into the dubious field of influencing Soviet-American relations had loomed large on HUAC's list of objectionable films. Jack Warner tried explaining it all away, adding a confusing layer to the rumours of the degree to which President Roosevelt had been involved, but it was all old-hat by now. Russia, the former ally, was one thing; reds under American beds were something else entirely.

The Red Menace uses a voice-over narration from a Los Angeles City Council member to create an impression of reality. Doubtless, audiences of the day were relieved to discover that commies were dim, crass, vulgar and could be defeated by traditional, all-American qualities such as honesty, integrity and a straight right to the jaw.

Red Planet Mars transferred the Manichean conflict to outer space, in a confusing melange of anti-communist cant and quasi-religious dogma that provides an unintentional laugh a minute.

Films of like nature and quality poured out. *The Iron Curtain* (1948) uses a true story, this time the Igor Gouzenko spy ring round-up in Canada. Despite the basic facts of the plot, links with past Hollywood exercises in depicting struggles against hidden, subversive enemies are inadvertently heightened by the presence of screenwriter Milton Krims who had co-written *Confessions of a Nazi Spy* a decade earlier.

My Son John (1952) shows how the menace can penetrate the average American home in the guise of every mother's clean-cut son. It also suggests that when it comes to beating off the reds blood, while still thicker than water, is a much weaker adhesive than the glutinous pap which binds together true believers in democracy and the American way. In some ways, *My Son John* is typical of what happens when reason flees the film-maker. The cast includes such stalwarts of the acting profession as Helen Hayes, Dean Jagger, Van Heflin, Frank McHugh and the irreplaceable Robert Walker, who died during production. With the cinematographer Harry Stradling and the director and co-writer Leo McCarey, this was the kind of Hollywood team that could turn poor material into good films and lift good material into memorable movies. The desperate attempt to match the prevailing mood of rampant paranoia was beyond even their undoubted talents. Highly forgettable though the film is, it stands as a warning example of what professional artists and craftsmen of the highest calibre can sink to when the pressure is on.

Pickup on South Street (1953) was much more ambiguous, as is to be expected of any film made by Sam Fuller. Here the good Americans are almost all low-life criminals existing on the edge of the criminal sink. The message, if indeed there is a message here, appears to be that any cheap and immoral American criminal is better than any communist. Latterday viewers of the film might well suspect that communism crept into the script only to give the story a topical flavour and that all Fuller wanted was to make a good, tight, gritty thriller. Political flavouring apart, that is what he succeeded in doing.

HUAC itself rarely featured in these films, neither did it often receive even a passing mention. One exception is *Big Jim McLain* (1952), in which John Wayne and James Arness, looking distinctly uncomfortable in wide-brimmed fedoras and floppy double-breasted suits, battle against communism in Hawaii. A line lugubriously delivered by Big Jim encapsulates the thinking behind the movie: 'We believe in fair play and all that sort of thing,' he declares.

An unintentional reflection of an earlier real-life incident is touched upon in a sub-plot concerning a student who wins a trip to Russia and returns suitably brainwashed. It was after a visit to Moscow in 1935, as a prize she had won as a student, that Frances Farmer first angered the authorities who would later destroy her.

Big Jim McLain pursued HUAC's less overt angle that the Constitution was being used as a defence by the very people who sought to destroy it. In such films, and in the words and actions of the Committee, belief in America as the land of the free is undermined by right-wing attitudes. These make it abundantly clear that subversives are those who believe in freedom of speech, thought and action. It is not surprising that John Wayne chose to make this film the way he did, instead of as a tale of a Texas cattle baron, which is how it was originally planned. As President of the Motion Picture Alliance for the Preservation of American Ideals, he was as much concerned with rooting out communists from behind Hollywood's screens as on them.

During this period J. Edgar Hoover was far from idle. His report on communist infiltration, *The Crime of the Century*, which was ghost-written for him, first saw the light of day in the pages of *Reader's Digest*. The report came to the screen as *Walk East on Beacon* (1952). The star of the film is George Murphy, whose personal political philosophy suited the part as well as any actor's, with the possible exceptions of only John Wayne and Ronald Reagan.

Of all the films of the era, none captured better the dangerously paranoic state of mind of the nation, exacerbated as it was by positive schizoid tendencies, than the low-budget science-fiction classic *The Invasion of the Body Snatchers* (1956). Unlike most of its sci-fi contemporaries, Don Siegel's film replaces bug-eyed monsters and little green men with a many-layered depiction of what was happening in the nation and to the people. The menace in the movie may come from another world, but not in the form of an alien being. The 'pod people' are look-alikes of the inhabitants of a small California town. They so exactly match the Americans they have replaced that no one can tell the difference, except where emotions are concerned.

Superbly ambiguous, the film can now be seen to have concerned itself with the danger of being taken over by those who seek to enforce observance of an ill-defined norm through extremism and intolerance in the guise of patriotism.

When the film was re-made in 1978 some of its impact was dissipated by a change of setting. A small Californian town could have been any American community. To many Americans in the 1970s San Francisco, where the re-make is set, was already in the hands of aliens.

In 1949 the search for reds under beds and in closets had received a disturbing fillip with the news that the USSR had its own atomic bomb. How had the Russians caught up so fast? It could not be that the communists were smarter; they must have an edge. If there were subversives in one government department then there might well be spies in another. Spies could be any-where, they could be anyone. They could even be an inoffensive couple like the Rosenbergs, who were arrested, tried, and eventually fried, to the accompaniment of gleeful applause. Today, that applause rings as sickeningly in the ears of many as it did at the time in those of a perceptive few.

Daniel (1983) takes a sideways look at the Rosenberg case. Concerned as it is with the after-effects of the trial of the 'Isaacsons' upon their children, the film does not seek to discover the real truth about the guilt or innocence of the couple who died. Indeed, it acknowledges that the full truth may never now emerge. What seems inescapable, whether deduced from the facts, fictions and surrounding circumstances of the Rosenberg case, or from *Daniel*, is that Julius and Ethel Rosenberg did not die in the electric chair because they were guilty (which he probably was, and she probably was not), but because they had the misfortune to go on trial at a time of acute national hysteria when scapegoats were needed.

However dangerous they might have looked at the time to fearful Americans, with hindsight the Rosenbergs were a pathetically innocuous choice of victim for such a powerful nation. Instead of finding scapegoats, America ended up roasting a pair of sacrificial lambs.

Had the temper of these times been different, anti-communist fears would never have gained the hold they did on American imaginations. As it was, the nation was rocked by scandal, revelation, innuendo and hysteria.

The effect of HUAC upon Hollywood revealed the shallow hypocrisy and insecurity of many who worked there. It also set back movie-making as writers and directors worried over the content of their screenplays and their cast lists. HUAC had made it clear that it was concerned about the effect on mass audiences of what it termed 'a drop of progressive thought' in 'an ordinary John-and-Mary picture'. In this context, progressive thought equated with hints of communism.

HUAC never displayed any doubts that it had done the nation a great service. In its report, issued at the end of 1952, it ringingly declared that 'Communist efforts to infiltrate this industry had been a full-scale and care-fully planned operation . . . Had these Communist efforts gone unexposed, it is almost inevitable that the content of motion pictures would have been influenced and slanted and become a medium for Communist propaganda.'

Whatever its averred patriotism, in retrospect HUAC can be seen for what it was – a cheap and scurrilous use of the great liberal tradition of American politics for the personal gain of the Committee's members.

Similarly, Joe McCarthy used the Committee upon which he served to advance both his career and his personal campaign funds. All along, McCarthy was stoppable, especially in the earlier months of his short stay on top of the muck-heap, and the man best placed to stop him was the President. Unfortunately, first Truman, then Eisenhower, had other things to worry about. Truman, especially, had his hands full with communists too; but in his case they were real, not imaginary. These communists were not in America, nor even in Russia, but lived in an obscure chunk of land which drooped off the eastern end of the Chinese mainland. This was a small country named Korea.

When, in mid-summer 1950, the North Koreans launched an attack on South Korea, America's attention was forcibly focused upon this previously little-known region of the world.

General Douglas MacArthur, who still had presidential ambitions, was busily re-shaping Japan. Perhaps surprisingly to any who did not know of his lifelong interest in and affection for the Orient, he made a remarkably good job of it and much of Japan's present-day success as a major manufacturing and trading nation can be accredited to him.

Whatever MacArthur's commitment to Japan, however, there is no doubt that he regarded as providential this new war which was practically on his doorstep. He was a soldier; he believed, as did many others, that he was America's greatest. Here was another opportunity to prove it.

At first it looked as if the old soldier was right about himself. From a shaky toe-hold around Pusan he launched a surprise outflanking manoeuvre which landed American forces at Inchon on the West coast of Korea. Pushing inland from there, MacArthur's army very nearly cut off the North Koreans, who rapidly retreated back over the 38th Parallel which divided the two halves of the country.

After confidently asserting to the President that there was no danger from the Chinese, MacArthur followed. The Chinese saw this as a positive danger to themselves and counterattacked with a force numbering one-third of a million men. MacArthur was ignominiously thrust back and America had to think again. Part of this new thinking centred upon the use of nuclear weapons now being built in ever-increasing numbers. The possibility of their use in Korea was neither an idle nor a passing thought but was actively considered at cabinet meetings, as Truman indicated in a November 1950 press conference.

MacArthur proved to be a great source of worry to President Truman, having already done deals with Chiang Kai Shek's Kuomintang and gone into print with comments which suggested that the American government was not only defeatist but actively sought appeasement with the communists.

Naturally enough this angered the President, and following a deterioration in their relationship, brought about partly by a mutual inability to see events through one another's eyes and partly as a result of some behind-the-scenes work from the Joint Chiefs of Staff who were gunning for MacArthur, he fired the General.

Now past seventy, MacArthur returned to America and was rapturously applauded by the people all across the country. A tickertape parade in New York was followed by a reverentially received speech to a joint session of Congress.

At the end of his life MacArthur still retained his views, as shown in an address he made to West Point cadets which brackets *MacArthur the Rebel*

155

General. In this address he exhorts a new generation of soldiers to uphold those qualities he holds most dear: duty, honour and country – the motto of West Point. When he died in 1964 at the age of eighty-four, those same young men were already being killed for those same misplaced ideals in another obscure South East Asian country.

At the outset of the Korean war Hollywood's response was largely that of the traditional war movie, although the first of the new batch was anything but a complacent gung-ho tale.

When the war flared up this first film was rattled out in under two weeks by the energetic Sam Fuller. *The Steel Helmet* (1951) does not tell a true story of the Korean War, yet, as with any film of Fuller's, it contains more truths than any random dozen standard Hollywood movies. Confusions abound, not just in events but also in the minds of the soldiers, who seldom seem to know why they are there – other than to kill the enemy. In this case the enemy appears to be anyone who is not wholly supportive of America and its ideology.

Predictably, the film met with very mixed response at the time of its release. Here are no heroic Americans; most are confused and frightened. One exception is platoon sergeant Zack (Gene Evans), who is viciously single-minded in his determination to kill rather than be killed. One scene, in which Zack shoots an unarmed prisoner, so incensed the US Army that Fuller received no co-operation in the film's making. Neither is Zack's attitude towards his own men very much different from that which he displays towards the enemy. American audiences were accustomed to seeing films about army sergeants who were tough survivors; they did not expect to see sergeants like Zack, who is no less crudely brutal than the worst of his enemies.

Unlike Fuller's film, *Pork Chop Hill* (1959) does purport to tell a true story of this war. As would be expected of a film by Lewis Milestone, the film was originally a balanced account of a futile battle to achieve a useless objective just before hostilities ceased. Edited drastically after Milestone had left the film following disagreements with the star, Gregory Peck, the film lost its balance and shows nothing of the other side of the battle. This is a pity, as the perception Milestone brought to his earlier war films would undoubtedly have given an edge to a film which otherwise has little to distinguish it from other Korean War stories. As it stands, however, there is still much that is creditable about *Pork Chop Hill*. For one thing, it shows something of the futility of war through its concentration upon one pointless event.

The assault on Pork Chop Hill is planned by Lt. Col. Davis (Barry Atwater), Lt. Clemons (Peck) and Lt. Tsugi Ohashi (George Shibeta). Clemons takes the hill with great loss of life and is then joined by reinforcements under the command of Lt. Russell (Rip Torn). Headquarters orders Russell and his men to pull out, leaving Clemons and the survivors of his command to hold the hill. Knowing the task is hopeless, Clemons asks for either support or permission to withdraw. He gets neither; Pork Chop Hill has become an issue at the Panmunjon peace talks. Militarily valueless, the hill has great propaganda use. Eventually relieved, Clemons and his weary band of survivors make their way back to HQ while the talks go on . . . and on.

The traditional, ethnically mixed platoon has its black soldier, Franklin (Woody Strode), who is much more forceful than his earlier counterparts. Excellently played by a fine but under-used actor, the character is brusquely dismissive of his superior's urging to fight alongside his fellow Americans. 'You ought to see where I live back home,' Franklin says. 'You son-of-a-bitch, I wouldn't die for that and I'll be goddamned if I'm going to fight for Korea.' The comment is a surprising pre-echo of how many black soldiers would respond in Vietnam.

This is only one of many elements present in combat films set in Korea which were notably absent from war films made in or about earlier times. It was no longer considered sweet and glorious to die for one's country.

Not all Korean War films were concerned with combat. The combination of political subversion and war proved irresistible to film-makers.

The Rack (1956) is a court-martial drama about an army major, played by Paul Newman, who broadcasts propaganda messages for the North Koreans. Essentially heroic, the film dodges a few issues by having it proved that he did so to save his fellow prisoners from torture and death.

Similarly concerned with subversion, and simultaneously over its head in psychology, is *The Manchurian Candidate* (1962), a highly entertaining if wildly impressionable drama about a problem which seemed very real to many people as veterans, now often dramatically changed men, returned to their homes. The film is a fascinating melange of blood and thunder, political posturing, sexual and moral corruption and more. It really has very little to say about the Korean War in which its central characters are brainwashed.

Neither does it say anything about McCarthyism, which, given its political content, is surprising. By the time this film was made McCarthyism was a thing of the past and the makers had nothing to fear from him.

The Senator himself had succumbed to a variety of complaints, not the least of which was an over-fondness for booze, and died in 1957. He did not die while still atop the muck-heap he had so carefully constructed. Overestimating his capabilities, he had taken on the might of the US Army, and although he had earlier destroyed the reputation of General George C. Marshall, who had become Secretary of Defense, the Army now helped destroy the malignant Senator. *Point of Order* (1964), a documentary, charts his downfall.

A motion to censure McCarthy was brought before the Senate in 1954, the first such step to be taken against one of the Senate's own since 1929. The blow was softened by one of his erstwhile supporters who had now become Vice President of the United States. Richard Nixon contrived to have the motion amended so that McCarthy was not censured but was merely condemned for conduct unbecoming a member of the Senate.

The Korean War had jolted Americans into awareness of the darker side of being a world power, but it was too late for another return to isolationism.

157

The nation was stuck with being the leader of the non-communist bloc – a situation which has caused it to look persistently over its shoulder in fear of what might be creeping up behind.

Fears of communism within the nation had divided Americans much more damagingly than was apparent at the time. The regularity with which film-makers return to this era is proof of their interest, yet the results fail to grasp the nettle.

Surprisingly, no one has yet seen fit to make a feature film about Joe McCarthy's few years of power. Perhaps the aftertaste remains too bitter to allow anyone, screenwriter, actor or director, to take on the task with an acceptable measure of detachment.

Indeed, this entire period of America's history has been inadequately served by Hollywood. The film industry of the time was active, of course, and not only with anti-communist claptrap. This was the period of the new sympathetic (and patronizing) approach to the Indian, the heydey of the sci-fi movie, and the last golden age of the big-budget musical.

There was much in the 1950s of which Hollywood could be proud; sadly, in its responses to what was happening closest to home, this was also a period about which the motion-picture industry should always feel ashamed.

The industry also faced severe financial crises at this time. Costs rose and audiences dwindled. The decline was blamed largely upon television: an easy target even if it was not the right one. Part of the industry's response was to try spending its way out of the decline. Bigger and more expensive techniques were used, CinemaScope, VistaVision and 3-D among them; bigger and more expensive stories were tackled and huge epic dramas lumbered on to the screen, usually vaguely biblical in origin and often in monumentally bad taste. It was not the right solution, as Hollywood eventually learned to its cost.

With the Korean War over, with or without honour, and the spectre of McCarthyism removed from newspapers and TV screens if not from minds, the time was right for change. It would take a few more years but it was in the air. Youth was finding a new voice, one which would serve to emphasize the estrangement of the generations.

When the new era dawned it provided much interesting material for Hollywood; understandably so, because much of it was already liberally coated with stardust.

CHAPTER TEN

'We stand today on the edge of a New Frontier: the
frontier of the 1960s . . . '
(President John F. Kennedy)

News that the USSR had launched an earth-orbiting satellite was received
with mixed feelings by Americans. Some thought it was all a pack of lies; these
doubters were possibly kin to those later sceptics who would claim that the
1969 moon landing was merely a well-staged television spectacular. One
senior army officer stated that the Americans should shoot Sputnik down, a
notion which overlooked the fact that whatever else American technology
could do, that was not included. Another army officer contemptuously declared
that anyone could put a load of old junk into orbit, omitting to add that
America could not. The overall feeling, however, once Sputnik's unearthly
bleeping was an established fact, was one of embarrassed outrage, mingled
with more than a smidgen of fear.

Embarrassment came from the fact that although the Soviet Union was
feared as the base of the worldwide communist conspiracy, the people there
had always been regarded as little more than a bunch of backward peasants.

One answer to the puzzle as to how they had managed it was to remark
sneeringly that all the real work had been done by German rocket scientists
captured by the Russians at the end of World War II.

Humorists were quick to point out that as America's space programme also
depended upon former enemy experts, the Russian success merely proved
that their German scientists were better than America's German scientists.

Outrage was generated by the knowledge that the vast amounts of money
being channelled somewhat unenthusiastically by the Eisenhower administration into space research had failed to produce the first manmade satellite.
What were they doing with all that money?

The touch of fear came from the realization that if the Russians had rockets
powerful enough to launch Sputnik, then they could also launch nuclear
warheads at targets almost anywhere in the world. Fortress America suddenly
had a very big hole in its defences.

Sputnik went up in October 1957, and soon afterwards the administration
made overtures to the Russians about disarmament talks. They did not get
very far, despite a momentary thawing in relations during which Premier
Khrushchev visited America, taking in such areas of military and political
importance as Disneyland and Hollywood.

The U-2 spy plane incident in 1960 and then the Berlin Wall quickly reversed such trends, causing the Cold War to plunge beneath the permafrost.

As if all this were not enough for Eisenhower's administration to cope with, there were problems much closer to home. Not least of these were dangerous conflicts between white and black Americans, an area of American life which will be dealt with in Chapter 11.

Even more pressing, or so it seemed to the government, was what was happening on a Caribbean island most Americans associated with sugar, cigars and rum. Early in 1959 Fidel Castro overthrew the corrupt Cuban dictator Fulgencio Batista.

Prodded by misjudgements on the part of Eisenhower and his advisers, Castro was forced into strengthening ties with local communists, which inevitably led towards a close relationship with Khrushchev. Once again, the United States backed the wrong horse in Latin America and before they knew it there was a communist-bloc nation within a pleasure-boat ride of Florida.

When Eisenhower's second term drew to its close, the ground was prepared for changes to be made. These changes, while they involved a switch from Republican to Democrat, were more concerned with a change in style and a move towards youth.

In 1960, the American political scene and its complex electoral procedures were not as interesting to non-Americans as they are in the 1980s. It is hard to imagine the average television viewer in Britain even knowing the names of any presidential hopeful in 1960, let alone seeing the extensive coverage lavished upon Gary Hart during his 1984 struggle with Walter Mondale for the Democratic nomination.

In America, of course, it was very different; massive viewing figures were achieved for the debates between the two candidates for the presidency in 1960, Vice President Richard M. Nixon and the young Senator from Massachusetts, John F. Kennedy.

Feature films about American politics have been around since D. W. Griffith, although most have centred upon issues rather than offices, with the obvious exception of the presidency itself.

There have been a few, however, and if most were fictitious there was enough of a realistic atmosphere about many to give a genuine feel for the smoke-filled rooms in which, often, the nation's future was forged.

Otto Preminger's *Advise and Consent* (1962), which was based upon Allen Drury's long and occasionally ponderous novel, manages to convey much of the in-fighting surrounding presidential appointments. As events proved to Presidents Nixon, Carter and Reagan, an injudicious recommendation can unleash all manner of previously well-hidden problems.

Although apparently well on-course for re-election, Reagan hit stormy waters in March 1984 when his recommendation of Edwin Meese for the post of Attorney-General raised issues of patronage and financial peculiarities.

A much more serious trap lay in the path of the President in *Advise and*

Consent. Here, the dying president (Franchot Tone) inadvertently opens up a can of worms that includes allegations of communism and homosexuality. The film is superbly acted throughout, with Henry Fonda, as Robert Leffingwell, the appointee, and Lew Ayres, as the ineffectual Vice President who ends up suddenly elevated to the Oval Office, in exceptionally good form. Surprisingly, given his origins on the north coast of Yorkshire, the star turn comes from Charles Laughton as Senator Seabright Cooley from the Deep South.

Another film of the 1960s which digs deeper than is usual into American political life is *The Best Man* (1964), which focuses on one party and the campaign for nomination as candidate for the presidential election. Once more the in-fighting is ruthless and unprincipled. Again a dying president is featured, this time endeavouring to leave his party in good shape. As President Hockstader Lee Tracy gives an outstanding performance in his first film since 1947. It was also his last role but he had the satisfaction of being nominated for an Academy Award.

The candidates, who wheel and deal energetically and deviously, are upright William Russell (Henry Fonda) and conniving Joe Cantwell (Cliff Robertson), who is so transparently venal that the chief surprise is that anyone nominated him in the first place. The film also features John Henry Faulk in the small role of T. T. Claypoole. Faulk had been a very highly-paid disc-jockey of national fame until he fell foul of red-baiters and was blacklisted. The blacklisting was unofficial, like so many others, but it was effective enough to ruin him and keep him virtually unemployed for the rest of his life.

Written by Gore Vidal, and based upon his own stage play, *The Best Man* remains one of the most persuasively honest views of American political life made by Hollywood.

In another of Vidal's works, his novel *Washington D.C.*, which was published in 1967, a character who rises to political influence is helped in part by his service in World War II. Vidal is especially cutting in his reference to a motion-picture made about his character's wartime experiences. It cannot be coincidental that a motion-picture was made about the wartime exploits of a young navy lieutenant (j.g.) who later achieved the pinnacle of political fame.

The young navy officer was John Kennedy and the film was *PT 109* (1963). Made at a time when World War II movies were not in demand, the only thing going for *PT 109* was that it told a more or less true account of the man who was then president. As Kennedy, Cliff Robertson plays well and there are some well-staged action sequences, but none of this was enough to prevent the box-office returns from being unexpectedly dismal.

There is about the Kennedy era a strange dichotomy made worse with the passage of time. Immediately following the assassination, and for perhaps a decade afterwards, the general impression created in the media suggests that Kennedy was the unanimous choice of the people who, as a consequence, were all diminished by his death.

True, there was a feeling of togetherness experienced by many, which

161

stemmed from a sense of collective guilt that such a dreadful act could have been committed in what almost everyone regarded as the most civilized nation on earth.

In some respects this response mirrors that which followed the assassination of President Lincoln. Then the nation was bound together in a collective purging of grief at the recently ended Civil War. Lincoln, it seemed, had paid with his life for the sins of the nation. Even the South held him in high esteem, especially when it became apparent that his generous terms for the treatment of the defeated Confederacy would not be followed by his political heirs.

Neither at the time of Kennedy's death, nor earlier, at his election, was the nation as one behind him. Although he had 56 per cent of the electoral vote, the popular vote was the narrowest margin in history: 49.7 per cent to Kennedy and 49.6 per cent to Nixon.

Elements of the story of John Kennedy have appeared in a number of films and TV plays; among them are *The Private Files of J. Edgar Hoover*, in which the role went to William Jordan, and *The Missiles of October* (1974), which deals with one specific event. William Devane and John Shea play the Kennedy brothers in this film, which, as its title suggests, concentrates on the Cuban missile crisis.

The assassination and its immediate aftermath have provided jumping-off points for a variety of films, of which *Executive Action* (1973) was reasonably thoughtful although hampered by being caught up in its own preconceptions.

The film begins with the unsubstantiated but promising theory that the assassination was plotted by ultra right-wing American businessmen whose financial interests are threatened by Kennedy's policies. Their leader, a man named Foster (Robert Ryan), hires a disaffected CIA operative named Farrington (Burt Lancaster) to set up a team to eliminate the President during a forthcoming visit to Dallas.

Teams of marksmen set to work, planning and practising, while elsewhere palms are crossed to ensure the gunmen's task will not be too hard: the motorcade is re-routed and a likely scapegoat, Lee Harvey Oswald, is set up.

The film uses an ingenious mixture of facts, reasonable assumptions and wild guesses. For the most part it works well as a conventional caper movie, but falls down badly in certain important areas.

The gunmen are shadowy and no sense of their motivation emerges; similarly unmotivated is Farrington, the assassins' leader. As for the rich businessmen, they appear almost casually unconcerned with anything other than getting the job over and done with. They seek not to establish power in other hands – no junta nor even a lackey in the White House. It is enough, the audience is expected to believe, that they need to remove a dangerous liberal from office.

In fact, despite the Democrats having good majorities in both Houses of Congress, Kennedy persistently had trouble getting policies through. Much of his most far-reaching legislation remained in the pipeline until Lyndon Johnson became President and brought his political expertise to bear on Congress.

Although scripted by Dalton Trumbo, the film relies too heavily upon the story by Donald Freed and Mark Lane. Lane's book *Rush to Judgement* rightly cast doubt upon the Warren Commission's report, and similarly the film removes all credibility from the official version of Kennedy's death.

Unfortunately, also like the book, the film fails to supply an alternative that is either stronger or more credible.

A closing title sequence lists all the people centrally or peripherally connected with the case who died in the decade between Dallas and the film's release. The list is impressively long but the implication contained in this passage, that a massive conspiracy persisted, is not substantiated.

The assassination brackets the most thorough examination of the Kennedy era so far brought to the screen. *Kennedy* (1983), made by Central Television in Britain, was screened simultaneously in 26 countries to an estimated quarter-million viewers on the three nights ending 22 November 1983, twenty years to the day after the assassination.

Written by the British historian and playwright Reg Gadney, the chronological section of the film picks up the Kennedys on the night of the 1960 election. The family, especially the three brothers, are swiftly delineated: John (Martin Sheen) is decisive and charming, Bobby (John Shea) is intense and explosive, Teddy (Kevin Conroy) is subdued and aware of his own shortcomings.

Once the film is under way, the characters of John and Bobby are extensively developed and all the major, together with several of the minor, events of Kennedy's administration are explored.

The first is the internal conflict developed as a result of the new President's wish to appoint Bobby as Attorney General. Bobby's initial reluctance, generated by a desire to avoid charges of nepotism which he feels might damage his brother, is eventually overcome.

Quickly following on the heels of this problem are a number of items left over from the outgoing administration which Kennedy has to pick up. Cuba is one, where clandestine CIA-backed operations are already well-advanced. Cuba soon develops into the President's first major crisis when the CIA's attempt to aid the overthrow of Castro is defeated ignominiously at the Bay of Pigs.

Kennedy makes a public statement, taking full responsibility, and finds public opinion beginning to move his way. Already, something of the magical glitter surrounding the new residents of the White House is rubbing off on almost everyone – hardcore opposition apart.

The Civil Rights movement comes next, but there is little the President can accomplish, hamstrung as he is by various elements inside Congress. The precise nature of this opposition is not clearly delineated in the film, leaving an uninformed member of its audience slightly at a loss to account for the President's (and the Attorney General's) inability to enforce observation of basic human entitlements denied to blacks in Southern states.

American involvement in South East Asia is another matter hanging over from the previous administration, but although he sends Vice President Lyndon Johnson (Nesbitt Blaisdell) to Vietnam, Kennedy fails to recognize the size of the problem. Commendably, the screenplay does not use hindsight in order to allow any character to make the kind of wise remark often tossed in unthinkingly by screenwriters.

At home the President has his hands full with his wife. Jackie Kennedy (Blair Brown) is busily redecorating herself and the White House with no regard for the expense. The complex personal relationship between the President and his wife is touched upon delicately. One of the concerns expressed by the writer during preparation of the film was that all dialogue should be known to have taken place, or could be logically and intelligently reconstructed from known events and circumstances. This disallowed invention of private conversations between Kennedy and Jackie: a commendable decision, but the resulting gap is none the less tantalizing.

Among the President's most pressing problems are those precipitated by J. Edgar Hoover (Vincent Gardenia). Apart from his outright refusal to help blacks being deprived of their rights in the South and his continued refusal to believe in organized crime, despite Bobby Kennedy's concern, Hoover is busily subjecting just about everyone in Washington to intensive surveillance. Interception of mail and wire-tapping are rife and not even the President is safe.

The sheer malevolence of Hoover is excellently realized by Gardenia, although the decision to add to his menace by lighting him from below so that he looks like a stage devil was an unnecessarily melodramatic measure. Gardenia's physical presence and dialogue delivery is more than adequate to convey Hoover's malignancy.

Hoover's interest in the President's private conversations has nothing to do with affairs of state: it is his personal affairs that concern the FBI Director.

By the time this film was made, everyone who cared to know was aware that John Kennedy was something of a ladies' man. The extent of his activities varies from source to source, the most outrageous of them suggesting a calling list long enough to turn him into a latterday Casanova with scarcely enough time between assignations to zip his pants, let alone attend to government matters.

Here, only one affair is highlighted, with a woman whose greatest flaw in Hoover's eyes is that she also consorts with a criminal.

The President's father (E. G. Marshall) suffers a massive stroke; then, in October 1962, Cuba once again emerges as a problem area. This time, evidence is found of a build-up of Russian nuclear missiles, with more on their way by sea.

Cuba is blockaded by the US Navy and international tension increases as the American president and Premier Khrushchev stand toe to toe. Eventually, it is the Russian who blinks first and orders his ships to turn back rather than run the blockade and risk precipitating God knows what kind of disaster.

President Kennedy and his wife arrive in Dallas on 22 November 1963.

The Kobal Collection

One of the most accurate reproductions of any period in American history. (*Kennedy*)

Kennedy's visit to Berlin is effectively intercut with newsreel shots of the occasion (as is the earlier sequence covering his Inauguration). Soon after Berlin the Kennedys' third child, Patrick, dies within a few hours of his birth. Jackie goes to Greece to recuperate, an episode which is tastefully underplayed. Anyone who wanted to wallow in Jackie Kennedy's subsequent interest in Greece and the Greeks could have had their fill with the execrable 1978 movie, *The Greek Tycoon*.

On her return home, Jackie agrees to accompany her husband on a forthcoming fence-building trip to Texas, of which a highlight is to be a visit to Dallas on 22 November 1963.

This section of *Kennedy* was shot in Richmond, Virginia, for twenty years had seen too many structural changes to the city of Dallas. The filming brought out latent fears and the production company's request for police protection was swiftly granted. No one wanted to risk some gun-happy lunatic trying to add a fatal touch of realism.

The meticulous research which clearly accompanied the writing and design of the film cannot be faulted and nowhere is history misrepresented. Necessarily, the accuracy of the depiction of some of the personal relationships had to rely upon one-sided evidence, but there is no sign of any liberties having been taken with probability.

The time, effort and money spent in giving the film the right look and atmosphere were well used. All this was fronted by flawless acting. An early production decision was made to select the cast on grounds other than physical resemblance, although in many instances a good match does occur.

Perhaps least like the character being portrayed is Martin Sheen as the President, but within moments of his first appearance it becomes a matter of no importance. In all but one respect he completely evokes the presence of John Kennedy. The support from John Shea, Blair Brown, E. G. Marshall and Geraldine Fitzgerald as Rose Kennedy is uniformly fine.

The one exception referred to above is something beyond the art of acting. John Kennedy made a remarkable impression upon his times and his death created an enormous sense of loss in the hearts and minds of millions, even in countries where the people had almost no knowledge of the man. Despite Martin Sheen's unflawed performance, and the actor's own characteristics of personal charm, the reason for this magical glow which Kennedy cast, and still casts, remains unexplained.

Neither does the opposite reaction become apparent. Some Americans hated Kennedy with such venom that news of his death was greeted in some quarters with undisguised glee; in one school the children joined with their teachers in cheers at the announcement.

No explanation of this sharp dichotomy among Americans emerges in *Kennedy*, yet despite this one failing the film stands as one of the most accurate reproductions of any period in American history. It may be significant that writer and producer and all major behind-the-screen participation was non-American. Perhaps the detachment this allowed was the factor missing from so many Hollywood ventures into the past.

In a fine film about American domestic politics which ranks alongside *Advise and Consent* and *The Best Man*, certain debts to the Kennedy legend can be observed. *The Candidate* (1972) stars Robert Redford as Bill McKay, a young lawyer with unformed political ambitions, and the film traces his campaign for election to the Senate.

Both in appearance and manner McKay is modelled upon Kennedy, but the character also shares his personality with Redford's own. The fact that the actor appears to have certain as yet unstated political interests suggests a possible future parallel between him and Ronald Reagan, albeit they are from opposite ends of the political spectrum. A career as a B-picture player did not harm Reagan; Redford's career as superstar should make any future bid for political office a cinch.

Once more, the unsuccessful 1984 campaign of Senator Gary Hart comes to mind. How much of his impact was due to his physical appearance? Certainly the images of John Kennedy, Robert Redford and Gary Hart do have a disquieting tendency to blur into one, even though detached study betrays almost no similarities at all.

The core of *The Candidate* is the ability of American political campaigners to manufacture a front-man who will serve their purpose. The plan is that McKay will be a blandly processed loser who goes through the motions merely to gain publicity for some of his conservationist interests. His campaign manager, Marvin Lucas (Peter Boyle), gives him a guarantee: he will lose. But then the system takes over and McKay proves to be as charismatic as a Kennedy. When his honesty is nudged aside by circumstances, his father (a savagely brilliant performance by Melvyn Douglas), an oldtime political warhorse, weighs in behind him. McKay wins as the film ends; and only here is he clearly unlike a Kennedy or a Hart (or a Redford). In the moment before a hotel door bursts open to admit a cheering throng of supporters, reporters and hangers-on, he turns to his campaign manager and plaintively asks: 'What do we do *now*?'

The lasting impression of the film is that of the TV and public appearances and the TV commercials made by McKay – put Redford's name on the buttons and banners in place of the character he is portraying and they could be the real thing.

The few bars of music played at the end of *The Candidate* are not accidental: they have a meaning within the context of the film. Perhaps, as time passes, 'Hail to the Chief', which figured in John Kennedy's life as it figures in the life of all American presidents, will have a meaning in the life of Robert Redford too.

When Lyndon Johnson was sworn in as president on board Air Force One in Dallas, it was the first move in a general closing of ranks. Despite his undoubted skills as a politician, Johnson was an unlikeable individual; the glamour and excitement associated with the Kennedy era, that bright new Camelot along the banks of the Potomac, were swiftly dissipated.

Nevertheless, Johnson made things happen; his political nous allowed him to achieve far more than had his predecessor. All the Kennedy plans that had languished due to his inability to push them through Congress were brought into effect with scarcely any resistance. Not least among them were the first serious steps towards establishing Civil Rights for black Americans. Another item that had bubbled gently on the back-burner during Kennedy's brief reign now began to boil up with unpleasant swiftness: Vietnam.

At this time Vietnam was little known, just as Korea had been unheard of before everything hit the fan back in 1950. In the early days, when the country's name was even written differently (Viet-Nam), the only Americans there were either businessmen or CIA operatives (often visually and practically indistinguishable) and a smattering of military advisers.

The Quiet American (1958), which stars Audie Murphy, makes changes to Graham Greene's novel of the same name and its central character becomes a representative of an American aid mission instead of a CIA man (another area where appearance and reality often overlapped). The film thus avoids any need to explain the political complexities which will eventually lead to the war.

Go Tell the Spartans (1978) is set in 1964 but its ambience is that of an America disillusioned by Watergate and the scrappy, no-win ending to the Vietnam war. At several moments in the film characters convey attitudes which probably owe much to hindsight. The repeated cry from several American soldiers 'It's *their* war' was unlikely to have been heard as early as 1964. There is, nevertheless, a touch of harsh reality at the moment of passing of the main character, Major Asa Barker (Burt Lancaster). On the point of death, Barker settles back against the alien ground for which he is about to die, and, instead of delivering one of those stiff-lipped statements so beloved of Hollywood screenwriters tackling war stories, murmurs: 'Ah, shit.' Hardly John Wayne's style.

Another untypical moment comes earlier in the film when an idealistic young soldier radios back to a bemused Major Barker to announce a successful mission: 'We have met the enemy and they are ours.' In one form or another, Oliver Hazard Perry's words have often been used in films, but always delivered straight. Here they are also delivered straight, but the effect is deliberately subversive. This is a soldier in a movie who talks like a movie soldier – and is mocked for it.

In the early 1960s, however, the grim reality of Vietnam had yet to impinge itself upon Americans. While Kennedy was still in the White House there were other things to think about. America was reaching for the stars and for a while nothing seemed beyond its reach.

The importance of the Frontier, an inherent challenge to American drive and ambition, had been stultified ever since that invisible barrier, against which the westward-advancing pioneers pushed, had ceased to exist. One result of this loss was the attention paid to the Frontier as a significant factor in American literature and film. Now it became real again.

In a speech given in July 1960, John Kennedy had declared: 'We stand today on the edge of a New Frontier: the frontier of the 1960s – a frontier of unknown opportunities and perils, a frontier of unfulfilled hopes and threats.' One part of that New Frontier was the Last Frontier for adventurous men: space.

Kennedy's decision to make the space programme a high priority brought mixed blessings to the Air Force and NASA. There were two schools of thought. One claimed that pilots were what counted and pressed for expansion of the rocket-powered aircraft programme already well-established in California. The other school favoured the rocket-launched capsules which could function perfectly well without men inside them.

The bulk of the new money went to NASA and their capsules, much to the chagrin of those who believed that it took men, not machines, to advance mankind: and not just ordinary men, but those blessed with a special quality, a quality that enabled a man to bring an out-of-control aircraft down safely by seat-of-the-pants flying when all the instruments were out; a quality evidenced by attitude, manner, even speech patterns. In the phrase used by Tom Wolfe as the title of his brilliant account of the Mercury space progamme, the men needed to fly high-powered aircraft and rocket ships higher and faster than anyone else had to have 'the right stuff'.

The film version of this account does not juggle much with history although it does, quite deliberately, pursue Wolfe's clear intention, which is to blend the legend of such men into the reality of their lives.

As in the book, the hero of *The Right Stuff* (1983) is not one of the magnificent seven astronauts but the man who preferred to stay with the Bell rocket planes out in the Western deserts, Colonel Charles E. 'Chuck' Yeager.

Oddly enough, this seemingly perverse step works admirably and none of the astronauts is downgraded by it. The effect is that the audience is given a hero with whom to identify much more readily. There are a number of reasons for this, some minor, one significant. The minor reasons include the knowledge that although all the Mercury Seven were individuals in their own right, they were subjected to a considerable degree of homogenizing. High spirits, fast car-driving, and drinking were all regulated; womanizing was severely frowned upon. It was not that the Seven necessarily wanted to indulge in these pastimes – well, not too much – but neither NASA nor *Life* magazine, which had an interest in their stories, was prepared to take any chances. Even a shaky marriage was forcibly healed.

The mixed bag of personalities comes over effectively in the film, with stolid, well-meaning, determined but dull John Glenn (Ed Harris) showing clearly why his bid for the Democratic nomination petered out during the 1984 primaries. Brave he might be, and honest, too, but there are too many shades of Eisenhower about him. Alan Shepard (Scott Glenn) displays the sharp-edged powerful personality that enabled him to divide work and play so decisively and satisfactorily.

Individuals or not, there is a tendency for these men to blend into one another and into the background of technical apparatus. It is this that sets the Seven apart from the real hero of *The Right Stuff*.

What is significant about Chuck Yeager (Sam Shepard) becoming the hero of the story is that unlike any of the others he could have stepped right out of any one of a hundred or more Hollywood movies. His appearance helps enormously. All the actors look remarkably like the men they are portraying, a production decision which for once has not resulted in inferior performances. Yeager, both in real life and as portrayed here, is lean and craggy and would have made an ideal stand-in for Gary Cooper or Randolph Scott.

Most important, however, is his manner. Laconic, laid-back – long before the term had currency – and utterly invincible Yeager is the Plainsman or the Virginian come to rawhide-tough life. It is no accident that the first time Yeager is seen in the film he is riding across the Mojave desert on horseback.

Taking only one discernible liberty with reality (and with Tom Wolfe's text), *The Right Stuff* ends with the launch of the final flight of the Mercury programme.

Earlier came the almost fatal accident suffered by Yeager, from which he emerged badly burned but still determinedly relaxed. In fact, Yeager's crash occurred many months after Mercury had ended. The critic Paul Taylor has suggested that this decision by the film's writer-director Philip Kaufman might well have been taken to avoid the effective and accurate, but seemingly improbable, bracketing of the film with images of the Lone Cowboy. Instead, Kaufman has decided to show the right stuff being taken nonchalantly into orbit as his finale.

The pervading nonchalance is demonstrated by Gordon Cooper (Dennis Quaid), who, before the final launch, is so relaxed he falls asleep in the capsule while waiting for the scurrying fussbudgets on the ground to get their act together and boost him into space.

The space programme, financed massively during John Kennedy's presidency, continued to move ahead and eventually fulfilled his prediction that before the decade was out America would put a man on the moon.

Despite occasional setbacks, which included the tragic deaths of Gus Grissom, one of the Seven, and two other astronauts, the American space programmes were remarkably successful. They helped Americans recover from the blow their pride had suffered when Sputnik went into orbit and which was still further damaged when the Russians fired the first man into space. The consistency of the Mercury programme and of those which followed convinced Americans that, as a nation, they too possessed the right stuff.

Eventually, the shift in emphasis towards the Space Shuttle proved that Yeager had been right all along. Men who can fly *are* needed.

The early 1960s, whether observed through the lives of the Kennedys or the Mercury astronauts, have received effective and accurate treatment at the hands of film-makers. Other 1960s events were less well served, perhaps largely due to their complexity, as when Civil Rights and Black Power ceased to be merely words and were translated into action.

Confusion also flourished as the counterculture of America's youth widened the gulf between the generations.

Worst of all for America was the growing realization that despite the euphemisms referring to police actions and military advisers the conflict in Vietnam was rapidly becoming a real war. Even so, few people in the mid-1960s suspected just how bad it would eventually become.

CHAPTER ELEVEN

> ' . . . a world from which every trace of
> genuine civilization has been merci-
> lessly expunged and replaced by its
> grotesque parody.'
> (Gilbert Adair on *Apocalypse Now*)

The fact that Hollywood's film-makers have never managed to come to terms with black Americans is not at all surprising. Neither has any other white-dominated section of the community.

From the earliest days, when blacks were portrayed on-screen by blacked-up white actors such as those in *The Birth of a Nation*, all the way through the painfully patronizing period when blacks had to fit into one or another of the acceptable stereotypes in order to be seen in a motion-picture at all, the film industry has failed to make a satisfactory response. The stereotypes into which blacks had to be jammed are summarized in the title of Donald Bogle's study of the black actor in Hollywood: *Toms, Coons, Mulattoes, Mammies and Bucks*. To which must be added the black as Entertainer. But by the mid-1960s these pigeon-holes were proving hopelessly inadequate for the rising tide of black consciousness.

The Civil Rights legislation John Kennedy had struggled to pass through Congress was enacted in 1964 by his successor, but that did not prevent riots in Watts, the black enclave in Los Angeles down at the southern end of Central Avenue, during the hot summer of 1965. Earlier that same year, conflict among the black community's manifold activists had led to the assassination in New York of Malcolm X; the following year saw the massive rise of the Black Power movement.

Clearly black Americans, no longer prepared to be called Negro let alone derided as 'nigger', were on the move. Their portrayal on-screen inevitably underwent marked changes; perhaps equally inevitable was the fact that the shift was often little more than a replacement of one form of extremism with another. The underlying mood was one of anger, regardless of the overt content of many of the films of this period and which, as often as not, depicted the contemporary scene.

Occasional thoughtful attempts had been made to produce films with an unpatronizing view of blacks in the late-1940s and early-1950s, but they were exceptions rather than the rule.

Home of the Brave (1949), which stars the excellent James Edwards, is a beginner's course in behavioural psychology dealing with a black World

War II veteran who suffers from hysterical paralysis. His condition has been brought on more by the way his fellow (white) soldiers treated him than by anything the Japs did. Essentially facile, the film ends with everything working out well, of course.

Edwards is a typical example of Hollywood's inability to find adequate roles for an actor of the highest calibre who also happens to be black. After *Home of the Brave* his career drifted along such tried and tested channels as the occasional Tarzan movie. In one of the more forgettable ape-man sagas, Edwards and another fine black actor, Woody Strode, were called upon to demonstrate their art by prancing around in animal skins. Understandably, neither looked especially happy about it all. Edwards' career ended with *Patton*, in which he was cast as the General's valet: a sad example of Hollywood recording the stereotyping of the military's own response to black Americans.

Blacks passing for white is a subject which fascinated film-makers in the 1940s and 1950s, perhaps because it got them off the hook by allowing white actors to be cast in leading roles. Most films of this period which dealt with blacks, however sympathetically, were made by whites, which irritated blacks because, well-meaning or not, they stemmed necessarily from an intellectualized approach to the problem. Whites were white, not black, and therefore could never really understand.

An attempt to get inside a black skin was made by the writer John Howard Griffin, who travelled in the South in the late-1950s posing as a black. His story became a film, *Black Like Me* (1964), but, like the book and the writer, it missed its own central point: being black is more than just having a black skin.

No Way Out (1950), which was Sidney Poitier's screen début, was less compromising than most films of the period and had sequences set in an unnamed northern city which in some way presaged the riots in Detroit, Newark and Watts in the 1960s.

The problem of increasing violence in black urban ghettoes was touched upon in *Take a Giant Step* (1958), while *The Intruder* (1961), produced and directed by Roger Corman, dealt with the problem of school de-segregation which harassed the Eisenhower administration. Both films have many qualities deserving of a wider audience than they received at the time of their original cinema release.

Even better were *Nothing But a Man* and *One Potato, Two Potato* (both 1964), which remain two of the most successful depictions of the realities of being black in America; the compliment is undermined by the fact that two decades have passed since their appearance.

In the early 1970s film-makers discovered that the black dollars which were coming into the box-office were the same as any other kind, except that in some areas there were more of them. The gradual disintegration of many inner cities forced whites out and blacks, and Spanish-Americans, in. These inner cities were also the location of the neighbourhood movie houses long fallen on hard times. The corresponding boom in takings led to black-orientated films, films which merely exploited the booming market created by the new black audience, and, occasionally, genuinely all–black films in which behind-the-scenes jobs were filled by black technicians and where production was funded by blacks.

Quality varied, for many black film-makers fell into the same traps their white counterparts had stumbled into in the past. Stereotyping was as prevalent in these movies as it had been in the days of Willie Best, Butterfiy McQueen and Stepin Fetchit. Even the usually high-quality films made by Sidney Poitier never fully escaped the stereotype as he was called upon to fulfil the expectations of white liberals who expected him to be 'their' man, not his own man.

Jim Brown, the former Cleveland Browns football star, began the shift away from this attitude, and by the time of the all-black movies of the mid-1960s even white audiences were prepared for change, albeit blacks still had to behave like them.

Raymond St Jacques also featured in a number of films which led towards general acceptance, although it was not until he was paired with Godfrey Cambridge, playing Coffin Ed Johnson and Grave Digger Jones respectively, in *Cotton Comes to Harlem* (1970), that a full-fledged black movie reached the quality towards which many had aspired. Nevertheless, despite its undoubted high standard this film, and its lesser sequel, *Come Back, Charleston Blue* (1972), failed to crack open the white market. This breakthrough was achieved in 1971 by *Shaft*, in which the supertough, supercool, superhuman private-eye was well played by Richard Roundtree. Sambo had become Superspade.

This success was due largely to the fact that it combined high production values with a storyline that had about it nothing that was especially 'black'. Every black face could have been replaced by whites, without the screenplay needing much alteration.

Despite the undoubted qualities of some of these films this was their essential problem: none of them told what it really meant to be black in America. Even in the 1970s, the only places where blacks could expect to rate highly were in unemployment and death-rate statistics.

Two films made by Melvin Van Peebles were very different matters, albeit failing to achieve the acceptance of *Shaft*. In *The Watermelon Man* (1970) Peebles uses comedy as his principal tool,and although the humour is uneven it is usually hard-edged. Jeff Gerber (Godfrey Cambridge) is a white insurance salesman who wakes up in the middle of the night feeling unwell. When he takes a look in the mirror he sees that he has become black. His attempts to continue with his life are met with resistance at all turns. Even his regular early-morning routine of running a couple of blocks before catching the bus takes on a new significance. As a white man his activity was harmlessly eccentric; as a black man he is promptly arrested. Alienated from his wife and family, his friends and colleagues (all except his boss, who sees an opportunity to break into the lucrative business available in the black community), Jeff Gerber takes to the ghetto and learns the militant's trade.

Essentially, however, compromises are made, not least of which is that although very different in its approach this is still a 'white' man in blackface.

The compromises Van Peebles had to make in order to raise funds for *The Watermelon Man* prompted him to commit himself totally next time out. This time he scored a direct hit on the exposed nerves of the nation's black community, although, given the film's content, it is not surprising that he failed to gain a white audience of equal proportions to the numbers of blacks who saw it.

Van Peebles produced, wrote, directed, edited, scored and starred in *Sweet Sweetback's Badassss Song* (1971). The movie begins with Sweetback (Van Peebles) as every white man's stereotypical black buck, performing as a stud in a Los Angeles sex show. Arrested by the police who need a face to prove they are working seriously on a murder case, Sweetback only resists when the cops who are taking him in also arrest and beat up a young black militant. Sweetback attacks the cops and then goes on a rampage of violence against the white establishment (and also against women of both races) before escaping across the border into Mexico. His final warning message looms large on the screen at the end: 'A badassss nigger is coming back to collect some dues.'

Undoubtedly, the film's relative failure with white audiences lies in the fact that for many the entire movie, and the final written message in particular, hits much too close to fears of what might be. Nevertheless, despite this restriction in its audience appeal, the film grossed $10 million in its first year of exhibition. Clearly, black audiences thought highly of it, and if it is not an accurate depiction of how the average black citizen behaves, it reflects alarmingly what many black Americans, outwardly average perhaps, think about their subordinate role in society.

Sweet Sweetback's Badassss Song does many things; among them, as James Monaco has suggested, it continues the line of protesting thought begun by Richard Wright in his 1940 novel *Native Son* (which became an unsuccessful film in 1950 with an over-age Wright himself playing the central role of Bigger Thomas), and continued brilliantly by Ralph Ellison in his novel *Invisible Man*, published in 1952. But *Sweetback* takes a harder physical line, caring nothing for intellectualizing the problems which face its protagonist. Neither does the film spend much time putting into words the forces which drive Sweetback. It is all fast, violent action, set in a hard and violent world in which no one questions the implicit assumption that the only response to violence which stands the faintest chance of success is even more violence.

The film has a message for all who see it, especially for whites. It is not always the same message, however. For white liberals, the message is that however much they might protest otherwise, they never really got the message in the first place. The message for white racists is 'Run'.

The death of Martin Luther King Jr. in April 1968 while visiting Memphis brought to an end a period of hope – hope that dialogue between certain elements in the black and white communities might somehow bridge the seemingly insuperable gap between them.

King's career was traced in the television documentary *King: a Filmed Record . . . Montgomery to Memphis* (1970), a powerful and frequently moving account of his involvement with the Civil Rights movement between 1955 and his death. A dramatized account of the same period is covered in *King* (1978), a 3-part TV film which stars Paul Winfield in the title role. Written and directed by Abby Mann, the film sticks close to known facts, there being no need for dramatization of any part of King's last years.

Whatever the difficulties of communication between blacks and whites and any failure, even on the part of the Kennedy brothers and their fellow liberals, no one can fail but to be impressed by the gathering of men and women of both races at the Washington Freedom March in August 1963. Similarly, it is hard to imagine anyone but a determined racist being unmoved by King's description of his visionary dream 'that one day the sons of former slaves and the sons of former slave-owners will be able to sit down together at the table of brotherhood'.

Coming as it did almost exactly one hundred years after Abraham Lincoln had reaffirmed that the nation had been 'conceived in liberty and dedicated to the proposition that all men are created equal', King's speech underlined how little had changed. In Washington he stressed how Lincoln's words had been forgotten when he was obliged to declare that ' . . . one day this nation will rise up and live out the true meaning of its own creed: "We hold these truths to be self-evident; that all men are created equal."'

Lip-service was no longer enough. Black Americans were not free at last; much remained to be done. A further twenty years on, there still remains much to do. Sadly, the motion-picture industry, despite a handful of honourable exceptions to the contrary, has failed to swing its undoubted ability to influence minds into action on this most important of all domestic issues.

One attempt to show how a black politician might achieve high political office comes in *The Man* (1972), a screen adaptation of the Irving Wallace novel. Entirely fictitious, the early convoluted stages of the plot require many coincidental deaths before a low-echelon black politician can be thrust into the Oval Office.

Such contrivances remain the only way, for despite his 1984 bid for his party's nomination as presidential candidate, Jesse Jackson could not make it, even by the back door. Cynicism prompts the thought that white politicians of all parties now have tucked away in a locked office drawer a copy of the screenplay of *The Man* to which they can refer when making appointments . . . just in case.

The high proportion of whites involved in the March on Washington which culminated in Martin Luther King's address was encouraging at the time, even though later events show that the high hopes raised were a shade premature.

Also encouraging was the high number of young people involved. Younger white Americans were at last beginning to show that being different from their parents was something more than merely growing pains, a desire to wear unusual clothes, grow their hair longer and listen to strange music. Radical new thinking was taking place which advised anyone who cared to interpret the messages correctly that despite the death of John Kennedy the future was still the place for the young.

The rebel has always played an important part in American society, and never more so than after World War II. The rebel can be a focus of discontent or can, conversely, serve to reinforce the strengths of old values. Post-war America's retreat into political and social orthodoxy ensured that those who rejected the mainstream of American life would perforce drift along its fringes.

Perhaps the most fearsome image of youth in the post-war period is that of the Hell's Angels. Symbolized on film by Brando's macho presence in *The Wild One* (1954), with its echo of the outlaws of the Old West, it became real at the Rolling Stones' Altamont concert, where, ostensibly present to control the crowds, Angels killed a man who rebelled against their rebellion. For middle-America they were a living nightmare, and for a while, especially in California, they replaced the blacks and the communists in paranoid fantasies.

The 1950s saw the first stirrings of the youth culture which would blossom in the 1960s. In stark contrast with the orthodoxy of the Truman and Eisenhower administrations, new icons emerged. The parents of this new generation were horrified when their kids looked to movie star James Dean or rock 'n' roll singer Elvis Presley for patterns of behaviour.

On a more esoteric level, Allen Ginsberg, Jack Kerouac and William Burroughs, the spokesmen of the Beat Generation, set the pace. In Norman Mailer's words, the young were rejecting 'the slow death by conformity'.

In 1960, students in San Francisco held protest demonstrations outside HUAC meetings at City Hall. The protests were broken up by club-wielding cops, a pattern to be repeated throughout the 1960s and culminating in the shootings at Kent State.

For big business, the growing emphasis upon a distinct and separate culture for the young meant new and often very lucrative opportunities. The Establishment saw only a potential for trouble and strife.

This counterculture of the 1960s represented a rejection of old values, which were replaced by radical attitudes towards sex, drugs and life in general. The 1960s became the decade of the inner man. At the beginning of the decade the use of marijuana spread. Increasingly, the use of an hallucinogenic drug – LSD – was interwoven in the counterculture.

The problems of the 1960s, from freedom of speech through to Vietnam, allowed the young to consider alternatives, to think for themselves. 'Make Love Not War' was at once a slogan and a course of action. More than at any other time in the nation's history, the young were politicized. They protested in support of Civil Rights and free speech, and they protested against the war. Natural leaders, who could sense the change in the air, arose. Among them were Tom Hayden, who later married Jane Fonda, Jerry Rubin and Abbie Hoffman. An alternative voice to be heard at the Democratic Party Convention in Chicago in 1968 was that of the Yippies, the Youth International Party, organized by Rubin and Hoffman. This voice was heard on the streets, and Mayor Daley's Chicago cops brought it into homes. A stunned nation saw their children on primetime TV being clubbed and kicked and arrested in droves.

Violence against the young was not confined to Chicago. Three students died in 1968 at Orangeburg, South Carolina when police opened fire. Another was shot at Berkeley in California in 1969, a killing which elicited from State Governor Ronald Reagan the comment that any blame should be laid at the doors of liberal college administrations.

The optimism was running out. It ended on 4 May 1970 at Kent State University when Ohio National Guardsmen opened fire on students demonstrating against the American invasion of Cambodia and four were killed.

An alert film-maker had noted the predictability of the confrontation at the 1968 Convention in Chicago. As a result, Haskell Wexler was there, ready, with a fictitious story which he interwove with what was happening on the streets, expertly catching the growing disenchantment of later-1960s America.

Medium Cool (1969) follows a Chicago TV news cameraman named John (Robert Foster), who gradually moves from being a detached, almost voyeuristic, observer of America's ills to being at least aware that changes must be made if the nation is to survive.

The run-up to the Convention had shattered the Democrats. L.B.J. had dropped out of the running, declaring that he would not seek re-election in order actively to pursue the cause of peace. At first it looked like a shoo-in for Eugene McCarthy, but then Bobby Kennedy announced his candidacy and McCarthy faded. With Hubert Humphrey rocky and uncertain, Kennedy gained strength until the California primaries. In Los Angeles he was gunned down and died on the floor of a hotel kitchen. With no one else to turn to, the Democrats reluctantly rallied behind Humphrey.

The growing disaffection of the young, especially over the Vietnam War, was exacerbated through realization that Humphrey would not overturn Johnson's policies. Chicago was the logical place to voice their protest.

The screenplay for *Medium Cool* was ready four months before the Convention, and Wexler took his cast there to film them among the demonstrations. Prescient or not, he can hardly have expected the show put on for his cameras, and the cameras of half the world's press, by Mayor Daley's boys.

The opening scene of *Medium Cool* is unpleasantly dislocating. John and his sound man, Gus (Peter Bonerz), are filming a car wreck on the freeway and it is only after a few moments that the audience realizes that the woman driver in the wrecked car is still alive. Unconscious, moaning and bleeding, but alive.

The two men leave her there, return to their own vehicle and call the studio for a messenger to pick up their film. Almost as an afterthought, they suggest the studio should call for an ambulance.

Later, John becomes involved with a black militant group and also with a young woman, Eileen (Verna Bloom), whose husband is in Vietnam. Through her, he discovers the city's Appalachian ghetto and begins filming that too. The combination of his involvement with militant blacks and Eileen and her young son, Harold (Harold Blankenship), gradually opens his eyes to some of the things around him he has previously seen only through the detaching lens of his camera.

When he learns that his film is being used by the authorities to help them track down the militants he explodes with anger and is fired. Later, hired to cover the Convention as a freelance, he is deep in among the demonstrations. So too is Eileen, who is looking for her runaway son.

The scenes in which Eileen wanders through Chicago's streets among thousands of demonstrators, hundreds of armed police and billowing clouds of tear-gas are remarkable. In one sense, the sense of the fiction being played out, Eileen is barely aware of all the activity around her as she seeks her son; in another sense, the sense of the facts unrolling before Wexler's camera, Verna Bloom, the actress, appears bemusedly distracted, as if she cannot really believe that all this is happening to her.

A further blending of fact and fiction occurs when John's film of the demonstrations is handed to the FBI; Wexler's footage, which he took for use in *Medium Cool*, was also requisitioned by the Justice Department.

Medium Cool shows an America many could not recognize from personal experience; even the TV news programmes showing the reality of the Chicago Convention were an experience of hitherto unsuspected forces at work in society. If few middle-Americans were prepared to support fully the younger generation, then equally few were prepared to accept the reactionary brutality with which youth was being crushed. None of this looked at all like the American Dream; or if it was, the dream was dying.

The death of the American Dream was especially attractive to film-makers in the late 1960s. Two highly contrasting films which took this as their theme were *The Swimmer* (1968) and *Easy Rider* (1969).

The Swimmer centres upon middle-aged, middle-class America while *Easy Rider* is concerned with conflict between middle-America and youth.

The Swimmer, a superb though much-underrated film, is set in Connecticut and follows Ned Merrill (Burt Lancaster) as he conducts a personal odyssey. Appearing unexpectedly at the poolside of some old friends, Ned, clad only in swimming trunks, decides to return to his home and his waiting wife and children by swimming through the pools of all his friends.

As Ned slowly traverses the valley in which his increasingly uneasy friends live, it emerges that he has not been around for a long time and that nothing is quite what it seems. As he progresses through this valley of affluence, Ned learns about himself – he is a bankrupt, he has cheated on friends and acquaintances and, maybe, his wife and family are not waiting at home.

When Ned finally reaches the end of his journey, his house is deserted and boarded up, his swimming pool is empty, the garden overgrown. Wherever he has been, whether in hospital or even in prison, he has been away a long time. Whatever he once had, wife, daughters, the house with its tennis court, he now has nothing. Neither has he any real friends, for the people he has met along the way have progressively shown their unease as he demonstrates all too sharply just how vulnerable they are. Their society, built as it is upon success, cannot tolerate failure.

For Ned Merrill, middle-aged and once successful, with all the material acquisitions any man could wish for, the American Dream has dissolved into nothing.

For Billy and Wyatt (Dennis Hopper and Peter Fonda) in *Easy Rider*, the Dream had disappeared before they set out on their odyssey.

Trailing casually across country from the Mexican border to New Orleans with a consignment of cocaine stashed in the fuel tank of Wyatt's motor-cycle, these two young men will never have the material benefits Ned Merrill has gained and lost. Also, unlike Merrill, Billy and Wyatt have never conformed, and never can. They are rebels without cause; more importantly, they are rebels without purpose.

Apart from the barbed sniping of Merrill's former friends, the only time he encounters hostility is when he tries to enter a public swimming pool and the ordinary people reject him. Billy and Wyatt are continually rejected, often violently, by middle-Americans because they assert their nonconformity through dress and speech, length of hair and ostentatious motorbikes.

This rejection does not take the relatively civilized form of Merrill's. Billy and Wyatt are thrown in jail, their new-found friend and temporary attorney, George Hanson (Jack Nicholson), is beaten to death by a lynch mob which resents the manner and appearance of the strangers in their midst. Finally, Billy and Wyatt are gunned down by an all-American good ol' boy who opens up on them from his truck because he has taken exception to the length of Billy's hair.

One similarity lies in the mood of the ending of both films. They are bleak and filled with despair. The America of middle-class, middle-aged, conforming Ned Merrill and the America of hippie drop-outs Billy and Wyatt is alien to all.

Wyatt's nickname is Captain America; the images this evokes, of a caped crusading man of steel, are simultaneously of a time that has gone forever and a time that, in truth, never really existed at all.

There is another similarity between these two outwardly different depictions of the disintegration of 1960s America. In both the audience is expected to sympathize with the protagonists. Yet Billy and Wyatt are cocaine-peddling iconoclasts, deliberately flouting the conventions of middle-America. Ned

Merrill also gains audience sympathy, yet for all that is known he too could be a criminal. Indeed, given the deliberate ambiguity of *The Swimmer*, he could even be a murderer. Where *are* his wife and daughters?

But none of this matters; both films, made in the decade they depict, know that whatever evils their protagonists might have committed it is American society which is at fault.

Among the differences between the two films is one which may, in the end, point to a greater truth. *Easy Rider* depicts a young, freewheeling, free-loving generation of Americans in conflict with an older, conventional, autocratic, gun-toting generation. Even though youth loses out, the film was enormously popular with younger audiences. *The Swimmer* depicts a snapped, middle-aged failure who has touched the American Dream and found it wanting; moreover, he is in conflict with his own kind, who are clinging desperately to society as they know it and are thus in imminent danger of sinking into their own swimming pools. This film was a box-office failure.

Youth, it seems, wanted to know about the revolution; their fathers preferred to look the other way.

Arising out of the changed attitudes of the young was a very different response from young and old alike to the continuing war in Vietnam. Anti-war sentiments ran high, producing some unexpected conflicts and, equally and encouragingly, some unexpected collaborations.

Film-makers' responses to Vietnam had followed a fairly predictable path given the pattern of Hollywood's reaction to other wars. The first films that dealt specifically with the war in Vietnam were typically gung-ho, with *The Green Berets* (1968) both archetypal and surprisingly late in its appearance. By 1968 most people knew enough of the reality not to be taken in by the numbing banality of a screenplay which assumed that no one had learned anything about war (or, for that matter, about making movies) since World War II ended.

As Gilbert Adair has indicated in his extensive examination of Hollywood's Vietnam, *The Green Berets* states, clumsily and for the most part entirely unconvincingly, all the pro-war tenets of an administration that had completely misunderstood America's role in South East Asia.

Not misunderstood, but entirely omitted from the film, is any indication of the nature of the war as actually fought by both sides in the conflict. In *The Green Berets* napalm is a handy gardening tool used to clear away stubborn undergrowth; bodies lie around gracefully and with remarkably little blood, just as they did in the old days of Custer and the Indians. There are no blown-up bits being scraped into a body bag, no search-and-destroy missions. Certainly there is no suggestion of the kind of behaviour by American soldiers that revelations about My Lai would show were frequent if not commonplace. True, there are atrocities in *The Green Berets*, but just as the Hun did all the dirty work in old movies about World War I, so here it is the Viet Cong who commit all the unspeakable acts. Of course, just to give a patina of realism, the South Vietnamese are allowed to indulge in some violence towards their cousins from the North. These are justified with some rather curious logic as being what the VC have asked for.

The differences between John Wayne's *The Green Berets* and Francis Ford Coppola's *Apocalypse Now* (1979) are extreme, and not only in their political ambience.

The Green Berets is an old-fashioned war movie, in many respects not all that much worse than several hundred of its predecessors. It just seems worse because everyone but its makers had moved on several aeons in their responses to war in general and this war in particular.

Apocalypse Now sought a new dimension for the war film in an attempt to make a definitive statement about war itself, its effect upon man, and, almost in passing, about Vietnam. That it does not quite achieve its aim is unimportant. Coppola aimed very high, very high indeed, and any failure of achievement is no more important than the failure of, say, *Holocaust* in fully evoking the horrors of the treatment of the Jews. It is the sincerity of the attempt which counts.

What causes the failure of *Apocalypse Now* is largely related to the final stages of the film. The earlier sections are all brilliantly conceived and realized: the preparation of Captain Benjamin L. Willard (Martin Sheen) for his mission; the fantastic vulgarity of the Playboy Bunnies sequence; the powerfully dramatic and disturbing firefights and napalm attacks organized by Lt. Col. Bill Kilgore (Robert Duvall in cracking form as a mutant General Custer with General Patton appendages).

Willard's journey up-river becomes steadily more unearthly, but loses no sense of the horrors of the war despite a simultaneous move into fantasy. Fact and fantasy blend in the sequence in which Willard witnesses the continual but senseless rebuilding of the Do Lung bridge complete with Christmas tree lights as, time after time, it is destroyed. Captured in this one mindlessly lethal exercise is the essence of the war in Vietnam. In a sense it can also be expanded to encapsulate all wars, as there are faint overtones, for those who choose to hear them, of World War I incidents where similar mindless persistence permitted the death toll to keep on rising long after everyone except the generals and the politicians had become aware of the futility of it all.

Once Willard reaches the quasi-religious dwelling-place of Colonel Walter E. Kurtz (Marlon Brando), the allegory surfaces and becomes indigestible. Kurtz's appearance is too long delayed, and once he does appear the wait seems not to have been worthwhile.

There is a strange, out-of-sync moment in this part of the film. A war photographer, played by Dennis Hooper, hangs around Kurtz's temple, looking like a refugee from a 1960s *Life* magazine report on campus unrest in some Californian university town. His appearance, brief though it is, suggests that another idea lurked at the back of the film-maker's mind but was somehow lost in the need to make an impact with Brando's brief appearance.

The presence of an American photo-journalist deep behind enemy lines

. . . a mutant Custer with Patton appendages.
(*Apocalypse Now*)

inevitably brings to mind Errol Flynn's son Sean. After taking advantage of the good looks he had inherited from his father, he made a handful of forgettable films in the 1960s, then became a news photographer, went to South East Asia in 1970, and vanished.

Fortunately, the point at which the brakes are abruptly jammed on happens so far into *Apocalypse Now* that it does not really matter. The earlier images – Valkyrie-helicopters, a water-skier amidst bomb-bursts, the napalmed jungles and villages, the slaughter of innocent people on land and in boats, the overpowering weight of the jungle's fetid air – added to powerful performances from Sheen and Duvall help carry this film over the last few moments of uncertainty.

Any doubts that this was the way Vietnam really was must have been stilled by publication of war correspondent Michael Herr's *Dispatches* in 1977. Herr wrote some of the voice-over passages spoken by Sheen, and knowledge that what is depicted here, and worse, had been seen by a detached, if not dispassionate, observer dispel any tendency to disbelieve.

Although later, Mark Baker's collection of reminiscences by the men who fought the war, *Nam*, published in 1981, also contributes, if only negatively, to the overall picture. Had Coppola been able to use some of this material, his vision of the Vietnam War might have been even more bleakly apocalyptic.

In the midst of the war in Vietnam, on 30 April 1970, President Nixon announced that he had ordered American troops into Cambodia in an effort to eliminate supply routes and sanctuaries used by the North Vietnamese. It was in demonstrations against this escalation of military activity that the Kent State shootings occurred. It was also an action which showed the American people just how far things had got out of hand. The war and the presidency had taken on life of their own, like crazed Frankenstein monsters.

The true nature of what happened in Cambodia has been slow in coming to the motion-picture screen. When it finally made it, it was with an impact more shattering than anything Vietnam had generated.

Under Prince Sihanouk Cambodia had tried to maintain a policy of neutrality towards events in Vietnam, despite the very obvious difficulties presented by an extensive border region which could not be patrolled. Eventually, with Sihanouk ousted by US-backed Marshal Lon Nol, the difficulties became insuperable. The American top-brass in Vietnam requested the bombing of so-called 'sanctuaries' in Cambodia in the mistaken belief that the Viet Cong was holed-up there and was using the country as a supply route. The original request was for 60 sorties (codename: Breakfast) by B-52 bombers, but there was a gradual and apparently uncontrollable escalation. Over a period of 14 months the Air Force flew a staggering total of 3,630 sorties.

Both the White House and the military clamped a blanket of security over the operation and neither Congress nor the public was informed. Maintenance of security was such a high priority that paranoia set in, resulting in falsification of information regarding targets and statistics.

The 1970 coup against Sihanouk drove him to side with his former enemies, the communist Khmer Rouge, and a savage civil war soon wracked the country. In April 1970 the extended bombing campaign was accompanied by the invasion of Cambodia by US and South Vietnamese forces which so angered university students back home.

The US government's mishandling of the situation in Cambodia – the bombings, invasions and general de-stabilization – allowed the Khmer Rouge, under Pol Pot, to become the ruling force. It took several years of fighting, which set brother against brother and son against father, before the heart, if not the soul, was torn out of the Cambodian people. By the time that the capital, Phnom Penh, was captured by the Khmer Rouge in April 1975, internal anger and bitterness and the internecine struggles had degenerated to the point that horrifyingly brutal excesses followed. In retrospect, they appear appallingly inevitable.

The Killing Fields (1984) is the first major feature film to examine this period of American history and it does so through the true story of two men, an American and a Cambodian, who suffered but, somehow, survived.

Sidney Schanberg (Sam Waterston) is a reporter working for *The New York Times* in Cambodia and is that rare breed of man – hard, almost ruthless in his determination to do his job, yet simultaneously sympathetic and caring. Schanberg's local associate is a Cambodian journalist named Dith Pran (Haing Ngor). Together, the two men manage to convey much information to readers in America, information which the military would have been happier to contain. This is especially true of revelations of the mistaken bombing of a harmless market town and the resulting deaths of many of its inhabitants.

By early 1975, with the Khmer Rouge takeover imminent, Americans and other foreigners are urged to leave, but a handful stay on in Phnom Penh. Among these are Schanberg, Al Rockoff (John Malkovich), a spaced-out photographer, and a British television reporter, Jon Swain (Julian Sands). Dith Pran stays with his colleagues even though his wife and children have been evacuated to safety.

When the Khmer Rouge enter the capital the journalists are witness to the violence which flows out of ideological differences between Cambodians and their lives are threatened. Only the fierce loyalty and determination of Dith Pran saves them from death. Eventually, Pran is separated from the others despite their efforts to take him with them as they leave the country. He has to stay behind, to what the foreigners believe to be certain death at the hands of his fellow countrymen.

But Pran displays an astonishing will to live, allied to remarkable ingenuity and sheer courage, and thus survives the mass slaughter taking place in Cambodia. Among the visible results of the massacres are the often-waterlogged tracts of land surrounding towns and villages where countless bodies lie rotting. These are known as 'the killing fields'.

The months stretch into years, and the dangers to Pran increase as the people are 'educated' into loyalty to the regime, but he survives as all about him his country dies. At one point Pran gets a message out to Schanberg, an action which almost costs him his life yet again. It is four years before the Cambodian reaches the border with Thailand and crosses to safety.

Pran's message eventually reaches Schanberg in New York. Feted for his reports from Cambodia, the American still bears an unshakable feeling of guilt at what he sees as his desertion of a friend and colleague, a man who saved his life. When he receives Pran's message Schanberg immediately returns to South East Asia and is finally reunited with Pran at a Red Cross refugee camp close to the border with Cambodia.

In telling Cambodia's grim and disturbing story through the medium of the astonishing tribulation of two men who formed an undying bond of friendship during conflict, *The Killing Fields* follows an established tradition of film-making. But here is none of the bravura and sentimentality which trivialized so many of Hollywood's recreations of real wartime events. Neither are the horrors of war, or of genocide, exploited for the sake of dramatic effect. One small moment is an indication of how this film's makers have approached their subject: as a town is shelled and buildings and people are shattered, the camera stays on a small child who screams at the terrifying noise. There is no need for blood and dismemberment. Nevertheless, at another moment, as Dith Pran wades through a swamp filled with bloated and rotting corpses, the film-makers do not shy from demonstrating what this man endured.

The man chosen to play the role of Dith Pran, Haing Ngor, is not an actor, but a Cambodian doctor who suffered tribulations of comparable magnitude to those of the man he portrays.

The makers of *The Killing Fields* achieve a most difficult stance. They are detached, yet they are neither disengaged nor unconcerned. Admiration for the capacity for humanity within an individual is allied to condemnation of the attitude of governments. This attitude, which combines indifference with acute if untargeted hostility towards anyone who contravenes an ill-defined normality, was rampant during the Vietnamese and Cambodian experiences. It still thrives in Central America in 1984, a fact which should ensure the film's impact upon America's conscience.

Cambodia was, and remains, a concealed and almost forgotten part of American political history. Most people remember the student deaths at Kent State; how many remember the hundreds of thousands of deaths which precipitated the Kent State demonstrations? Perhaps in 1984, a decade on and with a Presidential election at hand, this is the right moment to remember. It is fortunate that the film bringing this memory to life is of such extraordinarily high quality. Through *The Killing Fields* the tragedy of Cambodia has finally received the memorial it deserves.

When Vietnam veterans returned home to America the differences they found far outweighed those which had awaited their brothers-in-arms after earlier years. At least, that is the conclusion suggested by Hollywood's response to the post-Vietnam scene at home.

An inability to re-adjust to a society which had moved on at a different pace formed the basis as before, but instead of an Eddie Bartlett failing to find a job awaiting him or an Al Stephenson unable to reconcile banking with fighting, here were super-trained killing machines ready and willing to keep right on doing what a vet's gotta do.

Travis Bickle (Robert De Niro) in Martin Scorsese's *Taxi Driver* (1976) carries over his killing mission into civilian life without any discernible crisis of conscience. His only soul-searching is in deciding whom he should kill.

First Blood (1982) visits traditional small-town America, where the killing machine, John Rambo (Sylvester Stallone), tangles with the local lawman while trying to pass harmlessly through town. Refused the right of passage, he blitzes the town in the manner approved by the men who trained him for Vietnam. Rambo is a Green Beret, but despite some unnecessary special pleading, he is much more than a few thousand miles removed from John Wayne's view of this kind of man.

Although having no claim to be regarded as a message picture, *First Blood* does fit, albeit a trifle uncomfortably, into a line of tales about disaffected veterans which began after the formation in 1967 of the Vietnam Veterans Against the War. These veterans, all recipients of honourable discharges, spoke out at a time when it was considerably less than popular, or wise, to contradict the generals and the politicians in a formal, and identifiable, manner. A hearing, when several veterans admitted to appalling crimes against Vietnamese men, women and children, was filmed and released in 1972. *Winter Soldier* is a bleak record of a period in American history which refuses, rightly, to be forgotten.

Not all young Americans of draftable age experienced Vietnam. Some were lucky and drew a high draft number; others contrived to avoid the war through money and position; still more avoided an unwanted experience by refusing to serve even when drafted.

One batch of draft files was destroyed at Catonsville, Maryland, in 1968. The perpetrators were duly brought to trial, but the Catonsville Nine were very different from the Chicago Seven who had been tried earlier the same year on charges arising out of the Democratic Convention disturbances.

The Trial of the Catonsville Nine (1972) is an almost verbatim account of the trial, which was first turned into a stage play by one of the defendants, Father Daniel Berrigan. Berrigan's brother, another priest, was also one of the Nine, and the two women in the group were also in holy orders.

The trial attracted the attention of Gregory Peck, who produced the film, partly because the Department of Justice had taken great pains to ensure that there would be none of the suspicion of railroading that had accompanied the Chicago Seven trial. Additionally Peck, long identified with the Establishment wing in Hollywood, had been swayed by what Vietnam was doing to the nation and to the young.

The effect of the Vietnam War was profound, more so than any other conflict since the Civil War. Even after it was over, Americans remained divided by it and fumbled uncertainly for the required responses.

The period of American history which spans the end of Kennedy's administration and the end of the war is no more than a dozen years long, yet it covers more unrest at home than at any time since 1865.

Despite the wealth of material for film-makers to draw upon, little of the predictably huge output stands out as a worthy addition to the filmed history of the American nation. Those that are worthy are also condemnatory.

Twenty years on, some of the film-makers' efforts make the 1960s clearer, yet simultaneously show that not everyone wants to be reminded of that turbulent decade. Perhaps too little has really changed.

Black Americans remain disaffected, although the increase in registration brought about during Jesse Jackson's 1984 campaign suggests that sooner than many white politicians may care to accept the black vote may well hold the balance of power in marginal elections.

The young of the 1960s, the Hippies and Yippies and the wide-eyed radicals, are the middle-aged of the 1980s, and a corresponding drift away from early ideals has occurred. Film-makers have shown an interest in this with *The Big Chill* (1983) and its low-budget forerunner, *The Return of the Secaucus Seven* (1980), both of which examine the loss of idealism without successfully discovering what, if anything, has taken its place.

The Vietnam veterans are still around to nudge America's conscience occasionally, whether by way of a street-corner panhandler or an outburst of individual urban violence.

The majority of veterans have, however, returned to their former roles and have blended once more into society; just as the majority of long-haired, beaded children of the 1960s have become the neat, formally-suited executives that so exactly mirror their once-reviled parents. The majority of blacks have returned to resigned acceptance that, so far as they are concerned, nothing ever really changes for them, whatever may be happening elsewhere in American society.

Then, however, as the 1970s began, while there was general disaffection for the growingly limp adage, 'My country, right or wrong', there was still the smell of revolution in the air. Even that other majority, the Silent Majority in whom Richard Nixon vested whatever trust he was able to place in his fellow men, began to fall in line with their more vociferous countrymen: the blacks, the young and the veterans. The reason was their discovery of something which would readily seize hold of film-makers' interest.

This was the revelation that the nation's proudest office, the presidency, was itself a centre of discord, venality, corruption and criminality.

Surprisingly, it was the usually astute Nixon who himself precipitated the gravest constitutional crisis since the Civil War – Watergate.

CHAPTER TWELVE

> 'The journalist has a distant, cold relation
> with the reader. Film, theater, has to
> have a different approach.'
> (Costa-Gavras on *Missing*)

One of the most compelling examinations of the presidency of Richard Nixon came to the screen not from Hollywood but in a 6-part television series based upon John Ehrlichman's novel *The Company*.

Cumbersomely but more appositely entitled *Washington Behind Closed Doors* (1977), the series steered a neat course around the known facts and suppositions, both partially substantiated and otherwise. The script, by David Rintels and Eric Bercovici, improved greatly upon the novel, which was not itself of especial merit but gained good sales thanks to its author's participation in the events described.

The account was aided by splendid performances from Robert Vaughn, as the cryptically unemotional H. R. Haldeman-figure, and Andy Griffith, as a suitably vulgar Lyndon Johnson. The keynote of the entire production, however, was the brilliant performance of Jason Robards, who packaged all the paranoic malevolence of Richard Nixon into his portrayal of the besieged president.

One moment, as the President is about to leave a hotel to cross the sidewalk to his waiting limousine, is superbly done. Knowing the crowds await him, along with cameras by the score, the President turns from scowling misanthrope to beaming man of the people in less than the flick of an eye. Nothing could more accurately and aptly reflect the Nixon presidency.

The gradual collapse of the façade which the President had built up with the eager assistance of his henchmen began shortly after the Watergate break-in, when some Washington newsmen threw a little light into dark corners of the administration. Foremost among the journalists were two relatively undistinguished and almost unknown young reporters on the staff of the Washington *Post*. Their determination to dig to the bottom of the heap until they found whatever was buried there lifted them out of the ranks and placed them on a pedestal higher than that enjoyed by almost any other journalist in the history of American newspapers. They were Bob Woodward and Carl Bernstein.

The account of their efforts demanded more than just its appearance day by day in the newspaper for which they worked. A book appeared, in 1974, and, given the nature of the mess they had uncovered, a film version was sure to follow.

All the President's Men (1976) traces the book accurately, and as the book was itself a straightforward account of the events which sprang out of Watergate, the film is therefore a detailed record of a period in American political history most Americans, politicians and otherwise, would dearly like to forget.

The hearing in 1972 at which the Watergate burglars were arraigned, following their abortive break-in at the Watergate building offices of the Democratic party, produced information that an ex-CIA man was involved. This led Woodward and Bernstein to other, higher-up, CIA men, some with links to the White House. Unexpectedly aided by secret information from a highly-placed but disembodied telephone-caller, 'Deep Throat', the reporters picked up the trail of money flowing into and out of the office of the National Finance Chairman of the Committee to Re-elect the President.

Soon, Woodward and Bernstein were delving deep into a morass of dealing and double-dealing, the ultimate objective of which was to give the President's aides the dirt on anyone who could be seen as a threat to their boss.

As the movie displays, for Woodward (Robert Redford) and Bernstein (Dustin Hoffman) the gradual emergence of the extent of the conspiracy is almost beyond belief. Their immediate superiors at the *Post*, managing editor Howard Simons (Martin Balsam), executive editor Ben Bradlee (Jason Robards) and metropolitan editor Harry Rosenfeld (Jack Warden), hold on to the runaway enthusiasm of their younger and less-experienced colleagues. Everything has to be checked over and over again; nothing is to be printed, not even Deep Throat's revelations, without additional confirming sources. The caution is justified. This is too big a story to risk burial beneath an avalanche of lawsuits.

By the end of the film Nixon has been re-elected, but with Woodward and Bernstein clinging remorselessly to their task there is no chance that the President will avoid the inevitable.

The power behind the film stems largely from Robert Redford, who co-produced in addition to co-starring; quite clearly it was largely his determination to bring the story to the screen that resulted in the eventual making of *All the President's Men*.

In one respect the film came a little too soon. Had they waited until the end of 1975, Nixon would have narrowly avoided impeachment and resigned. No film could have asked for a better pay-off. *All the President's Men* does not end this way, but it ranks highly as one of Hollywood's most accurate depictions of the nation's political history.

The departure of Richard Nixon and his replacement by the accident-prone and determinedly unmagnetic Gerald Ford offered little for Americans to cheer at. The ending of the war in Vietnam in 1975 was at least a sign that some measure of sense had returned to politicians and the military, although the changing of these previously locked minds was no cause for rejoicing. This event, forced upon government by an increasingly disenchanted public, had come much too late to prevent deep and divisive wounds to the nation.

The new President's decision to pardon Richard Nixon for his sins but not to make a similarly generous offer to those young men who had evaded the draft practically guaranteed that next time out the electorate would try to keep out all vestiges of the old palace guard and try someone new.

Short of selecting Edward Kennedy as their candidate, the Democrats were sure to win. In the event, a small man appeared out of nowhere and took his place as front-runner. Grinning hugely at everything and everybody, Jimmy Carter became President and proved to be one of the few modern incumbents of the office who failed to grow in the job. In 1984, as the Reagan administration's juggernaut rumbles remorselessly towards military confrontation, the Carter years look increasingly golden.

The year of Carter's election, 1976, was also America's bicentennial year, but the occasion was barely glanced at by film-makers; perhaps they were aware that any such film could not help but date rapidly.

The new presidency got under way with a general if unstated hope that whatever happened now, it could be no worse than the recent past. These hopes were just about realized, but it was a close-run thing.

The main problems lay overseas, with Latin America looming large yet again, and an entirely unexpected crisis, blowing up as swiftly as a desert sandstorm, in Iran.

Two important films looked at different aspects of America's involvement in affairs to the south. Costa-Gavras's *Missing* (1982) is set in Chile after Allende, while Roger Spottiswode's *Under Fire* (1983) takes Nicaragua as its setting, shortly before the flight of President Somoza and the establishment of a new government of former rebels, the Sandinistas.

Missing is based upon the real case of a young American who went missing during the military coup against Allende's government. The film follows attempts by his wife and father to discover the truth.

In the film the missing man is Charles Horman (John Shea), who, although liberal in outlook, falls well short of being a dangerous radical. Yet this is what the authorities believe him to be. He disappears on a night of extreme violence during which his wife Beth (Sissy Spacek) cannot reach home before curfew. Her increasingly desperate attempts to trace Charles are thwarted both by local officials and by the American embassy staff.

Eventually Charles' father, Ed (Jack Lemmon), arrives in Santiago, having failed to gain any help from the State Department in Washington. Ed and Beth join forces, albeit reluctantly at first as there is both a generation and a political gap between them. He finds it hard to accept the slowly emerging truth: not only are the Americans in Santiago concealing facts about his son and other Americans who have vanished, but it also appears highly probable that American military aid was behind the coup. Worse still is Ed's realization that his son's disappearance came as a result of his having accidentally discovered the facts of American involvement. The implication is that, at best, the Americans turned a blind eye to his treatment. At worst, they connived at his disappearance.

Given the confusion which abounded at the time in Chile (and which has been mirrored in most other Latin American countries at times of political unrest), a precise knowledge of what happened must owe something to the imaginations of the makers of films like *Missing*. Just how much invention is present here is debatable, but the overriding impression is that it all happened exactly the way it is shown.

Eventually, Ed Horman is told that his son is dead. He has to pay for the body to be shipped home, but there is a seven-month delay before the coffin reaches the United States. Examination of the body to discover the cause of death is impossible. Horman's threat of legal action against the government comes to nothing as the documents relating to the case are classified.

In his depiction of the behaviour of American government officials towards their fellow citizens, whom they are supposed to represent and support, Costa-Gavras is utterly condemning. If the actions of the real-life individuals concerned were only one-tenth as obstructive and as culpable as this, then the entire American administration stands accused and, in this committed and impassioned film-maker's eyes, is found guilty of criminal abrogation of its responsibilities to the American people.

Under Fire, while largely fictitious, uses the factual setting of the circumstances leading up to the ousting of Somoza from Nicaragua to excellent effect. The film is also important in establishing the role played in real-life events by journalists and photographers, TV news gatherers and, by implication, film-makers too.

Photographs taken in Nicaragua by Russell Price (Nick Nolte) are used for a variety of purposes, only a few of which are why he took them in the first place. Persuaded to take a picture of a dead rebel leader in such a way that it makes the man appear to be still alive, Price knowingly, if at first reluctantly, commits himself to faking reality in defence of what he hopes will be a greater good. He persists with the deception even to the extent of concealing the truth from a colleague, Alex Grazier (Gene Hackman). Then the two men discover that earlier pictures Price has taken of rebels are being used to identify victims for Somoza's death squads.

When Grazier is shot by the army, Price films the murder, then goes into hiding. When the film is screened on television Somoza (René Enriquez) leaves the country as fast as he can, pausing only to collect his beautiful girlfriend and enough money to allow him to live a luxurious life in sunny Miami. Many years had elapsed since F.D.R. had remarked of his father, 'He may be a bastard, but he's *our* bastard.' Like father, like son.

More than any recent film, *Under Fire* raises intriguing and disturbing questions about the use of film in real-life political events. Here, film is used for good and for evil; it is used to show truth (as when Grazier is killed) and lies (the photographing of the dead rebel leader). Thus, the reliability of news reporting, whether in words, with still pictures, or on film, is seriously questioned. Many of the ramifications, the problems and decisions facing film-makers engaged in work on real events, whether for TV news programmes or for feature films, are therefore highlighted. Aside from all its other qualities as a motion-picture (and they are many) *Under Fire* sets out within its running-time most of the problems which confront the recorders of history, as well as some possible solutions.

By 1980, the man in the White House was on his way back to the inglorious obscurity from whence he had come. The ineffectualness of Jimmy Carter, allied to the affront to American dignity created by the treatment of the hostages in Iran, to say nothing of the failed rescue mission (surely never to become the subject of an *American* film), had swung the electorate back again. Once more they favoured a Republican, and this time they also got a movie actor, albeit one whose billing had rarely been above the title. For Ronald Reagan, the White House had become a personal Holy Grail replacing any ambitions he might once have cherished to star in a good-quality A-film.

It is easy, too easy perhaps, to criticize Ronald Reagan's foreign policy and notions on diplomacy by equating it to the kind of B-movie ambience in which he spent much of his Hollywood career.

On the credit side it has to be conceded that however unlikely it might seem, he managed to revert to the usual trend, which Jimmy Carter had temporarily altered, and grew with the job.

Unfortunately, in terms of his maturity in understanding world affairs and relationships with his allies, the new President had too far to grow for anyone to regard his improvement with equanimity.

As for Reagan's response to the communist threat, this showed that no more advances would be made. Indeed, from the standpoint of 1984, it can be seen that the atmosphere is as bad as it was in the 1950s. Even his *volte-face* over China and his visit there in April 1984 showed more concern for his forth-coming bid for a second term as President than for improving world relations.

His policies towards Latin American countries suggest that no one has learned anything since the days of Woodrow Wilson's responses to the Mexican revolution. Indeed, Reagan shows alarming similarities to Wilson in his inability to pick the right horse to back. Surely even Wilson would not have chosen to back reactionary elements against the Sandinistas.

Unfortunately for the cause of peace in Latin America, what is happening there is no horseback-riding, gun-slinging pursuit of a latterday Pancho Villa. Alarming though it is, Ronald Reagan really does seem to think that life, especially life below the Rio Grande,is just like the movies.

Back home in the 1980s, America became an even more hazardous place in which to live. If escalating street violence was not enough to contend with, nuclear power became as much a threat as its proponents claimed it to be a blessing.

The mishap at the Three-Mile Island nuclear power plant, and numerous other 'mishaps', have had sharp echoes in feature films. Some have been fictitious, some closely aligned with real cases, a few built entirely upon reality.

The China Syndrome (1979) is an account of how a TV journalist, Kimberley Wells (Jane Fonda), uncovers a dangerous incident at a nuclear plant in California. The construction company which built the plant has cut corners and there are flaws in a vital component. A technician at the plant, Jack Godell (Jack Lemmon), realizes this and tries to help expose what is happening.

The authorities clamp down on Jack and on the TV station which employs Kimberley. Attempts are made to bring evidence before a hearing which is considering the building of an even bigger nuclear plant by the same contractor. This evidence shows that the same X-ray has been repeatedly used in tests to short-circuit normal procedures on an important pumping unit. The unit is, in fact, approaching failure.

One of Kimberley's colleagues who is carrying the evidence to the hearing is run off the road. The cover-up almost succeeds but, following Jack Godell's death at the hands of a SWAT squad, another colleague speaks up, which suggests that, maybe, the truth will emerge.

There are some strong similarities between this story and that which forms the basis of *The Plutonium Incident* (1980) and *Silkwood* (1984).

Although ostensibly fictional, *The Plutonium Incident* is quite clearly based upon the case of Karen Silkwood. In the film, Judith Longden (Janet Margolin) pursues a quest for plant safety through union activities following the suspicious death of her union-activist lover. After discovering evidence of several mishaps at the Northern Oregon Nuclear Plant where she works, and of cover-ups, Judith learns that she has been contaminated by plutonium. She seeks help from a sympathetic Congressman but is lured back to the plant on the promise of more evidence, where she is trapped in the vaults used to store plutonium and left to suffocate.

Later, the Nuclear Regulatory Commission closes the plant down. Although vindicated, there is insufficient evidence to press charges against anyone for Judith's murder.

Silkwood tells the true story of Karen Silkwood, a 28-year-old worker at a Kerr-McGee plutonium-processing plant in Oklahoma. Although not politically motivated at first, Karen became concerned at the casual disregard for safety precautions at the plant and was soon involved in moves to unionize Kerr-McGee.

Discovering that X-rays showing flaws in the fuel rods being manufactured there have been tampered with, she collects evidence which she takes with her to a meeting with a reporter from the *New York Times*. She dies before reaching the meeting place, apparently driving off the road in a 'one-car accident'. The X-rays disappear. This was in November 1974.

Perhaps the most threatening aspect of these three films is the ability displayed by large corporations and government-backed bodies to conceal the truth, even at the cost of human lives, with such ruthlessly cold-blooded detachment.

Forensic evidence shows irrefutably that Karen Silkwood's car was pushed off the road from behind, yet no charges have been brought, nor are they ever likely to be.

If big business can do all this, and along the way corrupt and subvert government officers and others, and inhibit free speech, to say nothing of arranging disappearances and deaths, then how far can national government go when its toes are being stepped on?

Such speculations begin to make some of the fantastic tales of government manipulation and duplicity brought to the screen in recent years seem more likely by the minute. The fact that film-makers are prepared to tackle some of these issues head-on is one of the more encouraging signs of recent years. Back in the 1930s, during the heyday of the social-conscience movie, Hollywood brought forth some of its most creditable efforts. The 1980s are showing a similar awareness among film-makers; their efforts, one can but hope, will have some beneficial effect, just as did those earlier movies.

Unfortunately, one or two exceptions apart, few of those early films really changed the world; they did not, for example, prevent World War II. Can today's movies help prevent World War III, or some other grim fate for mankind?

Hollywood's view of where the world is headed has produced a wide range of possibilities. Many have been the simple, far–fetched meanderings of second-rate science-fiction writers; yet some visions of the future have been alarmingly believable.

CHAPTER THIRTEEN

Just as the past has fascinated film-makers throughout the history of the cinema, so too has the future provided a source of material – some whimsical, some extraordinarily pessimistic, and all, to a greater or lesser extent, highly speculative.

One of the earliest moving pictures ever was Georges Méliès' *A Trip To the Moon* (1902), a cheerful little film as enjoyable today as it was more than an average lifetime ago.

The science-fiction approach towards what the future might bring held sway until after the explosion of the first atomic bombs on Japan at the end of World War II. After that, science-fiction prophecies gave way to the grim reality of science-fact – or, at the very least, of science-probability. Later still, in a new era of potential for wars among the stars and close encounters with other kinds, many film-makers whizzed off into fantasyland once more, but serious observers of the future found little to be optimistic about.

Five (1951) is the first film to speculate upon what life might be like after nuclear war has devastated the civilized world. In this story, five people survive to battle out their personal problems and prejudices, principally those linked to racial discrimination, until only two are left – a new Adam and Eve intent on generating a new race which will not make the same mistakes as in the past. This piously optimistic note necessarily omits reference to certain matters which were virtually unknown at the time, mostly those relating to the long-term effects of radiation. The most forbidding of these, the 'nuclear winter', in which the entire ecological balance of nature will undergo changes likely to last for many years, may well effectively prevent regeneration of the human race.

In early-1950s movies of this type the Bomb did not always go off; often it became a commodity to be hunted or stolen, or used as a blackmail threat. Occasionally such treatment managed to transcend the inherent banality of the concept by means of a highly realistic setting. The British film *Seven Days To Noon* (1950) is one such example. In this, a nuclear scientist, worried at the long-term potential for harm that his work is creating, threatens to destroy Central London unless the government orders a halt to the development of nuclear weapons. He does not succeed, either in destroying London or in convincing the government.

Another film which uses nuclear weapons as a blackmail threat is *Twilight's Last Gleaming* (1977). The central theme of this film underwent a number of modifications between leaving Walter Wager's novel *Viper Three* and its final edited screen version.

In the novel, a mid-Western missile silo is taken over by an escaped convict, former Air Force Major Lawrence Dell. Apparently serving a sentence for his wife's murder, Dell demands money and safe passage out of the country. The original screenplay upgrades Dell to General (played by Burt Lancaster), and his incarceration is stated to be a military frame–up (something only tentatively hinted at in the novel) designed to keep him quiet. Dell, who has been highly critical of his country's involvement in South East Asia, demands money and safe passage for him and his helpers but, most significantly, wants the President to make public a top secret report which admits to the political machinations which kept America involved in Vietnam.

Somewhere along the way, the producers began to suffer from cold feet and after the film was completed drastic cuts were made which all but eliminated the political content. What is left therefore falters uneasily at some points where the motivation of the main characters appears less than realistic. It is encouraging to note that a recent British TV screening included the missing footage.

Dell's intention, to launch a nuclear strike at the USSR, thus precipitating a counter-offensive leading to World War III, is almost fulfilled. The manner in which he gains access to the underground control room of the missile silo has an authentic feel to it. Anyone who has thought much about those men who sit far beneath the farmlands of the mid-West with their guns ready to shoot any colleague who goes berserk is unlikely to be much comforted.

The fate of a small group of people facing life on an otherwise empty planet Earth was pursued in *The World, the Flesh and the Devil* (1959), which, like its predecessor, *Five*, is as much concerned with racial matters as with the implications of the political circumstances which have reduced the world to ashes.

On the Beach (1959) is similarly concerned with personal problems besetting the last living people on Earth as they sit out the days in Australia awaiting the approaching cloud of radiation which will wipe them out. Despite one sequence when the crew of the *USS Sawfish* under the command of Dwight Lionel Towers (Gregory Peck) surfaces off a silent and blasted San Francisco, the reality of the immediate effects of a nuclear strike upon a major urban centre is avoided.

Panic in Year Zero (1962) also avoids reality, by concentrating its attention upon one family, the Baldwins. They are vacationing in the hills above Los Angeles when the city is bombed. Naturally enough they stay in the hills, where they find themselves the only people prepared to live like human beings among half–crazed survivors bent on rape, robbery and murder. The film quickly degenerates into a pioneers-*versus*-Indians tale, with Harry Baldwin (Ray Milland, who also directs) eventually resorting to well–tried fictions such as that which suggests that a gun in a good man's hands is better than one in the hands of an evil-doer. The ending, as the Baldwin family are shepherded into an army compound, there to begin life again, leaves the cynical viewer suspecting that a better fate for them would be to have stayed home that week.

Testament (1983), which uses the almost *de rigueur* setting of a small California town, also shows the effect of nuclear war upon one family group. Eventually, the story devolves entirely upon the efforts of the mother, Carol Wetherly (Jane Alexander), to continue living a normal life despite the facts which stare her in the face at every turn. Ending ambiguously, but essentially optimistically, the film is simultaneously facile and deeply moving.

What is most disturbing about *Testament* is not so much the effect upon the fabric of life of a massive disaster (the film could work almost equally as well if the threat were not nuclear but, say, a plague or, given the location, a massive earthquake) but the unstated acceptance that no one in the town – and, by extension, no one in any town anywhere – can control what happens.

In reality as much as in fiction, the political and military establishments have what little control there is, but their grip appears even weaker in the 1980s than it was twenty years ago when film-makers made their first attempts to examine the reality (or unreality) of nuclear politics.

The politics of nuclear war are examined in three films all made in the early 1960s. Two of these offer a straightforward and relatively unhysterical view of how a nuclear holocaust might come about.

In *Fail Safe* (1964) the problem arises when the 'fail safe' device, which has been designed to prevent the accidental launch of a bombing mission against Russia, breaks down. A flight of aircraft sets out for Moscow; the President (Henry Fonda) tries desperately to call them back. Failing to do so, he contacts the Russian Premier to warn him and assure him that it is all a terrible mistake.

With the aid of secret American information passed on by the President, the Russians intercept the bombers, but one gets through. The President offers a deal: if the aircraft succeeds in bombing Moscow, he will order the bombing of an American city so that the Russians need not launch a retaliatory strike. When the President's hot-line to Moscow goes dead, he orders the bombing of New York.

The film stays close to what has since become steadily more probable although the ending, the bombing by Americans of their own most densely populated city as an act of contrition, seems less credible as time has passed. Today, while it is unpleasantly easy to imagine the launch of an accidental strike, it is much harder to visualize an American president pressing the button which will wipe out several millions of his fellow countrymen.

Today, of course, unlike those relatively slow-moving times depicted in *Fail*

Safe, bombing missions are not the danger. Missiles, which take only minutes to reach their targets, are what we have to worry about. Deciding to bomb New York is a question which requires rather more time than it takes for the President to shave.

The crisis which the US destroyer precipitates in *The Bedford Incident* (1965) does not lead to full-scale nuclear war, but the film's abrupt end leaves a big question-mark hanging in the air. The US *Bedford* is on anti-submarine patrol in the North Atlantic when she happens upon a Russian submarine inside Greenland's territorial waters. The *Bedford's* commander, Captain Eric Finlander (Richard Widmark), pursues the sub with gritty determination and his crew, a highly efficient and frighteningly well-motivated bunch, all co-operate fully. The only dissenting voices come from a German NATO observer and an American journalist, who are both along for the ride.

Commodore Wolfgang Schrepke (Eric Portman), a former World War II U-boat commander, thinks like the hunted Russian and is soon alarmed at the way the American commander is handling the incident.

The journalist, Ben Munceford (Sidney Poitier), sees past the surface intensity of Finlander and his crew. They have all become so obsessed with the hunt that they have lost sight of the wider implications.

Shipboard tension mounts until a keyed-up sailor mis-hears a command and launches the *Bedford's* nuclear missiles. In the split seconds before the missiles reach the submarine, the Russian vessel launches its retaliatory strike at the *Bedford*.

The question left hanging over the suddenly blank screen is – what happens next?

A realistic fear is that such an incident could mushroom, all too literally, into a nuclear war which would devastate mankind. The probability of such an incident occurring seems just as likely as that which overhangs *Fail Safe* or *Twilight's Last Gleaming*, while the narrow field of view heightens disquiet. There are unknown numbers of American and Russian warships at sea at all times. Pessimistic or not, logic insists that sooner or later such an incident will take place.

The remaining film of the three mid-1960s explorations into the politics of nuclear war is *Dr Strangelove, or How I Learned to Stop Worrying and Love the Bomb* (1964).

Although this British-made film takes its central plot line from a different novel, *Dr Strangelove* is basically very similar to *Fail Safe*, and even if it is pitched at a very different level, with deranged scientists and psychotic military officers rampant throughout, its dense black humour does not detract from the impact of its central message.

The crisis in this instance is deliberately set under way by General Jack D. Ripper (Sterling Hayden) after he has agonized long and hard over the reason for his impotence. Having concluded that he, and every other American, is being systematically poisoned by the Russians, he determines to save his country, and restore his personal potency, by launching a bomber raid on Moscow.

Once the aircraft are on their way, he seals himself into his base and prepares to sit out his own privately arranged Armageddon.

With President Merkin Muffley (Peter Sellers, in one of his three roles in the film) anxious to placate the Russians, the American Chiefs of Staff gather in the War Room. The President calls Moscow on the hot-line to assure his counterpart that this is all a dreadful mistake, but there is to be no simple exchange of blasted cities here. Group Captain Lionel Mandrake (Sellers), a British officer on Ripper's staff, discovers that the Russians have developed a new device, the Doomsday Machine, which will automatically trigger full-scale retaliation in the event of nuclear attack upon their country.

Eventually, a means of calling back the bombers is discovered and some are recalled. Those that cannot be reached are shot down by the Russians – all except one. Piloted by a demented survivor of the gung-ho era of sticks and flaps flying, Major 'King' Kong (Slim Pickens), this aircraft gets through.

For a while, when the hydrogen bomb's release mechanism malfunctions, there appears to be hope. But Kong climbs into the bomb bay, releases the catch, and with stetson in hand rides the bomb down towards Moscow a-whooping and a-hollering like a rodeo rider, but with the ultimate in male potency symbols between his legs.

By now the President and his staff have been joined in the War Room by Dr Strangelove (Sellers), a twisted, demonic survivor of Hitler's Germany. He assures the grim assembly that survival is possible if they take the best men into the deepest mineshafts in the country – along with ten times that number of women, an idea of particular appeal to Army Chief of Staff General Buck Turgidson (George C. Scott), who has none of Ripper's problems where women are concerned.

As they wait for the approaching retaliatory strike, mushroom clouds rise up and Vera Lynn sings her World War II message of hope and promise on the soundtrack: 'We'll meet again, don't know where, don't know when . . . '

The film's success has been maintained despite the passing of two decades during which too many people appear to have learned how to stop worrying and live with, if not actually love, the Bomb.

The reason for this success lies principally in the film's beautifully sustained balance between realism and satire. The realism of the action sequences and of the settings, especially the War Room, gives credibility to the principal characters, who owe more to the movies than to real life. What is most unsettling, however, is that as the film moves inexorably towards mankind's end, these comic-cartoon characters become steadily more recognizable as the men who control the world's destiny today.

When General Turgidson tries to convince the President that a nuclear attack on America might not be too bad (' . . . only ten to twenty million people killed, tops, depending on the breaks') an echo can be heard of the comments of men like Herman Kahn and his successors as they calmly weigh the balance, not in human life but in statistics.

If the maniacal ride to earth by Major Kong owes more to the movies than to reality there is no corresponding feeling that it could not happen. In spirit, if not in reality, a Major Kong lurks inside every Minuteman or cruise installation anywhere in the world.

Latterday audiences must bring to *Dr Strangelove* a higher level of acceptance than did the audience at the time of its release. Although the military potential remains broadly similar, given that the time-factor has diminished to minutes rather than hours and that the bombs are bigger and more numerous, the main difference is that audiences then only suspected their leaders might be less than perfect. Today's audiences *know* the world's leaders are hideously imperfect and seemingly confused on the subject of arms build-up and distribution.

If the fate of the world in *Dr Strangelove* rested in the hands of cartoon characters, now it rests in the hands of men whose minds appear to work no better than those of the leading players in a Tom and Jerry confrontation.

Ronald Reagan's glib approach to chemical warfare, his after-dinner jokes about nuclear weapons and his casual decision (based upon remarkably little scientific back-up) to order a multi-billion dollar 'Star Wars' defence programme for outer-space, suggests that his Hollywood background really has gone to his head. Unfortunately, proving whether or not he is right might well involve exploding the planet. Whereas disasters in the world of Tom and Jerry are temporary, those in the real world tend to be permanent, and the pieces will not all miraculously come together again later.

As the next generation of political leaders have never experienced life without a nuclear threat overhanging them, perhaps the advantages of younger and more questing minds will prove to be just as potentially dangerous.

The massive devastation caused by nuclear war and the resulting effect upon ordinary people have seldom been tackled realistically by film-makers; perhaps they have chiefly been deterred by the enormous cost of creating an impresson of what such scenes might look like.

The few successful attempts were made originally for showing on television although one, Peter Watkins' *The War Game* (1965), was promptly banned by the BBC for whom it was made. Watkins spared no one's sensitivities in his harrowing description of life after the Bomb. This was a factor, perhaps the only factor, which caused the ban on the screening of his film.

Earlier than Watkins' version of life in Britain after the Bomb came an almost forgotten play which *was* screened by the BBC, in 1959. This was *The Offshore Island*, which starred Ann Todd as Rachel Verney, a mother of two children who are among the tiny handful of survivors left in Britain after a nuclear war. This play was written by Marghanita Laski, and what makes it far more perceptive than most other tales of nuclear war survivors is that the rest of the world has not been subjected to the same disaster.

The war, between America and the USSR, has been carefully arranged to ensure neither side suffered undue damage to their own lands. Now they require a neutral zone between them and are co-operating in removing the last vestiges of life from Great Britain, the offshore island of the play's title. As one of the Americans declares in the play's closing moments: 'This is Operation Neutralizer, the neutralization of this offshore island so that neither side can try to hold it against the other.'

With their homeland laid waste by opposing sides in the war, the few survivors find themselves pursued with equal vigour by both Americans and Russians, and are additionally faced with the prospect that any chances they have of surviving through into another generation must inevitably be dogged by fears of the effects of radiation upon any future births.

Given the date of the play's transmission, it is not only remarkably perceptive but also unnervingly prescient of how America and the USSR have come to regard the buffer lands between them. With missiles in both countries, and in various locations in Europe, all poised for action, the message central to *The Offshore Island* is even more urgent than it was a quarter-century ago.

The after-effect of a nuclear strike is also examined in the American TV film *The Day After* (1983). The story is set in Lawrence, Kansas, just 36 miles outside Kansas City.

Beneath the region's peaceful farming lands lie missile silos ready for launching at targets in Russia. During the opening sequences, as the main characters are introduced and established, there is a permanent background hum of TV and radio broadcasts imparting news of a crisis in Europe. Berlin is blockaded, Russian forces advance, then they are attacked by a 'limited' nuclear strike.

Because of the presence of the missile silos, everyone knows that Kansas City is a prime target. Cellars are prepared as fall-out shelters; the supermarkets are stripped of food.

When the missiles are launched, the local people can only stand and watch helplessly as they soar upwards and set course for the USSR. They have half an hour: thirty minutes before the retaliatory strike will land. It no longer matters who is retaliating against whom. The whole shabby logic of the principle of deterrent is laid bare. The missiles have not deterred; they never could, and now everyone will lose the gamble that they might.

After the Russian missiles have fallen on Kansas City, which disappears under a pall of smoke, the effect upon Lawrence, while not as swiftly final, is just as catastrophic. Rows of shops and houses are destroyed by the blast; mud and rubble and ashes coat the area. Wrecked vehicles litter the streets, and everywhere lie the bodies of the dead and maimed.

For the survivors there is the task of trying to patch up themselves and their environment. The central character, Russell Oakes (Jason Robards), is a surgeon. He tries desperately to counter the after-effects, but his task is hopeless.

Water and power supplies fail; the sick grow worse as radiation spreads beneath clouds of settling dust.

Although the community has not been wiped out there is little of the false optimism which afflicted the endings of so many other nuclear disaster movies. Here there is an air of resignation which hangs over everyone and which casts grave doubts upon whether or not anyone will survive much longer.

Given that the effects of the nuclear strike depicted in *The Day After* are considerably less damaging than would really be the case – once again the nuclear winter effect is omitted – the film rightly caused many people to stop and think about the fragility of a future built upon an evergrowing stockpile of nuclear weapons.

Most critics were suitably impressed by *The Day After*, and many politicians and scientists applauded its realistic account of a future which was once merely possible but now appears highly probable.

Henry Kissinger was not overly impressed, however, commenting that the film is a 'simple-minded notion of the nuclear problem . . . The real issue is how to avoid a nuclear war.' Reflection upon events in Vietnam and Cambodia during his tenure as Secretary of State add a hollow ring to this remark.

Closer to the feeling of most people who saw the film, and the audience in America alone on the night it was transmitted exceeded 100 millions, was the comment of the physicist Dr Paul Sagan: 'I think we have all been sleepwalking in this country for the past thirty years. It is my unhappy duty to point out that the reality is much worse.'

Unfortunately, as tension grows and weapons proliferate and blind eyes are turned by politicians, military leaders, the Church and private individuals (like those who sought to have *The Day After* banned in Britain), the sleepwalking looks set to continue a while longer.

Just what the future holds is a matter for speculation (which might once have been saved for idle moments but which becomes steadily more urgent as the days pass). It is however certain that the Dr Strangelove-like behaviour of political and military leaders is just as steadily becoming more commonplace.

Who can tell if the Politburo has not already responded to the American Star Wars plans by allocating similarly vast funds and resources towards development of a Doomsday Machine which will take all control of mankind's future out of man's hands forever?

Hollywood and other film-makers have persistently interpreted the past ineptly and inaccurately, despite having resources of factual information upon which to base their stories. For their tales of what the future might hold they have information and speculation and the science of probability, all in similarly generous measures, allied to unlimited imagination.

Perhaps the best that anyone can hope for is that despite these facilities they are just as wrong about the future as they have been about the past.

AFTERWORD

Hollywood's interest in the American nation's past is laudable. Much less satisfactory is the haphazard and cavalier fashion in which it has treated individuals and events throughout history.

Examining idols for feet of clay, as Hollywood has done so often, is also a laudable activity, unless it is done merely to satisfy a whim or to cash in on audience curiosity. New and searching light *should* be cast into dark corners of the nation's past, but not merely to sensationalize. The muck-raking journalists of the past bore their tag with pride, and rightly so. Too often in films, muck-raking has taken on a more literal and completely dishonourable meaning.

Great events have been reduced to the level of horse-opera backcloths while other events, for which any nation should feel shame, have been glorified.

As indicated in the Foreword, the films examined in this book were not pre-judged or selected in order to make predetermined points, yet with few exceptions they have proved to be inaccurate, often inept, frequently grossly misleading, and offensive to the memories of some of the greatest figures in America's past. In the case of wars, the memories of ordinary men and women who suffered and died for their country are similarly offended.

Continually throughout Hollywood's history, noble figures have been trivialized while depraved killers have been elevated to folk-hero status.

Why did Hollywood and other film-makers think it necessary to make such changes?

As productions such as *The Story of GI Joe, Reds, Kennedy, All the President's Men* and *The Killing Fields* have shown, it is possible to make high-quality film dramas which are successful in both commercial and artistic terms, while simultaneously remaining faithful to the probable truth. For others, sadly the great majority, changes have been made to the truth which have been motivated by nothing more noble than a swift hatchet-job, to cash in on someone's fame or notoriety, to exploit the nation's response to great events in its past, or, as so often seems to be the case, to make a fast buck.

The effect this will have had upon the nation is a matter for speculation. Is the escalating street violence which terrorizes urban dwellers in so many cities a reflection of the glorification of outlaws such as Billy the Kid, Bonnie and Clyde or Al Capone?

204

Have the aspirations of black Americans been stultified by their difficulty in shaking off images of eye-rolling, shuffling coons which owe so much to generations of film-making?

Does the alacrity with which the nation still leaps to adopt a belligerent posture in world affairs owe much to those death-or-glory characters who stormed through countless gung-ho war movies?

People are not dramatically changed by films, television, books, magazines or newspapers, but it is not enough to say that none of this matters. While an individual who has never thought of becoming a criminal is unlikely to be turned into one by seeing a movie about a bank robbery, an individual who has already set foot on the path of crime might well see before him on the screen only the rosy side of such pursuits. The end, savagely punishing though it may often be, might justify the lifestyle needed to lead to it.

As for war, how many soldiers who went to Korea did so because life in movies about World War II did not seem so bad? How many went to Vietnam expecting bloodless wounds, camaraderie and an enemy who played by the same rules?

Does any of this matter? Does it matter if Hollywood has trivialized and adjusted and ennobled the ignoble? Does it matter if it has told lies about the nation's past, whether in the interests of dramatic effect or to make money?

Every nation draws upon its past, but progress is only possible if those areas of the past it uses have been clearly and accurately drawn, whether in history books or in popular entertainments such as the movies and television. To base decisions for the future on a false past is at best foolish and at worst potentially lethal.

No statesman, not even a Ronald Reagan, and no military leader consciously draws upon movie images in reaching decisions of such gravity that they might well effect the lives of every person on this planet. But, subconsciously, everyone who ever saw a movie or watched a television show or read a book has images, words, gestures and attitudes lodged in memory banks which can emerge at any time.

If any incumbent of the American presidency should ever pull out the wrong image from that flickering subconscious, filled as it must be with time-stopped frames from a thousand movies, the result might well be a hair-trigger response which owes nothing to the reality of the world in which we live today and everything to a long-forgotten movie: a movie which might have been made for no better reason than that its maker needed money with which to pay for a new automobile, or a bigger swimming pool, or to meet alimony payments. If the world has to end tomorrow, it would be sad to think that the reason could be as mundane as this.

Maybe the film-makers of today and tomorrow should take more careful stock of the past and be more thoughtful about how they use it in their works.

If they do not they might well have a lot to answer for – always assuming that there is anyone left to answer *to*.

BIBLIOGRAPHY

Adair, G., *Hollywood's Vietnam* (London: Proteus, 1981)

Alexander, C. C., *Nationalism in American Thought, 1930–1945* (Chicago: Rand McNally, 1969)

Alloway, L., *Violent America* (New York: Museum of Modern Art, 1971)

Allsop, K., *The Bootleggers* (London: Arrow, 1970)

Bataille, G. M. and Silet, C. L. P., eds., *The Pretend Indians: Images of Native Americans in the Movies* (Iowa State University Press, 1980)

Blevins, W., *Give Your Heart to the Hawks* (London: Futura, 1976)

Bogle, D., *Toms, Coons, Mulattoes, Mammies and Bucks* (New York: Viking, 1973)

Brown, D., *Bury My Heart at Wounded Knee* (London: Pan, 1974)

Brownlow, K., *The War, the West, and the Wilderness* (London: Secker & Warburg, 1979)

Cameron, I., *Adventure and the Cinema* (London: Studio Vista, 1973)

Clarens, C., *Crime Movies* (London: Secker & Warburg, 1980)

Culbert, D., ed., *Mission to Moscow* (Madison: University of Wisconsin Press, 1980)

Davies, P. and Neve, B., eds., *Cinema, Politics and Society in America* (Manchester: Manchester University Press, 1981)

Deer, I. and Deer, H. A., eds., *The Popular Arts: a Critical Reader* (New York: Scribners, 1967)

Degler, C., *Out of Our Past: the Forces That Shaped Modern America* (New York: Harper Colophon, 1970)

Denning, B., *Running Away From Myself: A Dream Portrait of America Drawn From the Films of the '40s* (New York: Grossman, 1969)

Faulk, J. H., *Fear on Trial* (New York: Tempo, 1976)

Friar, R. E. and Friar, N. A., *The Only Good Indian . . . the Hollywood Gospel* (New York: Drama Book Specialists, 1972)

Heston, C., *The Actor's Life* (London: Penguin, 1980)

Insdorf, A., *Indelible Shadows: Film and the Holocaust* (New York: Random House, 1983)

Isenberg, M. T., *War on Film: the American Cinema and World War One 1914–1941* (Rutherford: Farleigh Dickinson University Press, 1981)

Jones, K. D. and McClure, A. F., *Hollywood at War* (New York: Castle, 1973)

Kaminsky, S., *American Film Genres* (Dayton: Pflaum, 1974)

Laski, M., *The Offshore Island* (London: Mayfair Books, 1961)

Leab, D. J., *From Sambo to Superspade* (London: Secker & Warburg, 1975)

Lloyd, A., ed., *Movies of the Fifties* (London: Orbis, 1982)

McLoughlin, D., *The Encyclopedia of the Old West* (London: Routledge & Kegan Paul, 1977)

Manchester, W., *American Caesar* (London: Arrow, 1979)

Maynard, R. A., ed., *The American West on Film: Myth and Reality* (Rochelle Park: Hayden, 1974)

Milius, J., *The Life and Times of Judge Roy Bean* (New York: Bantam, 1973)

O'Connor, J. E. and Jackson, M. A., eds., *American History/American Film* (New York: Ungar, 1979)

Parks, R., *The Western Hero in Film and Television: Mass Media Mythology* (Ann Arbor: University of Michigan Institute Research Press, 1982)

Peary, G. and Shatzkin, R., eds., *The Classic American Novel and the Movies* (New York: Ungar, 1977)

Peary, G. and Shatzkin, R., eds., *The Modern American Novel and the Movies* (New York: Ungar, 1978)

Phillips, C., *From the Crash to the Blitz 1929–1939* (New York: New York Times, 1969)

Rhode, E., *A History of the Cinema* (London: Penguin/Pelican, 1979)

Roddick, N., *A New Deal in Entertainment: Warner Brothers in the 1930s* (London: British Film Institute, 1983)

Roffman, P. and Purdy, J., *The Hollywood Social Problem Film* (Indiana University Press, 1981)

Rozwenc, E. C., *The Making of American Society,* Vol. II (Boston: Allyn & Bacon, 1973)

Sayre, N., *Running Time: Films of the Cold War* (New York: Dial Press, 1982)

Shadoian, J., *Dreams and Dead Ends* (Boston: Massachusetts Institute of Technology, 1977)

Shaheen, J.G., ed., *Nuclear War Films* (Southern Illinois University Press, 1978)

Shindler, C., *Hollywood Goes to War: Films and American Society 1939–1952* (London: Routledge & Kegan Paul, 1979)

Sklar, R., *Movie-Made America* (London: Chappell, 1978)

Sorlin, P., *The Film in History* (Oxford: Blackwell, 1980)

Spoto, D., *Camerado: Hollywood and the American Man* (New York: New American Library, 1978)

Taylor, P., *The Distant Magnet* (London: Eyre & Spottiswoode, 1971)

Thomas, T., *Hollywood and the American Image* (Westport: Arlington House, 1981)

Tinkle, L., *The Alamo: 13 Days to Glory* (London: Landsborough, 1958)

Toland, J., *The Dillinger Days* (London: Arthur Barker, 1963)

Wake, S. and Hayden, N., *The Bonnie & Clyde Book* (London: Lorrimer, 1972)

White, J., *Reconstruction After the American Civil War* (London: Longman, 1977)

White, D. M. and Averson, R., *The Celluloid Weapon* (Boston: Beacon Press, 1972)

Wolf, W., *Landmark Films* (New York & London: Paddington Press, 1979)

Wolfe, T., *The Right Stuff* (New York: Bantam, 1981)

Woll, A. L., *The Hollywood Musical Goes to War* (Chicago: Nelson-Hall, 1983)

Additionally, reference has been made to various editions of the following magazines and journals: *Film and History, The Hollywood Reporter, The Journal of Popular Culture, Monthly Film Bulletin, The Movie* and *Sight & Sound*.

PICTURE ACKNOWLEDGEMENTS

Some of the illustrations in this book come from stills issued to publicize films made or distributed by the following companies: American International, Central Independent Television, Columbia, the Coppola Company, EMI, Paramount, Universal, Warner Bros., Zoetrope.

Pictures are reproduced courtesy of the Associated Press Ltd, the Bettmann Archive, the British Film Institute, Blair Brown, the Kobal Collection, the Museum of the City of New York, the National Archive Washington DC, the Netherlands State Institute for War Documentation courtesy Croom Helm Ltd, Popperfoto, Martin Sheen, Hilton Tims, United Press International, John White.

Although efforts have been made to trace present copyright holders of photographs, we apologize in advance for any unintentional omission or neglect and will be pleased to insert the appropriate acknowledgement to companies or individuals in any subsequent edition of this book.

INDEX

Figures in italics denote picture references.

216

218